THE
56TH
EVAC HOSPITAL

THE 56TH
EVAC HOSPITAL
Letters of a WWII Army Doctor

Lawrence D. Collins, M.D.
Introduction by Carlo W. D'Este

War and the Southwest Series
Number 4

First edition
General Series Editors for War and the Southwest series:
Richard G. Lowe
Gustav L. Seligmann
Calvin L. Christman

The paper in this book meets the minimum requirements of the American
National Standard for Permanence of paper for Printed Library Materials,
Z39.48-1984.

Library of Congress Cataloging-in-Publication Data

Collins, Lawrence D., 1907-
56th Evac Hospital: letters of a WWII army doctor / Lawrence D.
Collins.
p. cm. — (War and the Southwest series ; no. 4)
Includes index.
ISBN 0-929398-83-1 :
1. Collins, Lawrence D., 1907- —Correspondence. 2. United States.
Army. Evacuation Hospital, 56th—History. 3. United States. Army—
Biography. 4. World War, 1939-1945—Personal narratives, American. 5.
Soldiers—United States—Biography.
I. Title. II. Title: 56th Evacuation Hospital. III. Title: Fifty sixth
Evac. Hospital. IV. Series.
D807.U6C565 1994
940.54'7573'092—dc20   94-45516
                                                            CIP

Cover and interior design by Amy Layton

Photo on previous page: Sign for the 56th Evac Hospital. This and other
photos, unless otherwise noted, are taken from *The Story of the 56th Evac*, ed.
B.A. Merrick, printed around 1945, copy in the Texas Collection of Baylor
University, Waco, Texas.

WAR AND THE SOUTHWEST SERIES

The University of North Texas Press has undertaken to publish a series of significant books about War and the Southwest. This broad category includes first-hand accounts of military experiences by men and women of the Southwest, histories of warfare involving the people of the Southwest, and analyses of military life in the Southwest itself. The Southwest is defined loosely as those states of the United States west of the Mississippi River and south of a line from San Francisco to St. Louis as well as the borderlands straddling the Mexico-United States boundary. The series will include works involving military life in peacetime in addition to books on warfare itself. It will range chronologically from the first contact between indigenous tribes and Europeans to the present. The series is based on the belief that warfare is an important if unfortunate fact of life in human history and that understanding war is a requirement for a full understanding of the American past.

Books in the Series

FOO—A Japanese-American Prisoner of the Rising Son
Wen Bon: A Naval Air Intelligence Officer behind Japanese Lines in China
An Artist at War: The Journal of John Gaitha Browning

CONTENTS

PREFACE

This odyssey is a transcript of selected letters saved by the wife of a young doctor serving in World War II for thirty-two months in an affiliated army hospital unit overseas. The affiliation was with Baylor Medical College in Dallas, Texas.

Prior to Pearl Harbor Day, the surgeon general of the United States Army had approached the nation's major medical colleges with a request that they organize medical staffs for army hospital units. These staffs would be made up chiefly from their own roster, ready for mobilization as a unit whenever called. The army could provide administrative and enlisted personnel very quickly for such a nuclei of physicians, so the idea was a good one. Ours was such a unit.

On March 17, 1942, the Baylor Unit was ordered to active duty. Its medical officers and nurses reported to Fort Sam Houston, Texas, near San Antonio where its ranks were filled up. The Commanding Officer assigned to our unit had served twenty-odd years in the regular army and was convinced that a medical officer was qualified to serve in any capacity that conditions might require. He was prone to shift junior medical officers from one major service to the other from time to time—medicine to surgery and vice versa—to the general confusion of all concerned. In fairness to him, however, the reader should bear in mind that all any army requires of commanding officers is that their units function. The Baylor Unit did so in an exemplary manner. Years after this was written, the author learned from his former executive officer that theirs was the most highly decorated medical unit in the U.S. Army in World War II.

None of the letters refer to events between the unit's activation in March and its arrival a year later at Camp Shanks, New York, on April 3, 1943. The truth is that with the exception of three months on Louisiana maneuvers, the doctors and nurses had been practically idle for a year. The letters from overseas confirm my growing anxiety as a junior officer over frequent shifts from surgery to medicine and back to surgery. I had no desire to do surgery in civilian practice, and was ill-fitted for unsupervised surgery. After receiving our first casualties following an air raid in Bizerte, it seemed obvious that during times of stress we would have to break down our three-man surgical teams into single doctors assisted by a nurse. I dreaded the inevitable day and welcomed every opportunity to acquire any degree of surgical skill possible.

My own gripes were frequently judgmental and were particularly negative at times regarding my superiors. Please bear in mind that I usually held them in high esteem. But war is a miserable thing most of the time, and acutely so some of the time. War is too impersonal to blame for one's misery, and one's superiors who are right at hand catch the blame. This is probably a ventilatory mechanism to relieve the misery.

All letters mailed from overseas had to be censored by an officer. This tended to result in terse communications for we certainly did not want to tell anything we weren't supposed to. We had been told not to reveal our locations immediately after a move and never to reveal troop units in our sections at any time.

Thus, while short letters may not tell anything but the truth, they should always be viewed with some skepticism, since they did not tell the whole truth. Also, when the letter writer was in obvious personal danger, his letters might deny the fact in order to reassure home folks. Such denials were frequent in my own letters from Anzio. Associated Press releases had divulged our location and described our plight within a few days of our landing on the beachhead. The letters written between January 27, 1944, and April 9 do certainly demonstrate the denials when compared with the summary I wrote on April 15.

As to the importance of censoring, the commanders of German wolf packs (submarines) had nearly won the war of the Atlantic prior to March, 1943, from information leaked through the mail of soldiers and by longshoremen on the New York docks. German U-boats were taking a toll of Allied shipping that threatened the outcome of the war. The commanders knew the whereabouts and departure dates of almost every convoy out of New York. The source of their information had to be stopped at all costs. In March, the U.S. Secret Service decoded the German communication code known as "Enigma." Also in March, according to Sister Pascalina of the Vatican, a meeting between President Roosevelt and the head of the Mafia in New York was arranged by Cardinal Spellman. Sister Pascalina claimed a deal was made for the Allies not to bomb Rome in exchange for the Mafia's stopping leaks of information on the convoys.

Landing at Casablanca, some of us were greeted by our unit members who had crossed on a fast steamship, beating us by a couple of weeks. Two unusual experiences awaited us. The first was doing MP duty on the streets of Casablanca. Exuberant paratroopers had just returned to Casablanca after surviving the battles of Kasserine Pass and Mateur. They were whooping it up, and our assignments were to patrol until we each made ten arrests per day for misconduct of any sort, including such minor infringements as an unbuttoned pocket flap on a shirt.

The other experience was our learning to drive the 2 1/2-ton trucks we rode into Bizerte, Tunisia. The Atlantic base section (in addition to having a louse of a commanding general) had an assembly plant that was putting together the fleet of trucks needed to transport our unit's equipment and personnel. They had about finished the assembling but did not have the drivers equal to the task. Our CO rose to the occasion by ordering all officers below the rank of lieutenant colonel to learn to drive those trucks. Some enlisted men were also taught, thus providing some two hundred drivers. After we'd had a week's training, we got the convoy of trucks and were loaded and off in short order. Our route was over the Atlas Mountains and on to Bizerte, Tunisia, a thirteen hundred mile trip.

Sadly but clearly, the letters do reveal a progressive ennui as the months turned into years. Optimism did yield to pessimism, and idealism did yield to cynicism. It is a bit hard for me to accept that we who disembarked wet cheeked at Casablanca would cast dice for tokens of a grateful nation's appreciation just thirty months later, but we did. So be it. It was a war and General Sherman had a word for war, but every schoolboy knows about that.

Lawrence D. Collins

Introduction

The historiography of the Second World War is rich in first-hand accounts of its participants. Very few, however, depict war from the perspective of those whose task it was to treat the sick and wounded, and to save lives.

The dedicated men and women who staffed the evacuation hospitals were a key link in the medical chain. The seriously wounded who survived the first step of life-saving treatment by a medical corpsman at the front or at a nearby aid station were immediately transported to the rear area, where the U.S. Army field and evacuation hospitals were established to treat as many as 1000 patients per day.

From the time the first histories of the war began appearing in the 1950s and beyond, the Mediterranean Theater of Operations has never received the attention of historians that has been focused on the European Theater of Operations. The ETO began with what is arguably the best known military operation in military history, D-Day, June 6, 1944, when Allied forces invaded Normandy in the first important step in the liberation of France and the eventual defeat of Nazi Germany. Operation Market-Garden, the dramatic and costly Allied airborne operation to seize the Rhine bridges at Arnhem, and the Battle of the Bulge were all events which have attained an aura of mystique. Only in recent years has the Mediterranean begun to receive the historical attention it deserves.

By comparison, there was little in the bloody but otherwise undistinguished battles and campaigns in the Mediterranean to compare with those in the ETO. Yet, the war in the Mediterranean was the longest series of battles and campaigns fought by the Anglo-American alliance during the Second World War. It consumed two and one-half years, and was fought from French North Africa, to the island of Sicily and along the entire length of Italy from the boot to the Alps. Unfortunately, the Mediterranean remains as well known for its negatives as for its accomplishments: Kasserine Pass in February 1943; Sicily, where the Allies needlessly permitted the escape of a veteran German army corps to Italy; the near-run debacle of Salerno; and the tragedies of the Rapido, Monte Cassino and Anzio.

It is therefore appropriate that this book is set in the Mediterranean Theater of Operations, and coincides with the major campaigns fought in North Africa and Italy from early 1943 to the end of the war in May 1945. Lawrence D. Collins was a young doctor assigned to the 56th Evacuation Hospital, a Texas-based medical unit that was activated in March 1942 and largely staffed by men and women who trained at the Baylor University College of Medicine in Dallas. Often referred to as the "Baylor Unit," the 56th Evacuation Hospital was a mobile tent hospital (similar to the M*A*S*H units of Korean War fame), and one of several such army hospitals organized at various medical colleges for service during World War II. During its tenure in the Mediterranean, the 56th Evac treated over 73,000 casualties, which may have been a record for medical units in the Mediterranean and ETO. How many lives were saved by the men and women of the 56th Evac will never be known, but suffice to say, many were spared who might otherwise have died.

Dr. Collins chronicles his experiences in the 56th Evacuation Hospital from its training in Texas, to the relatively uncomplicated early months in the Mediterranean, first in Morocco, later in Bizerte, Tunisia. All were merely warm-up exercises for the Italian campaign which commenced in September 1943. The unit was sent to Paestum, near Salerno, and—following the progress of the Allies armies—north to Dragoni as the bitter, stalemated winter campaign of 1943-44 set in around Cassino, and along the Gustav Line. Disaster was narrowly averted during the relocation to Dragoni when a truck transporting nurses took a wrong turn, and ended up in the Allied front lines before being flagged down and saved by a military policeman who said, "If you go further here, the next MP you meet will be wearing a swastika!"

In January 1944, in an effort to unhinge the Germans at Cassino and break the deadly stalemate, the Allies launched an amphibious end- run at Anzio, thirty-five miles southwest of Rome. Its object was to so threaten Rome and the German lines of communication between the Italian capital and the Cassino front that the Germans would be compelled to abandon the Gustav Line. Anzio turned out to be a bluff that failed miserably. Instead of retreating, the Germans defended *both* Anzio and Cassino with a savagery unparalleled even in this terrible war. The result was continued stalemate, now on two fronts instead of one. Hitler was determined to crush the Anzio beachhead and drive the Allies back into the sea. In February 1944 the Germans launched a desperate counter-offensive to "lance the abscess" of Anzio. What turned out to be one of the most desperate campaigns fought by the western allies in the Second World War became the focus of Dr. Collins's life when the 56th Evacuation Hospital was sent to Anzio to reinforce the hard-pressed Allied medical services in the beachhead. What ensued forms the core of *56th Evac Hospital.*

The challenge facing the doctors, nurses, aid men, ambulance drivers, and others who comprised the medical service at Anzio was daunting. In no instance was the Hippocratic Oath more difficult to carry out than in the Anzio beachhead where the most significant part of Collins's story is set. As a Fifth Army medical historian has written:

> Despite the violence which surrounds them, medical personnel must offer the reassuring example of their own courage to grateful patients. They must stay rooted in a ward tent, speaking words of comfort, even though their own minds pound with the awareness of danger. In an operating room, they must hold their hands steady even though their own bodies might be shattered more critically than the one lying stripped before them. . . . There was no escape for a medical battalion, a surgical team . . . even an evacuation hospital from the artillery fire or bombing attacks. . . . The enemy could and did reach every part of the beachhead with his fire and the frequency with which he hit the congested corner occupied by the main medical installations were underscored in the name of "Hell's Half Acre" which the front line soldiers gave it.[1]

What Dr. Collins and his fellow medics of the 56th Evacuation Hospital endured at Anzio is beyond even his graphic descriptions of their existence in one of the most dangerous pieces of terrain on earth. In "Hell's Half Acre," the hospitals that patched the broken and shattered bodies sent to them were all in the line of around-the-clock fire from the heavy guns of the German artillery in the nearby Alban Hills. No place was considered safe from these guns which could reach every part of the Anzio beachhead, including the three hospitals. In one of the oddest Catch-22s of the war, patients were known to go A.W.O.L. from "Hell's Half Acre" and return to their units at the front, where it was considered "safer" to reside in the extreme discomfort of a foxhole than at the rear, in a hospital.

During the nearly five months of the Anzio campaign, 92 medical personnel were killed in action, 387 were wounded, 19 captured and 60 more missing in action. Among them were members of the 56th Evac. While the attacks on Allied medical facilities does not seem to have been deliberate, it was inevitable, given the negligible size of the beachhead and their proximity to nearby supply dumps that were prime targets. Thus, at Anzio even hospitals became casualties, such as February 10, 1944, when incoming shells wreaked havoc in the nearby 33d Field Hospital. Over the loudspeakers of the 56th Evac came the order: "All litter bearers report to the 33d Field Hospital area! All fire fighters proceed at once to check fire in that area!" The men and women of Dr. Collins's unit descended upon their crippled sister unit, from which there emerged a stream of patients, many of whom had been tending to the sick and wounded only moments earlier. In subsequent bombing raids and artillery bombardments, the 56th Evacuation Hospital was hit repeatedly, and suffered numerous casualties. After an artillery barrage rocked the hospital on April 4, it was decided to bring in a new hospital unit to replace the battered 56th. Despite their protests that they were ready and willing to carry on, they left the Anzio beachhead for new duty near Naples. As Dr. Collins writes,

> Shells from both sides, by the thousands, screamed over our heads twenty-four hours per day. . . . I think it unlikely that any of us will ever again work such hours and at such a pace. . . . Still, very few grumbled and very few cried in spite of the fact that a great many died. Least of all did the wounded grumble, delayed treatments notwithstanding. They were completely committed to their task at whatever the cost. You could read it in their eyes. They would not have traded their

country, their comrades, their officers, their medics, their nurses or their doctors during those hectic days. Not for anything would they, nor we, have traded off the other, for those were days of complete commitment, complete cooperation, complete teamwork, and intense pride. Small wonder Churchill rated the ordeal of the English during the blitz as their "finest hour"! I've no doubt our stint at Anzio will ever remain as ours.

These memoirs also show another side of war: the frequent boredom, the griping that characterizes all soldiers whether they be front line infantrymen or surgeons; the hazards characteristic of life in a war zone; the lack of sanitation and discomfort of military life; and the simple pleasures of mail from home or a hot meal. Dr. Collins offers some wonderfully evocative descriptions of visits to some of the world's most exotic places, and its peoples. But above all, *56th Evac Hospital*, despite its dark moments, is filled with examples of how the human spirit survives under the dreadful conditions of war. More than a tale of war, the book is a fitting tribute to the men and women who comprised the U.S. Army Medical Corps and the Nurse Corps.

During the commemorations of the fiftieth anniversary of the Second World War, I am pleased to be able to introduce *56th Evac Hospital* and to avail myself of this opportunity to publicly acknowledge the important contributions of the U.S. Army medical service. This worthy addition to the lexicon of war literature is opportune and will, I hope, endure as yet another testament to the stupidity and futility of war.

Carlo W. D'Este
Cape Cod, Massachusetts
April 1994

---

[1]Extracted from "The Medical Story of Anzio," written by the Fifth Army Surgeon's office in 1944, unpublished manuscript in the U. S. Army Center of Military History, Washington, D.C.

The Collins family at Turtle Creek in Dallas, April 1942. Photo courtesy Lawrence D. and Margaret Collins.

Officers and nurses of the 56th, sometime prior to leaving for Louisiana maneuvers in July, 1942.

Officers on training march at Fort Sam Houston.

Lawrence and Margaret Collins saying good-bye before the 56th boards the train for Louisiana in July, 1942. Photo courtesy Lawrence D. and Margaret Collins.

Scenes from 56th Evac quarters in Mansfield, Louisiana. Photos courtesy Lawrence D. and Margaret Collins.

New York

1

April 1943

A **PRIL 3, 1943.** Camp Shanks, New York. Pulled out of Fort Sam Houston promptly at 1:00 P.M. on March 31, 1943, right after you left us. We arrived here in a blizzard around 11:00 P.M. tonight. Except for the detail that prepared it, we were the first to occupy this brand new staging area. It had no heat when we arrived and we nearly froze to death before getting our blankets warm. We're comfortably located now with heat in our quarters and an outside temperature of around forty-five degrees with sunshine.

My overcoat and blouse are the most wrinkled things I've ever seen—this in spite of the care I took in packing them. Of course, wrinkles will come out of that heavy material after it hangs up a bit. These valpacs are certainly practical, if not overloaded, but they sure won't keep clothes nicely pressed. Mine came through all right, but many didn't. When too heavily loaded, the handles tear loose on quite a few.

APRIL 7, 1943. I've been to Waterbury, Connecticut, and met Mardi and Judy Collins. Judy is cute but hasn't yet taken her first step nor cut her first tooth. I sure did like Mardi, and brother Joe is well and happy.

Everyone in the unit except me has seen New York. I didn't get off the shuttle until we reached the New Haven train, and then had to run to catch it, so I didn't see much.

We're having our first warm day, and I'm sitting comfortably in my undershirt that was dyed khaki, remember? Incidentally, I've washed this stuff twice and can't see that it faded a bit. Martinak and I are planning to go into the city tomorrow to spend the day. I'll let you know if it's any bigger than your hometown.

Morale is high. There is no liquor available, our barracks are comfortable, the food is good, and our commanding officer looks better than I've ever seen him. Kiss Suzanne.

APRIL 8, 1943. I believe I didn't have time to write you about my first trip into town day before yesterday. I hate to admit that all I did was ride the Fifth Avenue bus from the Presbyterian Medical Center on 168th Street to town and back. That trip took up three hours and I had to get back to camp. But I did enjoy it and saw many of the sights along the way. These included Grant's Tomb, Fosdick's church, Soldier's (i.e., Yank's) Monument, Riverside Drive, Carnegie Hall, Broadway, and Fifth Avenue from 57th Street down to Washington Square. So altogether, I spent $1.10 on Camp Shanks bus fare plus twenty cents on city bus fare for my first visit to the great city.

Did a little better yesterday when Martinak, Fisher, Merrick, and I went back to New York. We stayed until 1:00 A.M., had a keen time, and only spent about $8 each. I was impressed with the view from the top of the Empire State Building, which looked much like a post card except the details were much clearer. We next took the East Ferry past Staten Island, the Statue of Liberty, etc. I was even more impressed with all of that than with the Empire State Building. And you might know, the lower Manhattan skyline is even prettier than the old hometown's.

We also went over on Broadway and ate at a flossy cafe and bar called Longchamp's. The wine was good, the food excellent, and they clipped us for most of what we spent—eight dollars. As regards boisterousness, the crowd was well behaved, but the guys and gals at the bar indulged themselves in considerable refined necking with their beer. I'll either eat at a hamburger joint from now on or at an automat. My finances won't really permit much else and I did see several such places.

We went to the Empire Theater to see *Life with Father,* and it was a scream. I hope you saw it when you were here, but if not, do be sure to see it the first chance you get. The theater's small size sure did surprise me, but we're told all of them are small. No wonder it takes New Yorkers several years to see a good show.

The lights of the entire city are dimmed out. We'll have to miss the famous bright lights until after the war. Broadway is no better lighted than the French Quarter in New Orleans. Remember how scared you were that night when the French Quarter bum asked me for a dime?

Back in camp, I hear hilarious Dunlap in the suite next to ours wrestling with his bedroll and cussing it. "Damn such a rearrangement job," he says. "It makes me want to vomit like a buzzard." His vehemence makes it all sound too, too funny. Small is in there, too, and we hear him griping about the sensuousness of *By Jupiter*, another Broadway show. "Why," he says, "they talk about an unmentionable subject every minute of the show." Hahn offers the information that *Sons o' Fun* is a wow. Kiss Suzanne.

APRIL 11, 1943. I was planning to go shopping in New York tomorrow and back up to Waterbury next Sunday, but guess I'll not be able to do so. I'd also planned to see Dr. Rappleye when I went by Columbia on the way in, but won't be able to do that, either.

I've had to undo my bedroll so many times since leaving the fort that I could now put it together with my eyes closed. Anyway, I had to unroll it again last night in order to get my duffle bag to take on a temporary duty assignment. Johnson, Brown, White, Bowyer, Jones, and I are going down into New Jersey for a day or two tomorrow to examine troops. We expect to be too occupied with the assignment to permit writing, so don't worry if you don't hear from me. Kiss Suzanne for me and take care of yourself.

APRIL 17, 1943. At sea. There is a great deal to tell, but because of censorship I'll have to curb a good many impulses. [For example, we were anchored in Bermuda awaiting a more propitious time to cross the Atlantic. A convoy a week or two ahead of us had been attacked by submarines and sustained many losses we were told. This information was dramatized by several damaged ships in Bermuda Harbor, all with large holes in their hulls above waterline as well as damage to superstructures. We were in an LST—landing ship tank—which was flat bottomed and shallow drafted for beach landings. We took comfort from the belief that we rode too high for submarine torpedoes to hurt us. Probably just wishful thinking.]

Those of us on this detached service detail went on to Bayonne, New Jersey, last Sunday and were shown a small craft anchored there. Brown took one look at the thing and announced confidently that it would be the tug for taking us out to the troop ship for our transport overseas. Hah! We're still on it, tiny as it is. We are also several hundred pitching, rolling, rocking, shaking, vibrating, cacophonous seasick miles from the U.S.A. Fact is, we're now in quite a beautiful harbor and no more than half a mile or so from a picturesque group of islands. We're still on our "tug," have come through some mighty rough seas, and are likely headed for some more as this is our "transport." Brown has naturally taken a good deal of kidding about his first impression of our ship.

Our trip to the port of embarkation was cold and wet and our introduction to our clean, warm, dry stateroom a welcome one. The ship is new and we're quite comfortable even if a little crowded. I did have trouble staying in my bunk the first two nights but have solved the problem. The bunk is a leather-covered studio couch with my mattress thrown on top of it. The leather is slick, allowing no traction for stabilizing my mattress. With each lurch and roll of the ship, my bedclothes, mattress, and I would all hit deck kerplunk! The solution was simply to turn the leather side of the couch cushion down. Now my mattress rests on the rough burlap undercover and can't slide. Stupid of me not to have thought of it sooner.

The only man on our ship who has ever been out of sight of land is our captain. None of the sailors have been to sea before. So by the end of the first day out, a good eighty-five percent of those aboard were seasick. Turnbow and I are among the few who have not upchucked so far, but when the ship rolls I never know whether I'll make it for another minute or not. And the green color that you've always heard about actually exists on those afflicted. Their faces turn the most nauseating aquamarine you ever saw, and they pray for just any sort of catastrophe to overtake the ship and get them out of their misery. Now I can't understand why any but a sadist would consider it so, but there seems to be something very funny about a poor devil who is seasick. Miserable as the victims are, they all laugh at whoever is heaving when they are not. Thus, the fun is rampant in rough weather, and Turnbow slithers around those providing it, bragging that his freedom from the curse is undoubtedly due to the clean, exemplary life he's always led—"ever since early childhood," he says.

It was yesterday afternoon when we ran out of the foul weather and into this semitropical climate. I came out of all my heavy underwear and walked the decks, a new man. Saw my first sundown on the ocean, where one can see the horizon clear around the compass. It was an experience in beauty—an indigo ocean as far as you could see, punctuated here and there by the ships of this convoy, and a lighter blue sky meeting the ocean eight miles or so all around. There were just enough clouds in the east to color up and reflect in the water. North and south of the sun, near the horizon, there were little islands of clouds that took on a brilliance in all conceivable colors. Most impressive!

And speaking of colors, the ship's wake seen from the stern is quite pretty. It is always there—fifty feet wide and a couple of hundred feet long—a healthier looking aquamarine than the faces of most of the men.

Today about 3:30 those on deck could see two misty looking knolls of land way past the east horizon. Some three hours later the sea became smooth. Its color changed from indigo to a deep sky blue. Color films do not exaggerate this color at all. The knolls of land became several small islands whose west coasts must be thirty feet high. Dwarf cedars and a few fir trees are seen and in the distance, of all things, a railroad. Various buildings are there also. And we're at anchor, all hoping we'll be here long enough to go ashore.

APRIL 19, 1943. By my time it's 9:30 P.M., but you and Suzanne may at this moment be watching the sun go down. Old Pappy would very much enjoy watching it with you, but there'll be time for that someday in the future.

We went swimming today in the prettiest place you ever saw, although the water was a bit chilly. After the swim we enjoyed a sun bath in the comfortable warm air. Had a fine time all in all.

Our activities are somewhat different from what they were when you were on hand. But our duties are exactly as they were when we got back from training maneuvers, if you will recall. [We did not have duties.]

APRIL 20, 1943. Bermuda. We were allowed ashore for five hours today. Learned that tourism is the island's chief industry and that no automobiles are allowed. The only store open today was a typically American Rexall drug store. I couldn't have done any shopping, anyway, as my total assets are the same as the day I left the States: $4.80.

Lots of lush flowers here; also lots of bicycles. Nasturtiums grow wild on the vacant lots, climbing any trees about like vines. All residents catch their own water from elaborate guttering on the rooftops. There are 35,000 inhabitants and ten doctors. Food for a family of three costs about eighty-five dollars per month, and a day laborer is paid about three dollars a day. There are no property taxes and no income taxes.

APRIL 22, 1943. We have practice alarms each day so we'll know what to do in case of a submarine attack. Each doctor is assigned a certain area of the ship, and Jabez Galt and I have the wardroom as our area. We are lucky, for we can talk or read until "all secure" is sounded.

On a typical day now that we are back at sea, the navy mess attendant wakes us up at 7:30, and we jump out of bed feeling like a million dollars, sure that we've whipped all trace of seasickness from our midriffs. Starting breakfast, we soon find that less has been whipped than we thought, and we all hurry to the rail where nothing really happens after all. For as soon as the view of the horizon confirms the fact that it isn't really rocking, our sickness leaves. There being no place to sit, we stand and fight the ship's rocking for a couple of hours. By then, we're so tired we go on warily back to our bunks. Having learned that lying flat on the back is about as effective an antinauseant as looking at the horizon, we stay put until noon and then go to the mess feeling okay. All nausea having departed, we go back on deck for a bit in the afternoons but must alternate between there and our bunks. By night, midriffs are all behaving again, and we spend the evenings in the wardroom where we read, play cards, or just talk. By 10:30, everyone except that lucky Turnbow is sick again. While he grins, muttering his refrain about clean living, the rest of us go back to bed. After much consultation we've decided Turnbow has a brain tumor that has destroyed his vestibular apparatus. We're trying to sell him on the idea of signing his own autopsy permit so we may document our conclusions. We just might perform that autopsy before his actual demise, too.

APRIL 26, 1943. Yesterday was Easter Sunday, the event being marked by a few more than the usual clean shaves.

We must be about in the middle of the Atlantic, and our time is now three hours ahead of yours.

Morale is pretty high, although we've no idea where we're headed or if we'll ever see the Baylor Unit again. Our only orders are the ones sending us to Bayonne, New Jersey, with which we've already complied. So now we're without current orders. As far as any of us knows, we'll not land at the same port as the rest of the outfit. We don't even know if they've left New York. While it does seem logical that we'd rejoin the same unit, logic isn't always what determines army commands.

APRIL 30, 1943. Ah, ha. We'll stay in our bunks today. It's cloudy and windy outside and the sea is rough. To go out on deck would be to risk going overboard, an irreparable catastrophe should it ever happen.

Did I say earlier that our stateroom was of ample size as well as new and clean? Do strike out any such intimations at once! My, my, my. How a man's viewpoint "do change" from time to time. And how bed linen "do change" after being wallowed upon eighteen to twenty hours per day without being laundered for seventeen days. [I'd likely not have been so scandalized had I known I was to sleep for two whole years in the same sleeping bag without its being laundered.]

And now the roar of the ship's motors have been in our ears day and night for the past eleven days, sounding for all the world like a fast train. One gets enough of it and enough of the swaying, rocking, and lurching. Jabez Galt says the distance from New York to anywhere across the Atlantic is an even thirteen thousand miles—three across, and ten up and down.

Practically everyone is growing a beard, and they don't really look as bad as you might think. I'm not growing one.

I've read *Oliver Wiswell, Popular Mechanics, The Unvanquished,* and countless "who-dunnits." One is the story of George Washington in which the author let him swear more heartily than one would expect from such a naive general. You know he did issue a general order to his army forbidding swearing, and that was naive.

MAY 4, 1943. A smooth sea again for the first time in a week. It's a fine world again.

The ship's orders have been changed three or four times in the past twenty-four hours, but we're expecting to reach a North African port before midnight. Nobody seems to know which port, nor do we know if our detail from the Baylor Unit will disembark if we get there. We still have no orders.

Being thankful as I am that we're so near land and a steady deck, I hate to inject a sour note. Still, I've not commented heretofore on the water supply aboard this ship. It is an outstanding item woven into the trip.

At the beginning of our journey, the water was relatively clear and tasted only a little like diesel fuel. Now it looks like orange juice and tastes like a glue factory's worst nightmare. As the days went by and the tanks rusted, the ship's vibratings and rollings kept the sides washed off and homogenized into the drinking water. None of us can drink half as much of the stuff as we should, so we're dehydrated and eternally thirsty. Had we only known, we could have brought bottled drinks or plain bottled water aboard instead of all those cheap cartons of Mars Bars, Snickers, and cigarettes. Incidentally, the latter only cost us forty-eight cents per carton, and the candy thirty-four cents for twenty-four bars. And no, we won't care for either type candy bar for some time. Thanks anyway!

What do you know? I went out on deck just now to see why we weren't moving, and I find we're anchored about two miles offshore opposite a very modern looking city about the size of Dallas. Such things as grain elevators, skyscrapers, and paved streets give evidence of a modern metropolis. I'm afraid the only impressions of Africa that I've carried since elementary school days have been of lions, tigers, and cannibals. The people who built this city haven't worn ornaments made from human bones in many generations. Neither have they fought with bow and arrow and spear. In fact, somebody around here has been fighting with sophisticated weaponry because over there to our right is a battleship with a large hole in its hull just above the waterline. It lists badly, and I believe I make out the name *Jean Bart* on her bow. This would identify her as French, scuttled by a loyal crew to keep her out of the hands of the Germans.[1]

Maybe our voyage is over. You may believe me—I hope so.

MAY 4, 1943 [second letter]. After a singularly uneventful trip, they say now that we're headed for a harbor that nobody has ever heard of. We may or may not leave the ship there. We expect to reach the port before midnight.

Referring to our trip as uneventful is true enough, only because we failed to encounter the dangers that might have been realistically looked for. In all other respects, it has been eventful enough to satisfy the inexperienced colonial-types that all of us certainly are. I have enough material to write a novel based upon it, I'm sure. I could either title the work "How Green Was My Voyage" or paraphrase Coleridge with "Water, Water Everywhere and Every Drop Did Stink"—and it wasn't the seawater that stank, but the drinking water. A sort of running account of the trip will be mailed to you later.

---

[1] The city was Casablanca and the French battleship was the *Jean Bart*, the newest warship in the French navy, which had never been completed and was unable to move from her berth. In Operation Torch, during the invasion of Casablanca by (then) Major General George S. Patton, Jr.'s, Western Task Force on November 8, 1942, the *Jean Bart* opened fire on the U.S. fleet with her four 15-inch guns, and was severely damaged and disabled by return fire from the battleship USS *Massachusetts*.

CASABLANCA 2
May 1943

MAY 8, 1943. We're ashore at last, and you'll never know how glad I was to find the unit, and with it six letters from my girls. I've fared very well, but my last letter was dated April 12. I'm already looking forward—more than you know—to whatever distant date finds me retracing my steps back home.

In spite of rumors and semiofficial notices to the contrary, we stayed in the first harbor approached for three days and nights. It was Casablanca, Morocco, and we were awakened the last night on board and told we'd disembark at 3:00 A.M. It was 5:30 before we actually walked down the gangplank, and that to the accompaniment of "God Bless America," sung by the beautiful voice of Kate Smith. With that rare insight as to how to best disturb army men—an insight given navy men in any situation—our erstwhile shipmates had put this recording on the ship's loudspeaker. Luckily, we couldn't get to them to deliver just retribution. Our eyesight had suddenly become too dim to find them, and we couldn't swallow well, either.

So in addition to those deliberately placed lumps in our throats, I'm sure we stepped onto the African continent with all of the misgivings any soldier might have had. For how were we to realize that all of the fighting we'd been hearing and reading about was taking place far to the east? The few soldiers we saw on shore did nothing to reassure us with their shouts of, "You'll be sorry!"

At 10:00 A.M., after sitting around on our luggage for five hours, a truck with a familiar driver came for us, and we learned the Baylor Unit was bivouacked, having arrived days earlier. Such a relief! We were tickled to death to finally see all of our own personnel, and they seemed even more glad to see us. F. J. Sebastian has just come in to bring me greetings from Dr. Leslie Sadler of Waco whom he'd run into in the city. Gee, we're all purring like kittens.

MAY 9, 1943. Camp Don B. Passage outside Casablanca. Here it is Mother's Day and I've no way to help Suzanne let you know we appreciate you, 'tho I'll be thinking about you all day—same as every day—plus a little bit more. I went to chapel this morning and was proud of the chaplain for not dwelling on sentimentalities even if this is the day for it. I find that a man's emotions stay pretty close to the surface under present circumstances and was proud our chaplain didn't take advantage of the fact.

The country around here is becoming Americanized pretty rapidly. Martinak, Merrick, and I went into town to the Red Cross show the other night, and as we left, a little ten-yearish Arab fell into step with us. He started singing "Souse of zee border" after the same manner of Bing Crosby and knew the words very well if not their proper pronunciation. His face lighted up as he saw the appreciation on ours and he did his utmost. Considering that we enjoyed him as much as we did seeing Leslie Howard in *Mister V*, the franc we each gave him was a gross underpayment. I'm sure we'll remember the boy longer than we do *Mister V*. Most of the little boys are picking up quite an English vocabulary although American obscenity seems to be what they learn the quickest and handle the best. Slang idioms seem to catch on, too, and we're told "Heigh ho, Silver!" rings out from Arab throats all over North Africa.

So far, the climate is quite fine. The temperature probably goes up into the low nineties during the day but drops quickly after sundown. I judge it gets into the fifties at night. I don't know what it is like the rest of the year, but May is mighty fine.

The soil here is red sand—not as red as that at Natchitoches, Louisiana, but redder than some. It seems productive enough to prevent hunger. It has rained once since my arrival three days ago, and oddly enough our bivouac area was not muddy for more than an hour.

I believe I told you we are living in tents, expecting to move on in the near future. We expect to head in the same direction that you take in going to Auntie Yard's and for a distance roughly three times that from your house to Jeanette's and back. [Such cryptic references to directions and distances was to circumvent censoring.]

Life here is just as convenient and just as comfortable as it was at Fort Jessup, Louisiana, last summer. If you and Suzanne were living in the nearby city, I'd like it better than Camp Shanks. The country is much more interesting, and we could eat our weekly meal out at Rick's American Cafe. [Still trying to identify our location. A film featuring Bogart and Bacall and called *Casablanca* had Bogart operating a cafe called Rick's American.] The one night I've been to town I did go to a French cafe, and the food was very good.

Food is perhaps not as plentiful here as it once was before the war, although for only twenty francs (forty cents) I had excellent fish, boiled potatoes, and a tart dessert that belied its cottage cheese appearance. There was all we could want, served family-style at our table set for three. The food we have at camp is just like that on maneuvers except the meat is much better. We get plenty of canned green food, and today we had locally grown green beans. We can only get three cartons of cigarettes per month at the local PX along with candy bars and toilet goods. We can't get any stationery. I should tell you, the franc is worth two cents in American money.

Barring the flora, fauna, and natives, this country looks exactly like parts of central Texas. It is gently rolling with fifty and one hundred-acre cereal crops interspersed with pastureland. There are no fences, and herds of scrubby black-faced sheep are herded along with scrubby looking Jersey cows by one or two Arab men aided by eight or ten youngsters of varying ages. Eucalyptus trees line a nearby blacktopped road. Their trunks look like sycamores, but the leaves look just like willow trees. They apparently thrive as well here as in Australia from whence they came. Palms are scattered here and there, and fig trees are actually large trees here. I also see what I believe are mesquite trees as well as some cactus that looks like prickly pear. Thistles grow three and four feet tall in the barley fields but not as thick as the brick-red poppies. Although the grain is still green, it is being harvested by hand with small sickles just like in Bible times.

These natives! It's downright hard to believe they are descendents of the race that conquered so much of the world in the seventh century. Did the ancestors of filthy, thieving pariah such as we see around here actually give us our system of numerals and invent algebra? Did they establish those universities that started the Renaissance in Europe? If what we're seeing are actual descendents of the Arabs, their ancestors certainly did all of those things. Of course, what we're calling Arabs just might be Berbers, whose origin and heritage remain a mystery. It seems both races occupy this area and may be hybridized beyond differentiation. Could be.

Never have I seen human beings so filthy. Their clothing looks like the movie version and is apparently of coarsely woven white or striped wool. Invariably, it looks greasy and dirty. Then some wear modifications of Europe garb, also dirty. Finally, a very hilarious modification is frequently seen, which combines Eastern garb above the waist with a GI barracks bag below. Leg holes are cut in the bottom of the bag, and its drawstring serves as a belt. A lot of natives are seen wearing these, and some American soldier's name and serial number is always emblazoned across the wearer's seat. I know of no way to tell whether these bags identify a native thief or an American culprit who bartered off his barracks bag for a couple of eggs or a night's fling of wine, women, and song.

About half of the men wear shoes, but women and children all go barefooted, and many of the children barebottomed as well. The women are no cleaner than the men and most wear the traditional veil. Many women have distinctive tattoos on their foreheads, which we understand mark them as the property of certain Berber tribes.

The children, always bright but filthy, have heads shaved except for a queue on top. They say this serves as a handle by which Allah pulls them up from sin during their tender years before accountability.

MAY 10, 1943. Money will certainly be no problem here, for there's no place in camp to spend it. I did have to write a check for $22.50 to pay my mess bill aboard ship. I wrote it on the Alvin State Bank where I last had an account in 1925 while in high school. Please warn them it is coming and see that they honor it.

I won't even have a laundry or cleaning bill, for neither service is available. On the trip over I learned that my wool shirts and trousers don't shrink when washed in cold water. Guess I'll do my own.

MAY 13, 1943. Baby, I didn't get to write yesterday because my duties took me into the nearby city where I patrolled the streets from 8:00 A.M. until 9:30 P.M. I was glad to observe our soldiers by and large are a fine lot and in excellent spirits. My assignment was of a policing nature, and I had to patrol until I had arrested ten paratroopers. They were in town on furlough after participating in the victorious battles of Kasserine Pass and Mateur in Tunisia. Their entire unit had been brought back to a rest area nearby, and all whom I arrested were sent back to their company commanders with revoked passes. Such a duty for a medical officer without military police training of any sort seems pretty farfetched, but the commander of the Atlantic base section ordered all local medical units to provide junior officers for the purpose.

Perhaps these paratroopers have been causing trouble for the commanding general, base section—I don't know. What I do know is that this particular base section demands considerable "spit and polish" of the type American soldiers generally resent. I also know that coming unscathed through an encounter with the enemy entitles them to a type of euphoria beyond the comprehension of those of us who don't experience such encounters. Our orders, nevertheless, were to arrest even for such minor infringements of discipline as a shirt unbuttoned at the neck or pocket flaps unbuttoned, as well as for major ones. The general evidently surmised such a duty would be distasteful for medical officers. He thwarted our overlooking minor infringements with the order to walk the streets until ten arrests were made. But I'm just going to keep walking them if ordered onto them again, until I see ten major infringements. [Of course, the above was considerably edited by me as I wrote it, for such things would have been censored in 1943.]

The streets are full of urchins—Arabs, I guess. They'll do anything to attract one's attention in hopes of getting a tip from "les Americaines." About half of them do this by pulling your sleeve and coming out with: "Me spik Mellican, see: scram, sonny bitch, he, he. See, me spik Mellican!" Such speech seems utterly without guile, and I believe the words are uttered in the belief that they constitute a flattering greeting. I'd like to bet that the original urchin who was taught that bit was primed by some GI who then pointed out an officer for the kid to pull it on. I could hope the officer might have been the base commander. It's rather startling upon hearing it the first few times.

I do wish I could watch Suzanne enjoy the sandpile along with pulling Tige's tail. I guess you won't spoil her too much, so go right ahead.

MAY 14, 1943. My manuscript came across the Atlantic for a minor correction today and will be approved for publication by the surgeon general. Mallory had damned it with the faint praise that it was well typed when I first submitted it, but palpable changes in attitude have attended the surgeon general's approval.

Bowyer and I worked on our tent floor and furnishings all morning and improved our home a lot. After leveling the dirt corrugated by last year's corn rows, we wet the entire mess down, temporarily settling the eternal dust by which we're blessed. It's quite livable now. White and Johnson will be surprised when they return from their tour of duty patrolling the streets. Johnson, who is hounded by few compulsions, kids Bowyer and me for demanding that things be "symmetrical." It has become a byword with all of us.

MAY 15, 1943. Yesterday, twenty of us took a trip to a good swimming place about an hour's drive from here. [Port Lyautey, where the first American landings were made.] We all thought it a beautiful place and enjoyed the swim a great deal. After a swim and a ball game, we went to a resort hotel and got the best meal I've had since leaving home. The cost for round steak, French fries, soup, wine, and some sort of marmalade dessert was $2.50. The wine, rum, cognac, and champagne around here are pretty terrible, and we'll not likely intoxicate ourselves on them even if so inclined. The waiters all apologize for it, saying the Germans confiscated the better grades along with their food, clothing, beef stock, and mares, and sent all to Germany. Still, they absolutely will not serve water with their meals. They seem to have as great an aversion to drinking it as the Arabs have for bathing in it. [We were to learn to be wary of native wines. They might not taste too bad but were said to contain hashish—cannabis sativa—and certainly had sudden and peculiar intoxicating qualities. The only time we became aware of this was once while leisurely drinking at the local Automobile Club, which had been confiscated for army use. Nothing happened until we got up to go and everyone's knees buckled. This seemed particularly hilarious at the time, and everyone laughed his way from dignified sobriety into a reeling drunkenness within a matter of two or three minutes. The intoxication lasted for an hour or two after we got back to camp and didn't do anything to endear us to our commanding officer.]

The following bit of doggerel is from a song the enlisted men are singing here. It is the only lyric I've heard that isn't too naughty to write down:

Dirty Gertie from Bizerte
Placed a mousetrap 'neath her skirty
Just above her kneecap purty;
Baited it with Fleur d'Flirty;

Made her boyfriend's fingers hurty.
Now the people of Bizerte
Have elected Dirty Gertie
Miss Latrine of 1930.

MAY 20, 1943. Whee! I'm tired and dirty and can't get a bath for two more hours. We're rationed and can only take three baths a week, and then only at specified hours. The officers played the enlisted men a game of baseball and beat them twelve to seven, much to our surprise. The unsettling thought has just this minute crossed my mind that we'd likely let a bunch of colonels and generals beat us worse than that! I guess it was really on the up-and-up, for we held them eleven to nothing until the last inning. Either the stamina of youth or their legitimate effort returned to give them those seven runs at the end of the game. Old Pappy got lucky once when the bases were loaded and brought two men in instead of striking out. Great fun. Great fun to be paid for with sore muscles for the next few days.

MAY 21, 1943. This is the third straight day with no mail. We never accord those days without mail with our recently acquired expression of approval, "symmetrical." Probably a stack of mail will come in a day or two, and the day will again become symmetrical. We hope. Morale always skyrockets on such days, as I've told you before. Johnson is over in a corner purring like a kitten in his enjoyment of a shave Bowyer is giving him. I enjoy those two very much.

I played volleyball yesterday with borrowed equipment, which a neighboring unit loaned us. They packed up and moved out last night, cancelling out any game for today. Maybe that's just as well, for most of us get pretty sore. At that, the games don't make us as sore as did the job of patrolling the streets in town the other day.

We saw a newsreel last night in one of the public theaters in town. I was struck by the reception the audience gave it, for it was a unique experience for us. About two dozen people clapped halfheartedly along at the first when pictures were shown of American Rangers in training. Then, about half of the audience clapped when pictures were shown of Canadian Air Cadets. But the audience went wild with applause when flashes of the British Eighth Army came on the screen. Of course, Montgomery's Eighth Army has been tenaciously pressing Rommel's Afrika Korps and with considerable publicity for some months now. Rommel has been defeated and pushed out regardless of who came to help, and the victory here will certainly be credited to Montgomery. One gets the impression that the local Europeans would just about as soon not have an American expeditionary force in their midst, but I don't know.

MAY 24, 1943. Several of us are planning to visit the Sultan's palace at Rabat this afternoon. Will tell you about it later.

We now have a new APO number 464, in care of the Postmaster in New York. Maybe the new number will straighten out our mail and we hope so. Delivery has been pretty poor. Many of the men have received no mail in more than two weeks and are pretty griped about it. They're moody, too, with wide swings of mood from day to day and even from hour to hour.

MAY 25, 1943. Well, the Sultan's palace is open to the public only on Fridays. We'll have to see it later and hope we're here long enough to get another chance at it.

You'll remember I told you Dr. Sadler was in Casablanca. He and Colonel Carter were classmates in medical school, and their meeting here was accidental. He is chief of surgery at a local station hospital, and I had dinner with him this evening. He reminded me that my brother Charley was best man at his wedding in 1924, a fact I'd forgotten. He also showed me some interesting cases and made me feel pretty much at home.

Still no mail, and we're told all new organizations in the area are having the same trouble.

MAY 26, 1943. I sent you a box of doodads today, but I didn't find anything for Suzanne. The silver pin is locally made and the Arab writing is said to wish the wearer good luck. Maybe when we move I'll be able to find something for little girls, but if they're in this city, I can't find them. I may have to compromise by sending something for a fifteen-year-old to be held until she grows into it. Incidentally, the Hershey box I shipped your things in is the third I've emptied since we got here. I buy twenty-four quarter-pound bars at the PX for forty cents.

Another baseball game today, but no mail for me. Mine came several days ago when the rest of the outfit got none. Thoughtful as always, Martinak let me read one he got from Macy and another from his brother Ernest.

MAY 27, 1943. Turnbow, who is a new father, has gone for more than two weeks without any mail. That sure is hard on him, but one of these mornings he'll get a couple of dozen letters in one batch.

[We had been cautioned never to mention our organization's movements, locations, or activities. My wife Margaret and baby were living with her parents in Brazoria County, Texas, and my sister Jeanette whom I mentioned below, lived some 650 miles to the west. I'd hoped the recent mention of "Dirty Girty" would at least plant the thought in her mind that we might go to Bizerte, a thirteen hundred-mile trip, partly through mountains and necessitating a ten-day truck ride westward. She made out the part that we'd take a trip, but had no idea where we'd go.]

How would you like to take a trip out to Jeanette's and back to see her sister Gertrude? By taking it easy, you could make it in about ten days. The roads are hard surfaced all of the way, and the trip would be a welcome change. I'm sure you'd find Gertrude very interesting. Think it over and let me know what you decide. I don't know if my letters reach you better than yours reach me at this point, but of course there'll be no mail before the end of the trip. Be sure to take warm clothes for the cold nights in the mountains.

MAY 30, 1943. Dallas and Waco papers for May 10 have arrived, confirming earlier news that Baylor will probably move to Houston. We're upset and feel orphaned. We also hold little hope for the school's future if it accepts Houston's offer. That would make it too close to Texas Medical College and a drawback for both of them. With no more population than the area has, they'd have to compete for the available clinical material. All of us are fond of Dean Moursund and fear he may have to preside over the demise of Baylor, and that after inflicting considerable damage to Texas Med's reputation.

JUNE 2, 1943. Am glad you're out to see Gertrude. You'll certainly enjoy the trip and will find Gertrude most interesting. Be sure to look down from those high mountains.

Happy day! I can walk into the post office in the nearby city and buy money orders. Am enclosing one for a Christmas present. Kiss the baby and your mirror.

CONVOY   3
June 1943

JUNE **11, 1943.** I've had quite a nice trip as you may have guessed. I'm so stimulated to tell you all about it that I may tell more than I'm supposed to. Please don't repeat any of it.

That request holds for everything I write, too, because there is no one to censor my mail except myself, and I'm still not too sure what shouldn't be mentioned. Also, you shouldn't divulge any information gathered by reading between my lines. [But the army didn't trust its medical officers as much as we'd been told. This letter had been gone over by a base censor somewhere along the line.]

Historians will probably record that the North African campaign ended along about the time of the fall of Bizerte. Being normally self-centered, I don't hold to that theory. I hold to the theory that the actual beginning of that campaign was on March 31, 1943, when I had to leave home. It got well under way on April 14, 1943, when I left the United States. I've already written to you of the trip across the Atlantic, which might be called Phase I of the campaign.

Phase II deals with Casablanca and Camp Don B. Passage, the staging area nearby. I couldn't write with much enthusiasm of Phase II, for that was one sorry bivouac area if I ever saw one, and that in spite of the nearby city with a population of half a million people.

It is of Phase III that I shall now write, and do remember that when I use the term "I" in describing movements or activities or even impressions, the chances are that my associates' activities and impressions are no different. I simply can't discuss organization activities, for that would be against army regulations.

Phase III did involve a move in the same direction as from Margaret's house to Auntie Pence Yard's [that is, from Alvin to Galveston] and covered the same distance as from Margaret's to Jeanette's and back. The highway was a tribute to French engineering all of the way, and the scenery a tribute to the Creator. Most of my first day's drive was through country typical of that around the staging area and characterized by gently rolling hills, many small truck farms, a few larger grain fields, and more interestingly, quite a large cork oak forest. We saw large stacks of cork oak bark in the small towns before we ever reached the forest. The bales were slightly smaller than bales of hay but looked to be tied by the same sort of baling wire. We also saw camels, burros, trucks, and ox-drawn carts, all bringing in bales of cork.

The forest, when we reached it, turned out to be several miles in width, made up of trees about the size of chinaberries. Green grass growing beneath the trees plus an absence of underbrush made the whole thing look like one very big park. A hilarious difference from any park was that stripping the bark left the tree trunks a pure white below but dark above, making the area remind one of a crowd of well-dressed men whose pants had dropped to their ankles.

Toward the end of the first day, I reached a very typical North African city [Fez] characterized, as most of them are, by an ancient native settlement called the medina, surrounded by a modern European city. In most of the cities, ancient walls built prior to 1000 A.D. surround the medinas. These walls are usually in good condition despite their age. This particular city is more beautiful than most because of its snow white houses built near the top of a rising slope above a fifteen hundred-foot canyon. From our position on the opposite slope, we could look across their red-tiled roofs and see both the European city and the medina. The latter's streets were narrow and crooked, having been designed for pedestrians, but the streets of the newer city were wide and beautiful. Both palm trees and flowers were along the borders everywhere.

The canyon was perhaps as much as six miles across the top but no more than a mile wide below. A river half the size of the Brazos meandered across the floor, its banks lined by oleanders in riotous bloom. These oleanders are along all North African streams so far encountered.

The Arabs seemed unaware of any inconveniences in cultivating the steep canyon walls and had right good-looking wheat growing on them from top to bottom. Some symmetrical patches had been cut over and were brown while some were still green, and others, ripe but not yet cut, were golden. Squares, rectangles, and triangles in the colors mentioned gave the impression of looking down across a huge canvas on which the geometrical designs had been painted. It made quite an impressive sight for this flatlander. [I do imagine the French residents rather than the Arabs were the motivating force behind North African agriculture, although Arabs or Berbers—we never learned to distinguish between them—did most of the labor.]

Leaving the valley, I crossed semiarid to actual desert for the next several days, making camp the first night just east of another typically walled, ancient Arab city [Meknes]. I can't really describe it, but then there's no need for me to try. It looked exactly like those you've seen so many times in the movies dealing with the French Foreign Legion. Its ancient wall was probably two miles to the side, twenty feet high, and three to five feet thick. There were five rows of narrow, slitted peepholes all along the walls, no doubt originally used to shoot arrows through, defending the city. Beyond the walls I spotted the domes of eight mosques rising above all other visible structures. Near one corner of the nearest wall was an immense gateway, which had been framed by wide mosaics of multicolored tiles. It was wide open, and through it I could see a narrow, winding street, which was soon blocked from view by ancient buildings. Whether a camel caravan was emerging as I drove past is immaterial, for no American eyes are likely to behold that gateway without either a real or an imagined caravan coming through it. Arabs were passing in and out and could also be seen in groups on the streets inside. They also look like the movie versions, except that movie directors neglect to put the lifetime accumulation of filth on their clothing and skin. Neither have movie directors obtained burros as small as the ones here. Without such small burros, it is impossible to visualize the ridiculousness of a tall, dignified Arab holding his legs parallel to the ground and his feet forward of the beast's shoulders as the poor thing trots along. Very tough and very useful are those tiny beasts hereabouts.

And I don't recall a movie showing a tall, solemn Arab mounted as above and followed at a respectful distance of two or three paces by two or three wives, who either walk or trot along on foot as the occasion may demand. Neither do movies show enough youngsters around Arab settlements. One is tempted to say that they are as thick as flies, but for one who has been in French restaurants in North Africa, such an exaggeration places too much license even upon the poetic. They are thick though—Arab children—and quite intelligent looking under the dirt. They are just dressed in any sort of rags or in nothing at all; it doesn't seem to matter.

Before leaving tall Arabs, wives, and burros, a digression is in order to recount that sometimes a wife is on the burro with the tall Arab walking alongside and another wife or two walking behind. In this case, the eyes seen looking over the woman's veil seem very young and very bright, and intuition suggests that perhaps you are beholding a honeymoon trip. Less romantic and more professional intuition then counters that it's more likely a pregnant wife who rides. Hang it all! You've no way to find out. You can't even stop and ask someone—not that your French 101 and 102 equipped you with a vocabulary equal to the task.

Not many days after starting our trip, we crossed an international frontier and entered a country that has profited by more than a century of French rule. This is in contrast to only thirty-five years of French rule in the first country. This second one is everywhere beautiful beyond the imagination and developed far beyond the first. Aside from the natural beauty, my interests lie in the agricultural crops and methods and the people whose living depended on them. The crops were grapes, wheat, barley, rye, tomatoes, beans, onions, corn, olives, oranges, apricots, apples, cherries, tobacco, flax, almonds, potatoes, soap lilies, and a few others I could not identify. Livestock was plentiful, and in contrast to that left by the Germans elsewhere, was fine looking. Hogs, cattle, horses, mules, sheep, and goats were plentiful, but there were fewer camels and burros.

Remembering how, as a boy during World War I, we were denied bread in order to send wheat to the French and other allies, I was soon irritated at all of the vineyards. Indeed, the greatest acreage in this French colony so near to France is planted in grapes. I estimated that several vineyards contained as many as a thousand acres, on land that could produce wheat and other foodstuffs. They moved the chaplain to preach a sermon based on the parable of the true vine, but moved me to condemn their wine-taking priority over a need for food. [I don't recall that any Algerian asked my opinion on the matter and will have to admit the vineyards were beautifully cared for and no doubt furnished adequate revenue for buying someone else's wheat.]

Agricultural methods in this country combine the ancient with the modern, but I believe the modern predominates. While oxen are more plentiful than trucks, tractors, or mules, they nevertheless pull modern disc plows, binders, and combines. They are also used by being driven over and over great stacks of grain sheaves, the most ancient of draft-animal thrashing methods. I don't remember seeing any old-fashioned thrashers but did see one modern combine.

The combine I saw was tractor-drawn and harvesting one area of a field at the same time hundreds of Arab women were harvesting another. All of the women were stooped over—some of them harvesting with small sickles, some cutting, and others gleaning—just as Ruth and Naomi did in the time of Boaz. Of course, modern machinery could not be used in some of the steep fields we saw.

The truck crops mentioned before were not only raised in kitchen gardens but in large fields as well. All are irrigated and well cared for; so are the fruit orchards. Some vineyards and some grain fields were also irrigated.

Fences in the area seem scarce indeed, and barbed wire such as we have is not seen. Such fences seen around small truck farms may simply consist of rows of either reeds or prickly pear, while a few of stone or concrete exist here and there. Large open ranges do not exist and would likely prove most impractical if they did, stealing natives driving off any unattended livestock within an hour. Wherever one sees livestock, it is being herded by a bunch of little Arab children to protect the crops. The children themselves are watched by an adult or two. An exception to this herding by children is seen in the mountains and on the rough terrain. In such areas, the plenteous herds of sheep and goats are under the watchful care of adult shepherds, all carrying a crooked stick as did their common ancestor Abraham.

The war would be over and Suzanne fretting over the absurdity of learning her ABCs before I could adequately describe the peoples I've seen. Maybe I can set down a few impressions. There are Europeans everywhere, but they are the "haves" attending to business and much less obvious than the have-nots. They live in nice to pretentious homes, drive good stallions and mares hitched to good buggies, and are clean and well dressed. In the large cities they do tend to mind their own business, paying little attention to us. In rural areas, as in our own, people are more cordial, stopping to watch us pass, holding up two fingers in Churchill's "V for victory" sign. The "haves" do not ask for "bom boms," and if displeased with our being here, are better actors than any in Hollywood. They have plastered posters of Mr. Roosevelt all over the country along with printed posters of De Gaulle's "Un seul but—la Victorie" ["Only one goal—Victory"]. They have also scrawled such graffiti as "Vive les Americaines" in many conspicuous places. The Arabs hereabouts? Well, whatever an American says about them is probably as wrong as what a Frenchman might say about Mississippi blacks if he should take a three-day trip across that state. The better class surely exists. One sees their homes in some cities, and the medinas were certainly not built by have-nots. But all in all, the natives seen by a soldier are pretty disgusting. They certainly couldn't give a hang who wins this war, and they try to ingratiate themselves to strangers for a few "bom boms." The things they'll do for a bit of candy include holding up a "V" for victory, saying, "Me spik Mellican; me Kamerad; me friend; gimme bom bom." Smiling all the while and gesticulating grotesquely, they may throw an obscenity at you whose meaning they're bound not to understand. Finally—and I've no idea why—they throw open their clothes where they certainly should not. One is vaguely reminded of the whipped dog who rolls over on his back, limp pawed, as his dominant animal snarls at him but no longer attacks him. And wherever convoys stop, they swarm down trying to sell all manner of items, mostly fresh fruit, vegetables, or eggs. By our standards, all of these are exorbitantly priced. For example, eggs go for as much as ten cents each.

We still don't know for sure how to differentiate the Berbers from the Arabs, but we think maybe Berbers are lighter skinned. It is said they were here before any invaders, even before Phoenicians or Romans. If I am really identifying them, there are many tribes, each differing a bit from all the others. In the cities they are among the have-nots, but in mountainous areas too rugged for exploitation I believe they are the haves. In one of these areas, they came out on the mountainside to sell us cherries in pretty baskets that looked awfully good. I couldn't stop, but a group of nurses did. A couple of them handed their money down to the hucksters only to see it disappear up the mountainside as fast as the legs of a small Berber burdened by two dollars and two baskets of cherries could carry him. An enlisted man, more wary than the nurses, got a hand on a basket before relinquishing his money. He was smart enough to get a basket, but it was filled with leaves and a single layer of cherries that hid them. The onlooking Berbers obviously enjoyed these two incidents, or so I'm told. Do remember these hucksters were children and youths aged about six to fifteen years, but those ages are mostly what a soldier sees.

It is too bad that my companion on the trip could not have been a Kenneth Roberts or Da Vinci or at least a camera addict with plenty of color film. I tell you frankly, it was so beautiful in spots that it would not only take your breath but put a lump in your throat and tears in your eyes as well. Aw, I must have been homesick 'cause how could anything have been that beautiful under ordinary circumstances? These mountains aren't as high as the Rockies, probably never more than a mile above sea level. This only made them more beautiful since there was no timberline, the trees becoming larger and thicker as one got higher and higher.

Winding up one hairpin turn after another, our narrow road jutted just far enough from the mountainside to allow two trucks to pass uncomfortably. A driver's discomfort is aggravated by the knowledge that neither an embankment nor a bannister stands between him and a sheer drop of a thousand or so feet in many areas along the way. Sergeant Liggett and I took two-hour shifts at driving, and the driver was always too intent on that to look at the scenery. But the passenger was also so intent on the scenery that he never noticed what the driver might be doing. Two hours in either position were quite enough, and our exchanges of duty were always welcome.

Fortunately, I was a passenger rather than a driver just as we reached the top of one particular segment of the mountains. Emerging across the divide, we could look down for perhaps fifteen or twenty miles on the other side from whence we'd come. It was at this spot that a narrator or an artist might have enabled himself to create such a masterpiece as would justify a lifetime of effort. It was also at this spot that I became more chagrined at not having cooperated better with the many teachers who tried to help me master the English language. From where we were, that particular valley looked like a miniature of itself, fashioned to perfection in detail and color. Being a gently rolling valley, the near side of each slope was presented to the eye as a picture on a colored page. The farms grew only wheat and grapes; but the gold of ripe grain, the green of the unripe patches, the tan of stubble, the brown and black of plowed plots, and the gray strata of rocks here and there, all against the blue sky, made a striking picture indeed. Still, not many would ever believe the reality of such a picture.

Liggett and I had other experiences than just viewing the scenery, and I'd better tell you about one of them. He happened to be driving one day, slowly as it happened, when he came to a hairpin turn. He started to make his turn when, guess what? His steering wheel spun loosely in

Convoy from Casablanca to Bizerte, 1300 miles through Africa, summer 1943.

his hand, but that heavy truck just kept going straight ahead toward the sharp drop-off over the edge. Slamming on all the brakes he had, all six wheels stopped turning and slid for ten seconds or so, which seemed like a lifetime. We stopped with our front wheels less than a foot from the drop-off, scared stiff, and in a cold sweat.

We found that whoever had assembled our truck had left the cotter pin out of a very important bolt in our steering apparatus. The bolt had vibrated its way out, allowing the tie rod to come loose from the drag link. If all that sounds too technical, just remember that when tie rod and drag link are firmly bolted together, the driver and his guardian angel steer the truck. When they come loose, only the guardian angel can steer. Our angel did very well, and the anticlimax to the experience was that we had to wire tie rod and drag link together and proceed another ten miles over mountain roads and fifty miles of coastal plains to a base truck maintenance shop for repairs.

Another anticlimax resulted from our separation from the convoy, for no clearly marked route led us back to the main highway. Liggett could speak only English, and my French wasn't serving us at all satisfactorily as we sought directions. Switching to my high school Spanish, I found I was understood by practically everyone I tried it on, and I could understand them enough to get back on the right road. This little vignette had taken place in Algeria, not far from Spain.

On the last day of the trip we crossed another frontier, entering a country that had recently seen war. Just before reaching it, we came to a large city that looked more Turkish than those we'd seen before. I'm unfamiliar with the history but was surprised to learn the city bore the name of a Roman ruler of the Christian era [Constantine]. We drove through without stopping, after driving over a bridge that spanned an unbelievably deep, narrow gorge. As we moved on, we met a group of Italian prisoners just outside the city who were being marched toward it. Their shoes were tattered, but they were otherwise well dressed. They also looked well fed and seemed pretty happy. As a matter of fact, they looked like they might have come off of almost any American campus a few weeks before, outfitted as they were. A few miles farther on, we met truckloads of German prisoners, also headed toward the city. I don't know why the Italians were walking while the Germans rode, and many of our companions were angry that the positions were not reversed. Some were angry at the Germans for looking so cocky—fully as cocky as our own average paratrooper or pilot. They did look like Americans and were quite young. They seemed to smile at us tolerantly rather than belligerently as we passed by.

It was near the end of my trip that I saw the first evidence of actual fighting having taken place [between Constantine and Mateur]. At first, there were only a few scattered, burned, or overturned trucks, but more and more evidence of war appeared as we proceeded. Barbed wire entanglements were next, along with groups of as many as eight or ten tanks all blown to smithereens. Finally, smashed farmhouses and roadside graves appeared with progressive frequency. Some graves were marked by unlettered white crosses of wood while others were in plots marked by iron crosses bearing German names. Empty gasoline cans were scattered everywhere as were various-sized shells of artillery caliber. Surrounding farms had not been as well cared for as the ones we'd passed earlier. A few bridges had been blown up and hastily replaced by temporary structures that served as well. But actually most of the bridges had not been blown up, and we could go a few miles at times without seeing any more evidence of recent conflict other than the signs on either side of the road reading, "Mines cleared for 20 feet on sides of road."

White-robed Arabs were again dotting the surrounding farms and hills as we passed, just like everywhere else. We concluded they'd probably watched every battle in the area as they were fought, unconcerned as to their outcome. While we'll never know what their thoughts may have been, a reasonable guess might be, "Oh, the inscrutable and silly ways of the infidel!"

The city at the end of my trip [Bizerte] really provided the first glimpse of what a hell this war really is, but even there we had to look twice to grasp what had happened to it. As we approached, it looked about like all of the others except that there were no children in streets that were usually overrun by hundreds. That seemed strange, but no adults could be seen, either, in spite of flowers and shrubbery still green or blossoming in the yards. Then you notice that most—no—all of the windows are broken out. Looking through a window in a wall that looks perfectly sound, you see too, too much light, and you realize there is a big hole in the roof. Checking every roof in sight, you then see not a single one intact. Passing more homes toward the center of the city, you see many have their walls blown out. One large, two-story building has its entire front missing, furniture still in place on slightly sagging floors, upstairs and down. [During one of his shows, Bob Hope, whose troupe came a few weeks later, referred to this as "Bizerte air conditioning."]

Large signs in English warned against pilfering in the city, one reading: "ANY ONE OF THESE MIGHT HAVE BEEN YOUR OWN HOME—PILFERING WILL NOT BE TOLERATED—STEALING IS PILFERING." Since these signs were in English rather than in Arabic or French, I'm sure we all understood to whom they were addressed.

An account of this trip would not be complete without a hurried mention of a few details. Each night was cool, and I spent all of them in my sleeping bag on a folding cot. I had a chance to bathe in some African oued (river) one night, at an artesian well on another, and once in a concrete-lined irrigation ditch. I washed out my clothes at these same places. I witnessed a very impressive cavalry formation at Tiemcen in Algeria. The squadron was native and was mounted on white horses. The men and their French officers were dressed in blue breeches, gray blouses, and red capes and caps. All were carrying sabers and made a very picturesque scene early one morning. I saw many women carrying water on their heads.

I saw an ingenious technique for letting an ox draw water from a well with a leather bag attached to rope and pulley. The ox was penned to a fixed path, letting him move out from the pulley with a full bag of water that automatically dumped into an irrigation ditch at the end of his trail. He'd evidently been trained to respond to the lightened load by backing again to the pulley, the empty bag falling back into the well to refill. The ox repeated the trip time after time. [Later we learned the "ox" was really a water buffalo, blinded by his master to make him docile.]

It was nesting time for the storks. I saw a lot of them in bulky nests on chimney tops. I saw the first rain to fall in this century at Setif in the Sahara Desert.

In conclusion, it might be noted that inexperienced truck drivers in a one hundred-plus truck convoy, led by an inexperienced convoy chief, have difficulty maintaining a proper space between vehicles, both upon entering and leaving towns. Unless every driver can be signaled to make simultaneous slowdowns to a prearranged speed when the lead truck enters a town, each following truck tends to ride hard on the tail of the one ahead. Conversely, after the lead truck resumes speed, those farther back must break rational speeds while still in the city limits. Arabs, having little experience in judging the speeds of motor vehicles bearing down upon them, were sometimes prone to step in front of a vehicle that was moving too fast to stop. A few were killed in this way absolutely unavoidably.

BIZERTE

4

June 1943

JUNE **12, 1943.** Well, we finished our long journey last night and are now in tents, bivouacked near a former permanent Foreign Legion camp of one-story barracks overlooking the sea. They are on a hill that must be seven or eight hundred feet in elevation, not far outside the destroyed city I wrote you about yesterday.

The buildings we are to occupy are undamaged, but have very recently been occupied by German soldiers who left them in the worst mess you can imagine. They had to move out in a hurry it seems. A company of engineers is here helping to get them cleaned up so we can move in quickly.

We are about six blocks from the crest of our hill, and by climbing to the top we get a good view of the surrounding countryside and of the nearby vacated city. We are surrounded by ancient olive trees and by dwarf pines, as well as eucalyptus trees. The latter are much larger than those around Casablanca. Maybe they've been here longer than those along the Atlantic coast.

Contrary to what I'd expected, the surrounding country is quite pretty and is not devastated. It does show a few signs of recent hostility, but numbers of Arabs are busily harvesting wheat while a few French are cultivating vineyards as though nothing had happened.

Camp Nador in Bizerte.

JUNE 15, 1943. I've been pretty busy for a change and haven't had a chance to write. We've been removing the filth from our buildings and then delousing them. They're beginning to look mighty nice, and we'll probably be able to move into our living area by tomorrow. Quarters were assigned from the roster rather than trying to match up previous roommates. Merrick, McClung, Turnbow, White, and I are in a three-room suite with all windows intact, smooth cement floors, and running cold water in a sink. These are certainly the best quarters the army has ever furnished me; too good to be true. Little do we care that our only furnishing will be our cot plus whatever we can scrounge or build. Hot showers are next door, which is also a comfort. Martinak, Fisher, McCauley, and Hahn are together next door; Small, Devereux, Johnson, Bowyer, and Dunlap next to them.

Old Pappy misses his gals more than you'll ever know, honey. Surely things will get better when we get a new APO and can get our mail regularly. Our present average is one mail delivery per month, and I'll tell you now that is far from satisfactory. One of these days they'll drive about three trucks up here, and all of our backlog will be on them. Kiss Suzanne for me.

JUNE 16, 1943. Jack Peyton of Dallas and another major from Boston came by to see us yesterday; so did Frank Connally of Waco. He and Devereux knew each other, but I didn't get to see him. They've all been on tour of detached service here and enjoyed the experience. They've also visited the French Foreign Legion museum at Sidi Bel Abbes, which we passed a week or so ago but could not visit. That museum contains relics from Mexico where the French sent troops to back up Maximilian when he sought to establish a monarchy in which "liberty, equality, and fraternity" would have had no part. They were told the legionnaires enlist for five years and are paid about forty cents a week.

We're still living in our pup tents in the medina, waiting for our quarters to be ready. Even in a twenty-mile wind there is no dust, and that's a welcome relief from Casablanca. We're allowed to name it now in case you hadn't already guessed.

Do you recall the Roman senator Cato who used to end every speech with a statement that a certain North African city must be destroyed? About fifteen of us visited a nearby city Sunday and drove by the site of the ancient ruins. Well, Scipio and Hannibal locked horns there many centuries ago, and Carthage was destroyed—still is. Not much remains except for a few hundred broken marble and stone pillars and a few pedestals and crowns. Oh yes, there is also an original Carthaginian bathtub of stone that once had running water and a drain. All of these wonderful souvenirs are sitting out there on the bald plains with no American tourists chipping them to pieces. Whatever polish the pieces had twenty centuries ago is long gone. The interesting thing to me was the perfect roundness of those very heavy pieces. I think this proves the ancients had a workable lathe of some sort going here.

We also saw olive groves in which every tree had been gnarled and twisted by the cumulative elements of centuries—no telling how many. It's fun to believe and really not too preposterous to assume that these trees had been there for twenty centuries. Be that as it may, whoever planted these trees knew all about straight lines, right angles, and accurate measurements, because they are all equally spaced in all directions so that any four make a perfect square. All of this is in Africa where I'm always shocked to see anything but circus animals, black natives, jungles, and desert. Sure, I knew better after eighteen years of formal schooling, but my provincial mind had never accepted the truth.

JUNE 17, 1943. Five letters came from you today, my first in weeks. One of those was dated April 14—two months and three days ago. Whoever that general was who noticed a connection between the mail received by a soldier and the soldier's morale was smarter than he knew.

I think practically everyone in this organization received mail today, and it certainly did raise the morale around here. Merrick got the first letter he'd had from Mattie in more than a month. He was about frantic before today's postman arrived.

I still don't know if anyone has heard that I arrived in the Casablanca area. You could be spared a lot of anxiety if the mail could be expedited, but don't ever worry about my safety. We're a bit too bulky to get nearer than a safe distance from the front and will always be safe enough.

If your allotment didn't come through in June, I'll try to get a local finance officer to cable in my resignation from the army, or something equally drastic that might get action. Check with the Red Cross for funds if you need them.

We're hoping to get into our quarters in another day or two. The apple of my eye at the moment is a pretty fine clothes cabinet I've built from scrap lumber stacked about. It is six feet tall and will serve the purpose very well. The shallow box I built in San Antonio to roll up in my bed roll was an inspiration, as were the tools I filled it with. I used every tool and could not have done anything without them. I'm sure carpenter's tools will always be at a premium whenever we move, for the unit's carpenters will need all of them at those times.

I'm not the least bit proud of whoever is responsible for our mail being so messed up but can imagine he's some old regular army sot who was given a high commission and the job at the same time just to get him out of the way. Even the regular army is embarrassed by its own sometimes and kicks them upstairs where they won't be seen by the guests. He's likely a medical officer.

JUNE 18, 1943. It's a fine world even if few of us ever leave it alive! For three days in a row we've received mail galore.

I do fine, and so do we all when we can keep busy. We all get homesick when we can't. I get fed up with an army that can't find anything for me to do, and it can't most of the time. We've all discussed this and believe we now know why the soldiers of World War I were so reticent to discuss their experiences. It was not because they'd seen too many horrors but rather because they'd seen so few and were ashamed to admit how bored they'd become.

Hudson Dunlap just came by, and seeing my clothes cabinet, is trying to bribe me into building him one. He is a gem of the finest, and if he can find the lumber, I'll surely build him one. I'm afraid he won't be able to, for our CO has declared the scrap pile off-limits until he's sure the hospital has all it needs.

We've had a twenty-five-mile-per-hour wind for four days now. Fortunately there's no dust in it, but it annoys, nonetheless. Even the chaplain gave a hearty "damn!" last night—sounded like his first as the tune wasn't good.

JUNE 19, 1943. So, it's Emancipation Day and the postman is still overwhelming us. Many of your letters speak of snapshots of Suzanne. Be sure to send along all you can of yourself, too.

A bunch of us went to the beach to swim this afternoon and had a good time. The beach is about a hundred yards long and is clean, smooth sand between a lot of rocks. Nature provided us with a fine freshwater spring coming out of the rocks. I may as well add, she also provided our swimsuits. We have to watch the undertow, which is the strongest I've ever seen, but it is fun. The coldness of African shade was particularly noticeable there, for as long as we remained in the sun, we were perfectly comfortable while wet. In the shade we nearly froze. North Africa really is a cold country with a hot sun, just as we were told.

Baby, I guess I shouldn't build up your hopes, but our table of organization has been changed so that no medical officer has to stay in the rank of lieutenant unless his colonel sees fit not to promote him. I suppose it's not unlikely that all of us will be promoted, but don't get too impatient about it.

Did I tell you one of the most impressive things about the convoy over here was the absolute absence of signboards along the highway? It was striking and might explain why the country was so beautiful.

JUNE 21, 1943. We've moved into our living quarters and have set up our wards. They're by far the best we've ever had in the army. Much better than Camp Joliff on maneuvers, and that was plenty good.

I'm assigned to a team with Dunlap and Devereux again, and that is a pleasure. We have a mess hall, where we sit at tables covered by clean, white sheets and set with tableware, so we don't have to use nor wash mess kits.

JUNE 22, 1943. I haven't done much today. There are eight or ten patients here, but none of them are mine.

The Red Cross brought a sound truck for movies to a beach about a mile from here last night, and a bunch of us went to see it. We have a big truck for transportation and we all pile in and go. The load last night was mostly nurses on the way over. Usually that's bad, for English soldiers have a way of attaching themselves as escorts to nurses, crowding us on the way home. (The CO, you'll remember, was sorry we had nurses in the organization, but he's probably changed his attitude by now. This is a good group and has been no trouble at all, so far.)

The show was one you and I had seen—Barbara Stanwyck and Gary Cooper in *Meet John Doe*. It seemed like a swell show when I saw it with you, but like the other tear-jerkers I see over here, it seemed pretty sticky last night.

You say I've never had to scold Suzanne, but I have and found it wasn't much fun. Don't you remember the time in San Antonio when I spanked her with the yardstick and you told me not to hurt her? It is rough for you to be saddled with all the responsibility for her during these early years. I'm lucky she has a mama who can describe her progress, and I do feel I'm watching her develop just as you are. I'd like to hear some of those phrases you write that she uses.

It doesn't get dark here until ten o'clock at night.

JUNE 25, 1943. I do hate to have to tell you about last night, but since I plan to divulge both the ups and the downs of the Baylor unit, I will try to. I believe I told you we'd moved into our wards. Well, we had. Everyone had identical cots, mattresses, pillows, blankets, and sheets, and all were lined up in two rows on each ward. But it had become obvious that orthopedics needed to be nearer the X-ray and fluoroscope than did medical wards or general surgical wards. It made sense to do some shifting. It also made sense to simply move personnel from location to location without disturbing any of the set up equipment. But guess what happened? You're probably correct as you realize this is the army. Anyway, what somebody in authority did—I'm not at all sure who—was have us move all equipment out of one ward and stack it up outside. Then we had to move the selected ward's equipment into the empty one. This was repeated four more times, moving identical equipment from a set up ward into each succeeding empty one. Finally, the last ward to be emptied was set up with the equipment that had been stacked outside. Two hours it took us, and everybody is about ready to spit in somebody's eye, but we don't know whose.

In spite of hopes for improvement over stupidities endured on maneuvers last summer, it looks like overseas duty will simply be a repetition of them. Morale is so low from one day to the next, it's hard to believe the moods swing by 180° from hour to hour. Do remember this and don't worry about it, but it must be a temporary, situational depression that comes to all of us overseas. I was talking to Merrick about my own introspection on the matter today. He confessed he'd written Mattie that he was a bit worried for fear his own periods of alternate depression and elation might be pathological. So it is with all of us and no cause for alarm.

JUNE 26, 1943. Well, we're busy again. Dunlap, Devereux, and I were busy until 8:30, and others until after midnight. So while ninety-five percent of us had been in the absolute depths of despair the other night, all spirits are soaring again. I did one case involving multiple shrapnel wounds myself and enjoyed the privilege. We've only been moderately busy today, but Dunlap and I repaired one case of hemorrhoids.

I don't know what you'll do about Suzanne's "Betty." Betty was showing considerable wear when I left home, and I guess she's really ragged by now. These little details about Suzanne are very welcome. I wish the snapshots of both of you would come.

Martinak got letters from Macy today with good pictures of her and Jean and the birthday cake. He told me Suzanne had remembered Jean's birthday, and that tickled him. He does get pretty homesick, and the pictures were cute enough to get to him.

It is twenty-five miles to the nearest place where we can spend money. I've spent a quarter in the past month, and that for a haircut.

JUNE 27, 1943. Seven airmails and two V-mails were waiting when I got through my work about 8:30 P.M. A mighty nice ending for another nice day. It begins to look like the days will be busy and pleasant in spite of all previous misgivings, that is if we never go more than five days without mail again.

And being away from you is a constant agony. I shan't dwell on it every time I'm conscious of it or my letters would contain nothing else.

Devereux and I designed a make-do fracture bed for our patient with a broken neck. The carpenters built it for us, and it serves the purpose satisfactorily, allowing for the traction the patient needs. All of us including Sid Galt, our orthopedic man, are pleased with it. And we got in another broken neck tonight, so I guess I'll build an even better table tomorrow if I can find time to do it myself. Pretty good for one internist and one obstetrician we think.

Whoops! Out went the lights and without a warning flicker. It's 10:15 and a guard will be by any minute telling us the candle has to be put out, too.

JUNE 28, 1943. About what to send me: please let it be something to eat. Candy, pecans, cookies would be fine—anything but Spam, corn beef, or dried carrots.

I'd never trade a career in internal medicine for one in surgery, but until I'm out of this war, I'd better learn as much surgery as I can. I'm really learning quite a lot and am enjoying the opportunity. We've been busy today and I'm tired.

JUNE 29, 1943. Go back to your June 29 newspaper and see where the entire crew of a flying fortress was awarded the DFC (Distinguished Flying Cross). They shot down eight out of fifteen Messerschmitts that attacked them over Sicily on June 27. That was the day Dunlap, Devereux, and I worked on the aviators. They were from that fortress, and their morale is very high tonight.

We took the head tongs out of one of our neck fracture cases today and put a plaster collar and jacket on him. He's comfortable and his greatest delight is in being able to walk to the latrine. He thinks we're pretty good doctors—we do, too.

Did I ever tell you promotions for Martinak and me had been requisitioned immediately after the unit was activated? Some time ago Colonel Winans told me he had done that while he was still our CO. We weren't promoted because the regular army captain who was acting as temporary adjutant at the time, couldn't stand seeing new men coming in as captains. Knowing the ropes gave him adequate advantage over Colonel Winans so that he could wire the surgeon general and get our table of organization filled with captains already in uniform but not from Baylor. Captains Ford and Pollard showed up before anyone else knew what had happened. That left no openings for Martinak's and my promotions. Nice fellow, eh?

Now today the CO told Brown that a blanket recommendation for the promotion of all lieutenants has gone in. He thinks we should have our captaincies within a couple of weeks. We all hope that the CO was sober at the time.

We got paid in francs again today. I drew 1,090 of what we call this Arab money. That figures out to $21.80 to add to my hoard.

Do you realize I left home three months ago today? I think I've been away for a great portion of my life. Still, it doesn't seem like I've been in North Africa more than a week. We're busy and the time really flies.

JULY 1, 1943. After fourteen months in the army, someone has finally decided to organize even our surgical section in such a way that we'll know what is expected of us. Remember how I fussed on maneuvers that identical routines were not established on each ward, and that nothing was ever put down in writing to preserve a consistency of rules? Well, it's being written out now, and copies are to be distributed. I can hardly believe it but do hope it's true. We'll see.

Be advised that soldiers sitting side by side on an army eight-holer are often inspired to share ideas and even confidences. It's true. Adams and I met in that position today and mutually agreed that none of us would need gardening, hiking, touring, or studying French to maintain morale as long as we stay busy. Adams is right fluent in several languages including Arabic and French.

We had a staff meeting last night, and good cases were presented. It was really about as good as the Tuesday night rounds used to be at Baylor. A difference here is that all presentations and discussions have to be extemporaneous, there being no literature available for reading up on a subject. It was always true at both Tennessee and Baylor that the subject of malaria was sure to cause a lot of arguments. We see a lot of the disease on the medical wards here, and their presentation last night caused the usual arguments. It was good.

JULY 3, 1943. I was OD again last night and again feel like an obstetrician from the lack of sleep.

There will always be paperwork to attend to each day, before patients can be considered. It is annoying and we gripe our heads off about it, but actually it does save lives in the long run. We should accept it more graciously. Our work is still holding up and we still enjoy being busy.

We're having frequent contacts with the English both as neighbors and as patients. They almost invariably leave you feeling like they're a mighty fine folk. Of course, they're not loquacious as a rule, opening up only after you've been around them for a bit. Pain that can leave an average American howling to the heavens they tolerate without a word. And they don't report on sick call unless they're sick. But then American boys over here don't either, although they goldbricked scandalously on maneuvers. A twenty-year-old English soldier was brought in the other night with acute appendicitis. We operated promptly and without thinking to tell him what his trouble was. He was delighted that he felt so much better the next morning and answered all of our questions but asked none himself. Three days later one of us happened to mention his diagnosis. "Oh," he said, "I'd wondered and am glad it was only appendicitis." Can you imagine anyone going to surgery without questioning the surgeon?

JULY 4, 1943. Happy firecracker to you, Suzanne, and all the folks! We did most of our "celebrating" with fireworks a couple of nights ago when I was OD. As usual, it was a safe distance away but was highly visible and audible.

Nearly everyone is griping about how sorry the food is, but they stow it away just the same. I can hardly wait for mealtime to come around and don't see how I keep from getting fat. Even the powdered eggs we have once a day and the corn beef we have at least twice don't bother me. The GI bread we've been getting is really good, being made from captured German flour that is not ersatz. Tonight I even ate some with our "butter-doesn't-melt-in-North-Africa" spread on it. Everything in that advertisement is true except the word "butter." It is neither butter, nor axle grease, nor castor oil, although having undesirable taste qualities from each of them. That stuff melts at a temperature well above that of hot cakes right off the fire, sticks inside your mouth like castor oil, and tastes like the Red Top axle grease of my boyhood.

A recent article in the *National Geographic* extolled the virtues of the dehydrated foods going "to our men overseas." Someone was reading it aloud and reached a phrase stating that very few people could tell powdered eggs from fresh scrambled ones. Ford was listening in another room and yelled out for the author's name to be sure he never went to that guy's house for breakfast.

So we eat and gripe and go back for seconds but still lose weight. Maybe we'll gain weight, even so, for we can't get half as many cigarettes as we're accustomed to getting. On the other hand, we can't get candy bars either.

You can't imagine the change in facial expressions on the doctors, nurses, and enlisted men whenever mail comes in regularly. The change is not unlike what I noticed in the faces of Waco fellow citizens the morning after Hoover was defeated in 1932. Amazing it was, then and now. But mail hasn't been very regular of late to any of us. [So here it was: not enough cigarettes, no mail, and sorry food. These were the factors General Lucas said broke soldiers' morale. I lost forty-five pounds before the logistics problem had been solved to keep the invasion forces supplied. Most of us lost.]

An American seaman discharged from Merrick's ward yesterday has just dropped by with a dirty pillowcase bulging with fourteen cans of tuna, four cans of peaches, and four big cans of boned chicken. Boy, oh boy! We'll certainly destroy the evidence of his felony for him!

HITTING OUR STRIDE   5
July 1943

JULY **5, 1943.** We've seen no fruit or fresh vegetables such as lettuce and tomatoes. And no meat, no eggs, no candy. Also, we've had no cigarettes in two weeks. However, as long as we go to the mess hall five minutes early for each meal and always go back for seconds, I guess we really shouldn't complain.

We admitted our first patient two weeks ago and have already seen more than half as many as we saw on maneuvers in three months. Our only battle casualties have been those few flyers admitted right after we opened. Since then we've been busy with the victims of jeep wrecks, malaria, diarrhea, and "desert rot" along with many casualties from what they thought were duds, booby traps, and captured ammunition.

JULY 6, 1943. Oh boy! The postman finally made it with all of your letters from June 1 through June 14. As you see, any answer to those questions in this mail may not reach you until after September 1.

Jerry staged the biggest raid we've seen from about 3:30 to 4:30 this morning. We all got up to watch it but had to go to work on the casualties we started receiving about 5:30 A.M. It's now 9:00 P.M., and I've just finished up. While there really wasn't that much work to be done, we're just not clicking as we should. We've lots of lost motion but will iron out some more wrinkles as a result of today's experience.

The British soldiers are a fine bunch of people. Let's never let propaganda make us doubt it for a minute. Today I heard a sergeant announce that he'd gladly have given his life for his "laddies." Some of them, he said, had wives and children at home while he did not. For that reason, he'd rather be maimed than see them so. Does sound pretty melodramatic, doesn't it? The only thing is, his legs had both been amputated. His remark was the first he made after being told what had been done in surgery while he was asleep. "This," he said, "is war, you know."

JULY 7, 1943. I was OD again last night and didn't get out of the operating room until 4:00 A.M. Very few traumatic cases this time—most of them about like those seen in private practice. And we're about to get the bugs out of our setup. We'll likely have a smoothly running organization within a week.

Things have been pretty dull around here for a couple of days, and I was caught up early this afternoon. This is a welcome letup, for I've been working long hours. It has never been as hard as an internship and certainly not as hard as the obstetrical service of an internship.

JULY 8, 1943. Walsh got his captaincy today and rustled up a whole keg of vin rouge from somewhere. Being afraid it might lack appropriate authority on full stomachs, he held his promotion party before supper. We all buzzed a bit until a better-than-average meal sobered everybody. The party was attended by a general from the surgeon general's office, and he seemed like a nice sort. I did notice an unusual thing when I shook his hand—it was as soft as a woman's. I doubt if he ever shoveled gravel or made hay for a living.

Merrick, Turnbow, and I went across the road to visit the neighboring British antiaircraft unit this evening. When their radio isn't in official use, they get the London newscast at 8:00 P.M. An alert sounded just as the news came on, and the broadcast was over before the incoming planes were identified as American.

Members of this particular unit have been away from home for as many as four years. They seem as philosophical about that as they are about everything else. One of their sergeants confided that our hospitals are less austere and our nurses more friendly than their British counterparts. Patients, too, make similar comments.

I suppose I've described the night battles sometimes seen when the German planes come over. The planes are met by tracer bullets, each tenth bullet through the machine guns being the tracer type. Whereas we maintain total blackout before and during these raids, the tracer bullets make a bright red trail in their flight. The German planes put out great magnesium flares at the moment the tracers start up, and they float very slowly down so that the entire area is as light as day. Then, as though on signal, dozens of searchlights come on to add more brightness. The whole area becomes a giant fireworks display, unimaginable unless seen, and accompanied by a great deal of noise. One puts on a helmet and being well above and some distance from the target area, heads for a nearby vantage point to watch and listen. Although there is a thundering of the anti-aircraft fire from the periphery of a five or ten-mile circle in which we're situated, the shooting becomes less intense from time to time, and we can hear the muffled roars of motors and propellers high above.

The searchlights send narrow ribbons of silver up into infinity. The magnesium flares, great balls of light, just seem to hang there for a time and then drift very slowly down toward earth. By now it seems all of the searchlights in the world have surely come on, their lights crisscrossing in all directions. They make the whole sky a latticework beyond which the flares are still seen. By now, more ack-acks than you'd believe exist add to the din, putting up tracers that parallel and crisscross the silver ribbons with broken lines of red. These red lines, of course, mark out the respective trajectories of bullets searching out enemy planes. They are radar controlled as are the searchlights. As soon as a single searchlight picks up what appears to be a black spot the size of a tomato tin, the other searchlights and all the tracers start intersecting at the same spot.

The spot turns out to be an easily recognizable German bomber with all of that light playing on it. It begins all sorts of gyrations to get out of those beams that have marked it with a kiss of death. Too late to escape, the bomber continues gyrations for a bit, even after being hit. By now, all of the searchlights and tracers have formed a great apex up into the sky, gradually working its way to the gyrating bomber. It gives off a puff of white smoke and then another and another, and its crazy gyrations result in an orderly movement to the ground. From a thousand throats of hospital personnel and patients, a great cheer goes up. It is as though these witnesses were seeing a fullback carrying a pigskin for a goal instead of that great bomber carrying a dozen young men to their death. The cheering continues, and white smoke seems to be jerked upward as it pours from the falling plane. The silver beams continue to intersect on the bomber, and the aircraft gets bigger and bigger as it speeds earthward. It shoots behind the crest of a hill, and we hear a big bang. A rumble is felt, and we know there is one less German bomber. [On a particular night at Bizerte, we saw a similar process repeated a couple of times and supposed two or three planes had been downed. The next day we learned that many more than a dozen had fallen during the raid. The buildup of ships and material for the invasion of Europe was being made on Lake Bizerte, the harbor, and the Germans were throwing everything they could muster into preventing it.]

JULY 9, 1943. Tell Suzanne her dad very much enjoyed receiving his first letter ever from her today. It had only been en route nineteen days, the fastest I have ever received. The postman must have sensed how important that letter was. Her handwriting is exactly like yours somehow.

You might also tell Suzy that if her dad was at home, he'd stay down at the pigpen with her to her heart's content. Those little wriggling blocks of pork are just about the cutest things yet, don't you think? I remember how it used to feel when I was a youngster and barefooted and six or seven of them would rub cold, exploring snouts against my feet and ankles. But, "quoth the raven," nostalgia.

Merrick, Turnbow, McClung, and I seem to be operating a menagerie in our quarters now. I've laughed at Merrick's anger at rodents in general ever since he waked up the other night with our friendly rat sitting upon his head. But since last night, I share his feelings. While lying awake reflecting on the paragon virtues of home, I felt a tentative nibble on my index finger. I slapped violently, knocking a furry body out into the middle of the floor. My flashlight picked up our rat hurrying for cover. He'd just been biting me. As I was about to fall asleep, something that turned out to be a spider ran across my chin, and thirty minutes later a mouse waked me up walking across my forehead. Maybe they don't like our taking over their habitat.

I wish I had one mousetrap, one rattrap, and cheese to bait them with. I'd eat the cheese and use the traps to throw at whatever moved in the night.

JULY 10, 1943. We've heard Baylor College of Medicine is definitely moving. All are anxious to hear just how both Baylor and the new school in Dallas—if any—will manage. I gather from the *Dallas News* clippings that the medical students aren't pleased with President Neff's action. But I imagine Baylor at Houston will be their only choice for finishing and graduating. I correspond with Dean Moursund sporadically but had no inkling of this change.

JULY 12, 1943. Three of the new patients I received today had taken a trip on the same ship on which I came overseas. They knew three of the young navy officers I'd come over with and reported they'd received minor injuries. They also knew Jack Peyton and said the last they'd seen of him, he'd been on the beach without a scratch, night before last. By contrast, things here are peaceful—as peaceful as at Alvin—and you'd think we'd be content with our good fortune in this respect. Conversely, a vague and restless discontent seems chronic, although alleviated whenever our time becomes completely structured by events. Surely it's true "man does not live by bread alone."

The General, "Uncle Fred," and I met at that generator of mutual down-to-earthness, the eight-holer, awhile ago. He'd just returned from an adjacent city sixty miles from here and said the temperature was 125 degrees. It seldom ever gets above 80 degrees here, but he said the bottom of our hill and its approaching slope only fifteen miles away gave the first relief he and his driver had from the heat.

JULY 13, 1943. We've been pretty busy today—real busy. If you'll check with your W. P. Hobby production [the *Houston Post*] on this date and yesterday, you'll know why. I didn't get away from the operating room until 9:00 P.M. and had been in a scrub suit all day. Evacuation back to the general hospitals was working so well, though, that by the time I'd finished, all but two of my patients had been moved out. Now I hope things don't start up again before morning. Today's patients have had very interesting stories for us that make us feel pretty good. [We were receiving battle casualties from Sicily.]

JULY 14, 1943. One of the patients received yesterday had been operated on by Jack Peyton. He's really working these days. We've been watching for his signature on emergency medical tags (EMTs) for several days but hadn't seen one before now. He really was on the LST I sailed on and I talked to several patients about that ship.

I guess I never did write you about Captain Salistean other than saying he was the only man on our ship who'd ever been out of sight of land before. Now I have several patients who think he's quite a sailor, and I do, too. He had been an enlisted man in the navy for fourteen years and was advanced after the war started. He was tough as a boot, but we all had him figured as a man who would get his job done come heck or high water. Whatever idiosyncrasies he may have had weren't hard to overlook, and we respected him. Now my patients tell me that bombers were recently strafing, making a target of his ship and doing considerable damage. Salistean took up his position on the bridge, a most unprotected place, and did not leave it until the attack was over and everything under control. The enlisted men thought his ship was disabled, but my officer-patient tells me the captain completed his mission and brought the vessel back to port. I guess he's quite a sailor and quite a guy, and I hope he gets proper commendation.

We learn from prisoners that New York City has been leveled to the ground. German bombers did it. From Italian prisoners who think they're still in Sicily, we learn that all Allied threats to North Africa have been removed. They think their side now controls the entire world except for this insignificant little area we're occupying. No amount of argument convinces them they're in North Africa. A wounded German lieutenant looked wild eyed at the wardman who tried to medicate him with sulfanilamide tablets. He thought we executed prisoners by poisoning them. Another decided it was foolish to submit to the pain of a hypo when he'd be executed in a few hours, anyway. He said as much.

I'm proud, mighty proud, of our soldiers. I'm proud of the sergeant who came in with his right hand mangled and bragged that the jerries hadn't known he was left-handed. The grenade he threw left-handed wiped out the machine gun nest that had fired on him. I'm proud of the lieutenant who has a break in each ankle and the captain in the adjoining bed who has a thigh wound and a broken arm. I'm proud of both of them for guying each other about goldbricking and for mustering up convincing argument that their casts would be no detriment to their duties if we returned them to work. Everyone's morale is high. We're winning.

JULY 16, 1943. Jack Peyton is still a couple of hundred miles from us, but I get his patients. I don't know how happy he is for having transferred from the Baylor unit, but I see patients who are happy he did.

JULY 17, 1943. The postman failed us today for the first time in more than a week. Another quiet day, but probably the last for awhile. We are to start functioning as a station hospital temporarily. That means we will be allowed to keep patients for three weeks rather than three days. This change permits us to do elective surgery, which sounds pretty good to me.

I didn't keep mum about Baylor. If my letters reach you, you'll see that my first reaction was disgust at the trustees for making the move. I believed it would simply prolong the college's death agonies. After thinking it over, it might prove beneficial to get it away from the cliques and petty jealousies existing in Dallas. Of course, these same things will develop in the Houston medical community if they don't already exist. "Town and gown" pull apart around medical schools just as they do around undergraduate institutions.

They tell me that as my allotment is already awarded, you should not expect a change in banks or in amount until July 1. Be sure to send me the figures on your June and July receipts.

I hope to be able to go to Tunis after some souvenirs pretty soon. Started to trade my binoculars to Turnbow for vases he'd bought but decided I'd better get some from the merchants if they were to have much value as souvenirs.

I got so griped at the lack of organization on the surgical service that I handed Colonel Carter a very militarylike communication, which could have been taken as an indictment for inefficiency on his part. I was at the point of not caring how mad it made him, but tolerant gentleman that he is, he took it well and promised to consider my recommendations. [April, 1985: I have a hard time believing I'd have been guilty of such boorishness thirty-five years ago, but it's in the letter, plain to see. I do remember my anger and disappointment over having to accept assignment to the surgical service, and as my chief, he'd always reminded me that I was more mature than the other lieutenants, with nearly two years more postgraduate training than the lieutenants on the medical service.]

JULY 18, 1943. Please call Mrs. Jack Peyton and tell her Jack is with the invasion forces, in case she doesn't know. Several of my patients had been treated by him, and their wounds gave evidence of what a good surgeon he is. These soldiers all thought he was probably the best doctor in the army.

JULY 19, 1943. This being Sunday, it might be well to comment that it is usually no different from other days. This one is different. Although it took me until noon to change dressings and apply casts, the PA system carried this morning's chapel services with organ music.

I've not set foot off the hospital grounds since the day we opened up. We were discouraged from any unnecessary wanderings at first because the cleanup squads had not finished removing the booby traps and land mines. That is no longer a valid reason for staying around. Of course there is nothing in Bizerte to justify a visit, and the sight of its torn-up homes depressed me when we came through. I'll try to get away to Tunis one of these days.

JULY 20, 1943. Turnbow, Hahn, Arnold, my team leader Dunlap, and I climbed up on the highest hill in the neighborhood to look around. I have acquired an excellent pair of Carl Zeiss 8x30 binoculars for surveying the countryside. From this hilltop we can look north and see the Mediterranean about a mile away. Looking east is Bizerte and the harbor, Lake Bizerte, with its narrow connection to the Mediterranean. Looking west we see hills much like west Texas and home. We also see similar sunsets. Valleys to the east are in vineyards, olives, figs, green corn, and wheat stubble. All is pretty and peaceful now, the utter devastation of Bizerte not obvious from where we stand. Those fields to the east were unkempt last month when we came through but are carefully cultivated now.

Lake Bizerte, like Digby Gut in Nova Scotia, is a tidewater lake connected with the Mediterranean by a narrow inlet only a few hundred yards long that goes right through Bizerte. It has been dredged by French engineers so that it is large enough and deep enough to accommodate practically any-sized ship. The lake then provides a very large and protected harbor some twenty miles long. What an excellent place for the buildup of a large invasion fleet!

A word about the binoculars referred to on the previous page. One of my patients confiscated them from a German lieutenant at Licata, Sicily. He practically gave them to me two days later as he was on his way to a general hospital to recuperate from his wounds. He had no money and thought he might need some back at the general hospital. He was glad to take the ten dollars I gave him.

JULY 21, 1943. On only two days since our arrival here have we noticed any heat. Today is one of them, although I don't suppose the temperature is more than 85 degrees. We're used to lower than that, so it seems sultry.

Rose Craig brought me a letter she'd received from Irby Holland. Irby was in Dallas and watched Baylor Medical College equipment being moved out, depressing her. She reported her husband's chief duties were simply improving his golf game and said his heart is still with the unit.

Quoting Rose again—she substituted on my ward today—she says the *National Geographic* for June 6 had a nice article on North Africa and with good pictures, too. Honey, if you can get two copies, please send me one. If you can get even one, hold onto it until I get back, please.

JULY 22, 1943. The medical service is still having excellent meetings at frequent intervals. I attend every chance I get, for they are about as good as the regular Tuesday night ward rounds were at Baylor. Medical officers from surrounding organizations are showing up in increasing numbers, but Peterson and I are the only members of our surgical section who attend. I continue to learn a lot from them, particularly about malaria, of which every ward here houses a few to many cases all the time. I wish our surgical service had such meetings on surgical cases. We never do.

Some of the fellows went to Tunis today, and Turnbow found some brass candlesticks inlaid somehow with silver. I covet them but will get over there myself before too long and pick up something.

JULY 26, 1943. To quote Dunlap, "She's a fine day." Even if sand from the Sahara is blowing outside, it's fine inside. On the other hand, when the euphoria of my shower wears off, maybe "she" won't seem so good.

A two-bit copy of Dale Carnegie's *How to Win Friends and Influence People* has fallen into my hands, and I've been reading it today. I feel like he'd been following me for days on end, eavesdropping on my own personal contacts with people. He must have been, or how in the world could he use me as such a horrible example of how not to influence people? He as much as called me a fool in one paragraph, and he'd certainly better watch his step if I ever get close to him. His copyright antedates my entrance into the army, so how could he know? What he said was, "Any fool can criticize, condemn, and complain—and most fools do." The nerve of that man!

A plague on our postman who is still on strike. Gordon has not heard from Evelyn, and Merrick is getting touchy from not hearing from Mattie. Martinak did get a couple of very old letters from Macy, but I've not heard from my gals in days.

We heard yesterday that Mussolini resigned. Wouldn't that be fine? It does begin to look like the Sicilian campaign will soon be over, and maybe Italy won't have to be taken by force. Golly, won't it be something when Germany gives in? Maybe that day is not too distant.

JULY 28, 1943. Old Pappy feels like a big shot tonight. Dunlap stood back today and looked over my shoulder while I took out the first appendix I'd ever gone after. He voluntarily submitted to the nurses, putting his gown on backwards so that he couldn't get his arms and hands out. Nonetheless, I was proud of old Dunlap for exercising the willpower that that degree of retirement on his part required. Not only was the case his keenly felt responsibility, but his is a temperament that demands he never pass a light switch without trying it out, never sit still more than a minute at a time, never see a new car without raising the hood, and ordinarily never see an opened belly without getting his hands bloodied. Also, this case turned out to be one of the tougher types with the very hot organ lying back of the caecum, where approach and removal is technically difficult.

Thus he not only had to restrain his natural temperament but also the natural urge of a teacher to help a student when the going got tougher than had been anticipated. I stumbled through all right, and the patient is getting along satisfactorily. Dunlap was very patient, not to say complimentary, after it was over.

The medical service hosted another good meeting last night. Colonel Carter attended, along with several other members of our service. Two visiting British medical officers attended and added instructive comments for the gathering. Colonel Winans, Rippy, Merrick, and McClung each presented interesting cases that were well discussed. We all had a good and worthwhile evening.

Devereux went to Tunis today, and I had both our wards to care for. I probably spent three hours rather than the usual thirty minutes on the job. So war certainly is an inefficient and wasteful plague that humanity can't seem to escape. Millions of men wait months or years to perform their particular function, perform for a few hours or days, and then the survivors wait some more. And those men draw full pay the whole time, just as we do. War, the inexplicable, for sure!

JULY 30, 1943. Letters mean very much. I hope you can write every day. I knew Dean Moursund would be glad to see you. In case the clipping he sent me doesn't reach you, the University of Tennessee started the July pharmacy class as a combined course in pharmacy and laboratory technology, just like my article suggests. I do believe the combination is badly needed in rural areas.

I rode to Tunis in a weapons carrier yesterday. Walking the streets from 11:00 A.M. until 5:00 P.M. didn't result in my finding much I could afford to buy. It is about like Casablanca in this regard. The shops in the native souk were interesting, and I visited them in spite of signs warning that they were off-limits. I've never seen so much brass anywhere else. The smaller pieces had been pretty well picked over, and larger ones, many of them beautiful, were from sixty-five dollars and up. I did buy a cloisonne and brass vase for Suzanne, which she'll be too young to despise. It is allegedly Persian, but if so, it must have been made on a machine from Waterbury, Connecticut. I did find a cute little Arab costume of some sort that I hope will reach her in time for her birthday. It should be large enough.

We passed by the olive grove again that impressed me so on our convoy trip over here—I wrote you about the precision of the plantings. Also passed an ancient viaduct built by the Romans no telling how many centuries ago, but doubtless plenty. It is in an unbelievably good state of repair, reminding us again that the Romans certainly knew how to leave permanent marks on the landscape wherever they went.

The souk really was interesting, dirty shops notwithstanding. Its streets, barely wide enough to squeeze a single carriage through, are very crooked. In my two hours within it, I saw only one horse-drawn vehicle and no motorcars. All classes of people milled about the streets, predominantly Arab. But there were other nationalities, too, and no doubt some French.

The streets are so narrow that one can tell very little about the architecture except that shops have no show windows, which renders them all "dark and mysterious" to coin a cliche. I did go by a church, of all things, and one whose doors were open. Too bad it wasn't a mosque, but the inside was conventional Roman Catholic like Catholic churches everywhere. It was a pretty red and white. The striking thing about it was that it was in the souk. On the outside it looked no different than the shops surrounding it, but this only made the inside more beautiful by contrast.

I said the doors of the church were open, the occasion being a wedding. The bride passed right by me as I passed the door. How lucky could a once-in-a-lifetime visitor be? She was wearing a cream-colored satin gown and carrying a bouquet. She also wore long white gloves. I think she'd not have been taken for a foreigner walking down the aisle of any church in Dallas or Alvin, Texas. And guess what? The groom wore a conventional dark dress suit, but all the men of the party had on tuxedos. It was before six o'clock, too. I can't imagine where in the world all of those clothes came from, for I've been through the shops in two of the largest cities over here without ever seeing such merchandise. Shipped in from Paris is my hunch.

Back to the shops: they look something like the sorrier ones in the French Quarter in New Orleans, except dirtier and darker. Another difference is that in the medina each shop is specialized, exclusively brass or china, rugs or furniture. You'd have a ball in the place.

JULY 31, 1943. White just brought me another book by Kenneth Roberts, *Rabble in Arms.* In contrast to *Oliver Wiswell* that presented the loyalist's side of the Revolutionary War, this one's hero is an American patriot—I see in script on the flyleaf "Byrd White, Jr., Rabble Without Arms." I think we should get these two books for our library. They're very interesting.

Things are pretty slow. I have two circumcisions scheduled for in the morning. Not much surgery, but some, anyway. I see no way that we junior officers will ever be prepared for any major surgery in case we ever have to do it on our own. I've a premonition that in time it is inevitable. We'll have to perform major surgery on our own, ready or not. Whether we or the wounded will be the victims, I'm afraid to suggest.

AUGUST 2, 1943. My former roommate, former housemate, and even former tentmate Martinak, has gone sissy and is ironing his clothes. The fact would hardly be worth comment except that he is doing it on the table I'm trying to write on. His shaking gives my handwriting that same fine tremor that our neurology professor palmed off on us as diagnostic of Parkinsonism. Reading over my shoulder, he requests that I admit he was invited in here. I admit he was invited to avail himself of both the table and the electric outlet, neither of which is available in his own quarters. I also have to admit his shirt and trousers look better than any I've seen since leaving the States, and they smell even better than they look. He made an ersatz starch out of flour and water that works just fine but smells exactly like hot homemade biscuits! Boy! Could I ever go for some hot biscuits right now. I may take a bite out of his shirt sleeve!

Unmarried and unharried, Dunlap hasn't had a letter in so long he takes delight in the fact that most of us aren't getting many these days. Martinak did get a letter today that was mailed in Dallas only ten days ago, but that is very unusual for most of our mail.

I was OD again last night and couldn't write. We got in a shipload of wounded from Sicily, and all of them had been capably and thoroughly handled by Jack Peyton's outfit. Drat the field surgical units! They are so much smaller and more mobile than we that they might eventually take the place of evacuation hospitals. I just don't know. Such an idea may provide better and more prompt surgery to the battle-wounded where front lines are moving fast enough. Right now, however, Peyton's outfit is doing all of the surgery and sending the patients to us for postoperative care. Mostly we equate them with doing the interesting part and leaving us to attend to the "scut work." Of course, our next move will put us close to the front again, and the later hospitals will be making the same beef against us.

There goes the 7:15 P.M. newscast over our PA system. The first item is that there has been a mass bombing of the Rumanian oil fields. The attack was made by squadrons led by a man who attended Baylor University for the two years that I was there. It seems to me he was in law school at the time, but I remember him slightly. New sponsors have been invented for the amusement of our patients: Arab Rodent Repellent Co.; Camp Nador Health Resort; Dry-Run, a new exciting game; Lady Gloss-Over Creme for men at the front; Disposable Straddle Trenches; Gyp-You Travel Tours, and others. The patients love it.

AUGUST 3, 1943. Today's most interesting is again a British soldier, a private. He isn't very sick and so is able to relate his unique story. He was captured by the Germans at Dunkirk and held captive in Belgium for six months. He did not consider himself mistreated at all, though he was given but one meal per day, and that solely of rice. He was allowed to work twelve hours a day on a voluntary basis digging trenches. He said the Belgians slipped cigarettes, food, and candy to him and the other prisoners rather regularly. After six months, he and four others managed to escape into France where they were hidden for another six months in a French home. He crossed into unoccupied France but was put into a stockade there. Escaping with forty others, he reached Spain. I believe he went from there to Portugal, but in any event, he reached England nine months after having been captured by the Germans. In England he was immediately reassigned to the British Eighth Army, which he accompanied to North Africa. I'm not sure he even had time for a furlough home before coming here. Interesting. He was favorably impressed by the French, particularly by one named Blanche whom he pronounces "Blawnshay." He is anxious to get back to England when Germany has been defeated.

Before I dismiss this man, Goldstein by name, I must find out exactly how he escaped and what part Blanche, who lived in the first French home, played in the affair. Getting details from an English enlisted man will be about like picking thorns from a little kid who sat down in a cactus bed, but I'll try. Most British soldiers are very rank-conscious, no doubt from growing up class-conscious.

Gordon got five letters today but still doesn't know if he is a papa.

Devereux heard today that he and Sebastian have been named on the ob-gyn faculty of the new Baylor Medical College at Dallas. He isn't sure he'll go back to Dallas, but who of us is? Could be I'll have no choice but to go back to Baylor.

AUGUST 4, 1943. Today is sister Ruth's birthday and more than any of my siblings, she'd appreciate being remembered. But even if I had a card to send her, it would be a month late by the time she received it. Things being like that, let me wish you a merry Christmas now.

We had another good medical meeting today. A neighboring medical laboratory has invited us to their clinical pathological conference next Friday night. At such meetings in civilian life, several doctors read up on available literature on the case to be presented and are ready with prepared comments that are always instructive. Since no literature is available here, those who comment will likely give testimonials on cases they've treated that bear similarities to the one being presented. I do believe it's more interesting this way, but it isn't as instructive. We usually have a good sprinkling of both British and American doctors at our meetings. The comments are always entertaining, and if British doctors are a fair example, our English cousins really have a very good sense of humor.

Well, wonder of wonders. A good old tortoiseshell alley cat just strolled by my desk, rubbing against my leg in passing. It's been so long since I've seen a cat, I'd forgotten they existed. I hope she (tortoiseshells are always female, aren't they?) will pay a visit to our quarters and rid us of less-welcome fellow creatures.

Back to our anecdotal medical comments at today's meeting, I had an opportunity to tell of the case of an elderly tenant farmer. He'd been brought screaming into the emergency room in the predawn hours, thinking a rattler had bit him on the scrotum. As I was preparing to examine him, his middle-aged son who had followed in another car came in timidly but determined to set the old man straight. "Aw, Paw," he said, "that warn't no rattlesnake. I took a flashlight out and looked, and you'd messed right on top of a terrapin turtle." The old man had decided to relieve himself before going all the way to the outhouse, and the reptile had done all that he could. His action was applauded by the audience of doctors. One of the Britishers brought up the old wives' tale of a turtle not turning a victim loose until it thunders. Well, of course that old patient had thundered adequately as soon as struck, and I so informed the meeting. I must remember to report that interesting case again sometime.

AUGUST 5, 1943. You surely must read Kenneth Roberts' novels. He claims to be from Maine and also claims all of his research was limited to the American Revolutionary War. Don't you believe it! He's bound to have followed the Baylor unit, from the day it was organized at home, to have described us so perfectly. It's uncanny. Could be his name is just a nom de plume for some junior officer, noncom, or enlisted man right here in our midst, or a senior officer for all I know. Do read them. They're exceptionally good.

Our supply officer Captain Clarence E. Soper flew with our CO to Palermo in a two-motored transport today. Soper says the country is even prettier than Algeria—hard to believe. He also reports that the cities are not badly damaged and that the people are friendly and nice looking. He found a soda fountain in Palermo as clean as any at home and says he walked right up and got a chocolate malted milk. He also says he and the CO had a four-course dinner at a civilian cafe for $1.80—thick steak, new potatoes, sliced tomatoes, etc. Could be, I guess, but maybe Soper is just inventorying what he's missing back at home. All of us surely do miss such things.

THE LONG HAUL 6
August 1943

AUGUST 6, 1943. I rejoice that Johne D and Randolph are "expecting." But even if Suzanne does think the little bitties are pretty nice, I'm glad her siblings are to be delayed. Gordon still hasn't heard from Evelyn whether he is a papa or that things are going well. Her last letter was about the middle of July, and her obstetrician had decided she'd not likely deliver before August. Gordon doesn't seem upset, but I'd be if I hadn't heard from you by three weeks after you were supposed to deliver. The uncertainties are a strain on the expectant fathers here.

We can send cablegrams now but on a priority basis. Only a few prefabricated phrases are accepted such as "am well," "received your letters," etc. Martinak got one from Macy the other day, and the three prefabricated phrases weren't even typed out, just cut out of printed forms and pasted on a sheet. They sometimes travel no faster than letters, so I'll reserve my quota for better days. The method is available, however, in case of emergency.

Each day here has become much as the one before. That fact does lay a pall upon reportable current events. This frequently restricts a soldier's comments exclusively to the homely happenings. I guess that's why I so frequently find myself commenting on latrine events. Of course, it is a meeting place for the community. Any given resident is bound to meet the others of his own sex there at frequent intervals, about like the post office lobbies in every small town in America.

Recently Arnold, with that sharp mind that must have filled all of his teachers with delight, made a noteworthy addition to our community meeting place. He has invented a very simple device that adds to everyone's comfort. By bending a hook at each end of a short piece of wire, one is able to hook each lid of opposite latrine holes open against the other, instead of against the user's spine. Those hinged lids are heavy and most uncomfortable against the back, as all soldiers learn. This may well have been where the original expression "Oh, my poor aching back!" came from, and the army is blind to talent if Arnold doesn't get promoted for his invention.

My pants still fit like a sack gathered in at the waist, regardless of how much I eat. We had corn beef at noon today for the first time in two or three weeks, and it tasted good. Unbelievable!

I'd better get back to the ward and finish up what little work I have for the afternoon. Goldstein, the British soldier from Dunkirk, is still here. Did I tell you the Germans paid him the same salary they paid their own soldiers of equal rank while he was captive?

AUGUST 7, 1943 [to Mama].Things are about as quiet as a July Sunday afternoon in Alvin. We sometimes work pretty hard for a day or two then drift along for a week or so. However, in my fifteen months of army life, I've never put in a day that would compare to work on my quietest day at the Baylor Clinic. I believe I did more for the war effort in the eight days of truckdriving than I've ever done for it professionally. Maybe I missed my calling, or maybe wars and armies are funny things. Maybe my patriotic urge is the primitive sort, which can only be satisfied by clawing and biting and taking scalps. Whatever the score, I'm more at peace with it than I've ever been, even if my life is a quiet one.

Mrs. Rose Craig, a former division nurse at Baylor, is one of our nurses here. She's written some rather presentable poetry since we've been over here, the following being a less serious poem:

Nostalgic waves encompass me
'Tho I'm still patriotic—
Tonight, my friends, I long to see
A land that ain't exotic.

I doubt that any member of this unit has been entirely free from such sentiments for a whole twenty-four hours since we left New York, although McClung, one of my suitemates who writes every two or three weeks, says he hasn't been homesick. He's a psychiatrist, internist, chess player, and a good fellow, but he isn't married.

AUGUST 8, 1943. A carton of twenty-four almond Hershey bars arrived today in perfect condition. Regulations require that they be requested by us and the request confirmed by the U.S. postmaster at the point of departure. The box reached me in the surgery dressing room where Dunlap, Devereux, Bussey, and I made short work of it. All remarked how well it carried.

Dr. Randolph Jones of Houston just finished his postgraduate training at Hermann Hospital and is going into practice there with a neurosurgeon. I certainly see no reason why he should do otherwise. If I were in his place and knew what I know now, I'd do no differently, even though I'd hate to miss what I've seen in the past two months. I do think he'll probably do more good there than I'll ever do here. If more doctors are needed by the army, younger men even without internships are amply qualified for the jobs junior medical officers are doing here. I cannot see for the life of me how the senior officers and those in administrative positions can be so sure we'll never be in catastrophic situations. Even a meager imagination should visualize situations where senior medical men were casualties. They could very well become the patients of anxious and unqualified junior officers. Every one of us could become immediately responsible for major surgery, and Bowyer is the only lieutenant who has had any formal surgical training. I hope it never happens, but can't shake my premonitions that were branded as preposterous in the Fort Sam days. I'll never go near an operating room if I ever get back home, but here I must go as frequently as possible out of self-defense.

Funny things, these armies! But ours always seems to function well, at that. It seems to be doing all right this time, too.

Major Dunlap sure is popular with our patients, and I hope I can stay on his team. He is a real good surgeon and is a character as well. Even the sick men on the ward got a good laugh today. After he'd finished a serious talk with one of the sickest, he turned to the next patient, a black man from Waco, and greeted, "Well, Mose, are you hitting on six again?"

AUGUST 10, 1943. A Red Cross cinema is a recent addition to Bizerte. Bowyer, Turnbow, Johnson, Arnold, Gordon, and I went in to see *Reno*, a pretty sorry show. But the trip in by way of the Bizerte harbor and back through the empty medina was not sorry. Our route carried us through the narrow streets of the medina and out through the nearby French village of attractive homes. These had been spared damage from the shellings and were nice to see.

We also saw some pretty vegetable gardens, and at one, irrigation was going on. An ox pulled up a large leather tubful of water, and a man dumped it into an irrigation ditch. You'll remember that the ox can only walk the short distance necessary to bring the tub to the surface and out to where it is dumped. He stops a moment, apparently without a signal, then backs up the incline to the well to repeat the process. Ruminating aloud, Johnson wondered what might be the thoughts of the beast about the process. Quick as a flash, Arnold voiced them for the poor ox: "Dadgum, but humans are certainly crazy as well as a nuisance."

I probably should let that irrigation story lie and say no more about it, but I can't. The first time I saw it, I do remember thinking to myself how stupid a method for irrigating. Then I remembered quite distinctly the hand pumping of water into a bucket when I was a boy down in Gulf Coast country. I'd pump those bucketfuls by the dozen, carrying each one into the field to water tomato plants or sweet potato slips. Now I don't rightly know what to think, so I'll let it lie.

AUGUST 11, 1943. Had a letter from brother Joe in Waterbury this week. One sentence bears comment, and I quote it verbatim: "We at home probably can't conceive of the situation as you fellows see it." He was referring to the war and the war news. If he only knew it, New England is seeing as much of the war as I am. And of course he gets a lot more news than I do. By the time we've reached areas that have seen fighting, the fight is over. Our situation is much more comfortable than it was in Louisiana, and except for such grandstand views of distant bombings as I've previously described, our area is as quiet as Alvin, Texas. So far, I'm just as much an outsider in the fighting as Joe, but I guess folks can't believe that. I can remember how, with a twelve-year-old's curiosity for gory details, I'd pick at the returning veterans of World War I for their stories. I got nowhere, the town's elders telling me in asides that the soldier's experiences were all too horrible for them to relate.

Now we see soldiers who've experienced the horrors of war, but they aren't at all reticent to talk about it. And most of them are most anxious to leave us and get back to their fighting outfits. One gets the impression that they, too, feel that they're outsiders and that the outfits other than their own are having the rougher time. We've still not seen the civilians, but I believe they likely suffer far more than do the soldiers.

AUGUST 12, 1943. I received two letters yesterday that had been mailed on July 8. I didn't get any today, but a lot of the group did. One had been mailed on August 6, just six days ago—a record.

McCauley, Lebermann, and Willis got commendations from the Eastern base section today for "meritorious action on the morning of July 6 for anticipating and preparing to care for unusual numbers of casualties, etc." Lebermann and Willis were the ODs that night, and of course McCauley was in charge of the receiving section, where he does an admirable job always. So my remarks that follow are in no way to be interpreted as deprecatory of the commendations.

July 6th was the morning I wrote you about, when all surgical teams were aroused to care for the large numbers that failed to materialize. This was the night when any group as green as we, would have expected a thousand casualties from the action. We got in fifty and were so inefficient in our handling of them that my morale still plunges to the depths when I think about it. It will gradually work out I'm sure, and Colonel Carter has been more than a prince for not pinching my head off for the gripes I directed toward him. I suggested to him that even his own belly was not secure against the possibility of surgery, under the woefully inexperienced hand of one of his lieutenants. He said he agreed but that nothing could be done about it. Two days later I performed my first appendectomy under the welcome supervision of Dunlap and Devereux. Within the same week, every lieutenant on the service had performed major surgery.

AUGUST 13, 1943. Six years as a pharmacist running my own business during the Great Depression; four years as a medical student plus almost three in postgraduate work at Baylor; now, sixteen months in the Army Medical Corps, and yesterday my thirty-sixth birthday. It was a pretty good one, all in all. The fact that I'm not the army's oldest lieutenant is adequate compensation for being the Baylor unit's oldest. H'mmmmmm.

Goldstein, my Dunkirk survivor, has finished a twelve-page letter to you, written on both sides. I've mailed it in two separate envelopes and do hope it arrives safely. The other men on the ward have guyed him a great deal about writing to his ward officer's young wife, but he kept at it anyway. By the time he'd finished, half the patients and a good many men of our outfit had read it. Tonight, four typed copies are in existence with more to follow. If they could ever interview him, some feature writer could really get a good story out of Goldstein.

It was quite a coincidence that you saw the newsreel on North Africa on the day you got my long letter describing it. Nope, you didn't see me with the French nurses. In fact, the only French nurses I've seen over here were driving French ambulances. We passed them high in the Atlas Mountains in Algeria, and they simply would not yield us as much room as we felt they should. But then, nobody gives enough room on those roads.

And speaking of nurses, I suppose we can thank our CO for keeping his officers and nurses pretty well in hand. Our nurses are rushed to death by officers from other organizations but very few by our own. The result is we like each other and work well enough together. I suppose, really, we can thank our CO with the same degree of enthusiasm mustered when we criticize. Anyway, the lot of the CO over unindoctrinated civilian doctors isn't necessarily the answer to any career officer's fervent prayers.

AUGUST 14, 1943. Well, my German field glasses add considerably to the interest we are developing in the surrounding hills. Devereux, Dunlap, Johnson, and I just got back from the top of a previously unexplored one. I could see for the first time that our hospital is located on a little peninsula that juts out some four or five miles. We're really at North Africa's most northern tip, Cape Bon, and from today's hilltop we can look east to see the moonrise over the Mediterranean, after looking west a little earlier to watch the sunset.

Too bad so much of that particular letter—July 14—was censored. I probably mentioned things I should not have, either about the buildup for the invasion of Sicily or certain gossip among our wounded. I do recall mentioning one time something about American atrocities somewhere in Sicily, when it was the common gossip on the wards. If a censor got hold of that one, he scratched out such information as being possibly demoralizing for the home folks. It seems that both sides are doing a remarkably good job of preventing such things. Isolated instances are inevitable when the function of the fighting man is to kill. That function can most readily be insured by teaching him to hate—not a difficult task when he is chronically frustrated and frequently miserable. War just isn't peaches and cream, anyway, so whose moral and religious armament can be expected to keep the soldier's reactions compatible with humanity's highest ideals, in every situation? None but the bleeding hearts would expect it of fighting men, I think.

As it turned out, it didn't amount to much, but I had my first experience with insubordination today. We routinely use ambulatory patients as helpers with the housekeeping on the wards and could not get along without them. Today in my absence, one patient flatly refused to "do somebody else's work." I had to do something about it as soon as I returned and just offered him a choice. He'd either get right along with a remopping job over the entire ward, or he'd be on complete bed rest, bedpan and all, until he was returned to duty. He immediately chose mopping and everyone was happy.

AUGUST 15, 1943. Goldstein, whom I returned to duty the day after he finished the letter to you, was back to see us today. On my recommendation, he had been transferred back to his old driver's job where he could keep off his feet. He was all grins. I asked him to elaborate a bit more on Blanche, whom you'll find mentioned in your letter. He declined, saying, "Sir, I said all I could about her. You see, her husband was a prisoner at the time, and I've married since then, too. So, you see, really . . . ."

Incidentally, Goldstein's speech isn't much different from ours, nor that of better-classed Londoners generally. Lower-class Londoners, rural English, Scotch, and Irish all have such brogues as to make communication difficult at times. Sometimes I have to ask for so many repetitions that we all laugh.

Had an interesting little side trip today. Went with Soper, Turnbow, and Sergeant Dutton to try to find some wheels for Turnbow's anesthetic machines. Turnbow has largely built them himself out of whatever material he could bird-dog here and there, but needs them on pneumatic-tired wheels so they'll roll over our dirt floors. So we went to the nearby junkyard of downed German planes. Sure enough, Dutton found what was needed—three good Messerschmitt tail wheels.

Dutton is our motor pool sergeant and a good mechanic. His interest in today's trip was to see if he could find some parts for a German motorcycle that he got from some French marines. They'll let him keep it while we're here if he gets it running for them. He found what he was looking for, so maybe I can borrow the machine and break a leg sometime.

AUGUST 16, 1943. Well, this has been a second birthday for me. Mail came today! Several birthday cards and the Shanklin Studio pictures of you and Suzanne. They were a sensation all over the place. I simply can't imagine the little bug having grown so. I'd say Shanklin's caught both of you at exactly the right second.

Whoops! I'm OD and there goes my page. Probably won't amount to much, but one never knows.

AUGUST 17, 1943. OD call on surgery comes every fifth night. Last night I worked until 1:00 A.M. on the usual run of minor accident victims.

Captain Devereux, a well-trained gynecological and obstetrical surgeon, is the logical man on our team to first assist Major Dunlap. Today he relinquished the place to me, and I assisted Dunlap on a hernia operation. He had me do part of the repair, and I expect he'll oversee me doing the entire operation on our next case. I appreciate their taking that much trouble with me for it is a sacrifice on their part. The surgeon enjoys doing it himself and tends to become fidgety over the fumbling fingers of the novice. Still, I must not be entirely wrong in my assumption that any day or any hour could give rise to situations demanding more of my fumbling fingers than required in appendectomies, hemorrhoidectomies, and hernial repairs. And there is absolutely no way for the novice to correct his fumbling under our circumstances except by operating time after time, and day after day. The novice's overseer, the surgeon, must assume absolute responsibility for the work performed by that novice, certainly a sacrifice of himself. I do appreciate it. I should.

I've been gone for an hour, answering a call for all officers on surgery to report to their wards. That usually means a hospital ship has docked and we'll be receiving their patients for a good part of the night. It was a ship, but we're already overflowing. After seeing there were no emergencies aboard, our CO had them shuttled elsewhere. As usual when assembled and freed of duties, we had a bull session.

Colonel Carter joined our session tonight, telling about rooming with Dr. Bedford Sullivan when they were medical students. It seems these two weren't always medical college professors or lieutenant colonels. Sullivan used to torment him by putting toads and lizards in Carter's bed.

That story reminded Devereux of Sullivan's obsession to apply poison ivy extract to human skin so that he might study the allergic responses and time them accurately. Being frustrated by a lack of volunteers, he turned to applying it clandestinely to the earlobes or hands of faculty friends. It was months and months before they caught him at it, and many were wondering at the high incidence of unseasonal cases of poison ivy at Baylor Medical College.

I told of the highly embellished and animated account of old John, a black Baylor orderly. He had a hilarious encounter with Dr. Speight Johnson about the time I arrived in 1939. You will recall that Dr. Johnson was among the earliest physicians west of the Mississippi specializing exclusively in ophthalmology. In addition to being an impressive gentle-man, he was held in high esteem by his students, the hospital staffs, and Dallas citizenry in general. But on the day in question, a bit of careless-ness on John's part nearly caused the doctor an accident and did cause him embarrassment. His usually impeccable decorum was temporarily suspended by more pressing matters.

As John told the story, he had been sent to wipe up some spilled cosmetics from the bedside table in one of the hospital's more expensive private rooms. Armed as usual with a pan of sudsy water and sponge, he'd set them down to open the door only to encounter Dr. Johnson's back. He noted the doctor bowing and reassuring the patient as he backed toward the door. Somewhat intimidated, John simply stepped back away from the door, forgetting the pan of soapsuds. It would be unkind to Dr. Johnson to describe all that took place after he planted his foot in that pan of water, but John claims he turned a nearby corner out of sight before hearing, "Wheah is that damned awedly?"

Ford, our roentgenologist [in charge of x-rays] without whom we'd be in a bad way, tells about asking McCauley down in the receiving section how many patients had come in one day. McCauley, speaking right up with, "Oh, we've been busy as hades. I'd guess somewhere between 180 and 225. Just how many, Sergeant Abell?" From the sergeant: "Seventy-two, Sir."

As always at such gatherings, it becomes the audience for admiring anyone's recent pictures from home. Alessandra brought out a very cute one of Sarah for all to see, and I showed two of Suzanne. Alessandra confessed he'd been so overcome by Sarah's growth and change that he became misty eyed when he got the picture. I guess I mumbled something, but I confessed nothing. Still, North African weather can get us pretty sentimental at times.

Chaplain and Gordon both got telegrams today, telling them of new babies. Both were boys. I've no details on the chaplain's new son, but Gordon and Evelyn's was about a month late and weighed eight pounds. I believe they named him Terry Dennis. Gordon tells me Jewish people do not name a child for any person still alive.

Oh, yes, I heard from the surgeon general's office today, just nine months after I'd sent my paper in for approval. It could have been published without delay if I'd submitted it as a civilian, but I let Mallory talk me out of that route. The subject of premedical education was much more timely at the time I wrote it than it is now. No one knew then how radical the changes desired by the armed services would be. Dean Moursund has the manuscript and will submit it to various journals for me. I do hope somebody will proofread it, if it ever gets that far. They seldom come out as written.

AUGUST 18, 1943. Bob Hope, Frances Langford, and party spent the night with us last night and will make the Baylor unit their headquarters while in the area. Of course, ours is the pleasant spot of all North Africa, the temperature rising some 40 degrees as soon as one drops down off our promontory. I look forward to seeing them.

Our war news has been awfully good as of late. In spite of this, our nearest English neighbors predict at least another eighteen months of fighting in Europe. I sure hope they're overestimating. Two of their officers want us to consider "union now." They are very much in favor of such a union, regardless of whether they become our forty-ninth state or we become a British dominion. They do muster up good argument for their point of view. Too bad about bumbling old George III, maybe?

AUGUST 19, 1943. The Bob Hope Show went on at 10:00 A.M. and lasted until nearly noon. It was exactly what the soldiers in this area seemed to want and need. I shared with them on both counts. While it might have been risque for a high school chapel exercise, most of us thought it the best show we'd ever seen anywhere. And how the patients did go for it! Regardless of their illnesses or other mitigating circumstances, they all went for it in a big way. After watching for ten minutes, I forgot all about the nap I was intending to take, although I'd only had two hours sleep in the previous thirty-six hours.

Of one thing there can certainly be no doubt: the work Bob and the rest of his cast are doing is a great thing for morale. Their job is not an easy one, and they deserve a lot of credit. Bob had on a gray Palm Beach suit that gave evidence of the scarcity of cleaning and pressing shops over here. Both the collar and back of his coat were wrinkled and soiled, and his trousers were even worse. I'm sure everyone felt each wrinkle was a merit badge. And in common with sane people everywhere, air raids scare the heck out of the man. Still, he's here when he doesn't have to be. And that, in my humble judgment, passes very well for patriotism of a high order.

Hope's opening statement telling the men how glad he was to be with them made way for his first quip. "Fact is," he said, "I'm awfully glad to be anywhere this morning." He got a terrific hand. His next quip was after his statement that he'd spent the past two nights with us—"Bob

Hope knows where it's safe." Of course that's right, but he could be in the U.S.A. had he chosen to be.

Frances Langford made a big hit with her songs and also with her figure. Her pulchritude was accentuated by that sort of slack suit in which the pants and shirt fail to meet. You know the kind.

For our nurses, the climax of the program must have been when Bob Hope got Miss Ruth Hungerford, our smallest nurse, to dance with him while Frances sang. She was perfectly poised, and we all were proud of her for maintaining it when Hope just picked her up and started clowning.

Some kid whose temperature had been 104.8 with malaria yesterday and up to 105 this afternoon, yelled out about this time. He said that if Hope would sing, he'd dance with Frances Langford. Hope set Miss Hungerford down, grabbed the microphone, and called for the guy to step forward. Unable to withstand the uproar from the crowd, this eighteen-year-old New Yorker stepped up on the stage. The song he asked for at Bob's query was "something that will take me back to New York." Hope immediately admitted that his singing, great as it was, could bring neither a transport nor a subway into existence.

Hope sang and the kid danced rather poorly with Miss Langford, every soldier in the audience empathizing enviously, I'm sure. At the end, the kid kissed Miss Langford smack in the mouth and to heck with his malaria. "Now go back to your cold bed," quipped Hope. The patients yelled.

Jack Pepper, a good entertainer from Dallas, was in the show. Also the best guitar player I ever heard was with them, but I can't recall his name. Pepper says he will phone all of our folks when he gets back to Dallas and tell them how well we're situated. If he keeps that commitment, he'll make more than two hundred calls.

AUGUST 20, 1943. After two of the hardest days we've ever had, idleness for twenty-four hours has been most welcome. I think the hard work pepped everybody up, but we're still tired.

Bob Hope and party are still with us and stood with the officers and nurses for a picture. Jack Pepper is taking it back to the *Dallas News*.

Bowyer, a pretty good gagman himself, had the luck to eavesdrop on Hope and his gagman today. They were working up a program under a large tree that stands just outside Bowyer's window. As he relates it, the gagman would read off something as Hope listened solemn faced. Still with a solemn face he might say, "Yeah, that's funny," or, "Naw, that's no good." Rarely they'd laugh at their gags. Once Hope said, "If they don't laugh at that, I'll just bark 'wuff, wuff!'" Another time Hope said, "Leave it in, and if it doesn't get a laugh, I'll just say who in hell wrote that, anyway?"

Martinak is in here ironing again and smelling like hot biscuits. Every few weeks, he recalls the time in San Antonio when I was washing the car and Vic Linsey and his bride came over. Remember? He just giggles as the recollection hits him, but invariably he bursts out into a guffaw after reflection. I always thought your shielding of my exposure had been prompt and adequate, but Martinak still laughs. Do be blamed certain you burn those swimming trunks!

AUGUST 21, 1943. Boy! I got three letters today—your airmails of July 18 and July 30, and your V-mail of August 1. I've no way of telling which sort of mail is fastest, for they aren't consistent. More than once, a Dallas airmail reaches me on the same day as an Alvin V-mail, dated as much as a week earlier than the Dallas one. The exact reverse also happens, without rhyme or reason it seems. I do like airmail better, but there are days when nothing gets through except V-mails.

I'm glad I learned about your Gulf hurricane after the fact instead of before. Three weeks waiting to learn whether you'd survived one could be pretty tough. I don't remember what was in our big box in the storeroom, but I can't work up much excitement about its getting wet. I'll never forget when the roof blew off our house in the 1915 Galveston storm. Even the mattresses were soaked through, and we had to sleep on them, anyway. Of course, every stitch of clothing and bedding, and all mattresses, were carried out for days and days on end to get them dried. We all survived, and carpenters and family worked together replacing the roof. No Red Cross in those days. Blamed few, whether affluent or in poverty, would have accepted "charity," anyway.

Honey, you needn't get your dander up over who is and who isn't in uniform. In my own case, it's just a matter of misery loving company. If the army needs a young, healthy, unestablished medico badly enough, they'll take him. What really gets our dander up over here is that when they do take him, they frequently keep him in a hospital in the States and promote him right up to lieutenant colonel, while promotions with us are frozen. According to Kenneth Roberts, Gibbons, and others, it has been so in each army of recorded history. Why should it be any different now?

I hope you will edit my letter thoroughly if you're sending it to Mrs. Winans. I'm sure I was unusually impressionable at the time I wrote. Not only was it my first time out of sight of land, but none of us had the slightest idea where we were going or whether we'd ever see the Baylor unit again. Someone simply forgot to tell us that little detail. And of course, the beautiful voice of Kate Smith making an inventory of all of the things we were leaving didn't help. I did tell you the blasted navy slipped "God Bless America" onto the PA system as we walked off the ship into the darkness?

Too bad my typewriter turned out "not so good." I'd rather have mail in your own handwriting, of course, but thought you wanted to practice. I guess Suzanne is more of a handicap to typing now than she used to be in San Antonio. I always had to lock her out of the dining room while I worked on that paper. I'll never forget how mean she made me feel, flattening her nose against the glass in the French doors. She did want so badly to come in!

Mommy, you're right about being missed. The longer I stay away, the worse it gets. Nothing short of hard work seems to help. Happily, lots of work is available these days and my morale is good. But old Pappy does get pretty lonesome.

The July 2nd *Alvin Sun* came today, addressed to Camp Shanks, New York. I enjoy getting it and wish it came every week. *Time* is also sporadic in its arrival. The July 12 issue came two weeks ago, the July 5 just today. They're nonetheless welcome whenever they come.

Speaking of news, we hear a number of officers are being fined for writing items that should be restricted. The only information we've ever had dealing with the subject has come by way of rumor. We've never had any offical instructions. Kiss Suzanne. All my love always.

AUGUST 22, 1943. McClung and I climbed another high hill tonight with binoculars. The view was splendid, but when I got back at 8:00 P.M., one of my surgical cases had spiked a temperature of 104 following a chill. I've been hanging around the laboratory proving his trouble to be malaria. It seems Atabrine prophylaxis prevents malaria as long as the men get their pills every day. Anything that prevents their getting the drug every day results in their coming down promptly. By the time men reach us, most have missed Atabrine for a day or two, so they get a good case of malaria on top of whatever brought them to the hospital.

Bad news today! The surgical teams are being scrambled. There are fine men and fine surgeons here, but they don't necessarily come in compatible pairs like Dunlap and Devereux. They've charitably developed tolerance to my idiosyncrasies when they didn't have to do it. Tolerating any they may have is a pleasure for me, for I hold both in high esteem. Only the captains are moving this time, but our morales will plunge.

Martinak is pleased. He's been on the shock ward all this time with practically nothing to do. He will go on Small's team, and he admires Small, as almost everybody who knows him does.

AUGUST 23, 1943. Had a letter from sister Ruth this week selling me on the virtues of our daughter. She must have done a pretty good job, for I'm well sold.

Ruth still seems to think I'm in India, but I've no idea what made her imagine so. Probably an overly protective reaction that refuses to accept the reality of her youngest brother being in a war area. Her thought processes, unfortunately, don't always lead her to rational conclusions it seems. Although I've said it before, I now understand that we may say we're also in Tunisia. In addition to visits in Carthage, Bizerte, and Tunis, I came through Mateur and by famous Hill 609 on the way over here. Bob Hope described this area as "Texas with Arabs on it." Pretty accurate.

AUGUST 24, 1943. This is our third day without mail, and we get pretty mean after three such days. The mail orderly had better watch his step in the morning. On checking, I find I've received several June letters this month and am still short many July ones. Thus, the day has been very subdued—until this very minute when our PA system blared out with "Take It Off." That hit is high on the popularity list here.

I've done a circumcision today but little else. My experience with British soldiers could lead one to believe the United Kingdom is devoid of both rabbis and surgeons. Seriously, several patients have expressed delight in getting into an American hospital. Also, the French provincials and the Arabs accept our services rather readily. We get pepped up with the idea we're something special at times.

Jones, Alessandra, Brown, and La Due share the same room. I just went by to see Jones and found him taking the others to task for not joining him for a shower. Their valid reply was that they weren't going anywhere. Reasonable attitude.

AUGUST 25, 1943. Dadgum! Our team is broken up. Devereux was transferred to Bussey's, and Rowe to ours. Martinak is on Small's, and Galt is on Sebastian's. Lebermann goes to shock ward, and Alessandra to Willis' team. For some quarters, there is rejoicing. But by and large, the moves entail the weeping and wailing that goes with breaking up groups that have learned to work together with mutual respect and understanding. Carter's stated reasoning is that the shuffle will give all captains and lieutenants a chance to work with and learn from the majors. More likely, the real reason is that we're blessed in the unit with one major whose unquestioned competence as a surgeon is no help to subordinates who must work under him. Carter, I'm sure, realizes something will explode unless those subordinates are rotated.

Having said more than I'd intended to, I must explain that the major in question is simply not material for military command, for he has no concept of chain of command. On the other hand, he is a very talented musician with a personality befitting such a talent. He is a tireless volunteer of his time at the piano or accordion in our recreation areas the moment he leaves the operating room. Thus, he is a blessing to patients and personnel. Too bad he's not a hospital chaplain instead of a leader of a surgical team, for he does constitute a problem for both subordinates and superiors. He practically never visits a ward, and the few times he does, he is just as likely to pat the lowest ranking ward personnel on the back with instructions to "run this ward any way you want to," with no thought or realization that he has relinquished his own authority and denied it to those responsible for the patients. The ranking personnel on such wards seethe in frustration, the major going happily on his way, completely unaware. I do hope my luck holds out and I'm never on that team.

I've been most fortunate that my own immediate superiors, including Carter, have tolerated my shortcomings, as well as hostilities I've failed to cover up from time to time. As far as learning is concerned, most of us believe Sid Galt and Devereux can teach as much in a professional way as they're likely to learn from their superiors. Armies always were, and I'm sure always will be, funny things. It is remarkable how well they function in the face of the flagrant injustices, however unavoidable they admittedly are. War's victims are by no means limited to its vanquished side, never were, and I'm sure never will be.

Dunlap tells me that we lieutenants will be juggled next week, but he doesn't know where. I hate like poison to have to leave Dunlap, notwithstanding times past when I could have throttled him. He is much like a brother—one you fuss at and who fusses back but against whom no grudges and hard feelings seem to build up. No matter what the conflicts of the day, there's never anyone with whom you'd rather climb a hill after supper. In short, he is patient and tolerant to an unbelievable degree, held in high esteem by both subordinates and superiors, alike.

AUGUST 26, 1943. Honey, I hate to tell you the things that might worry you. I do it, though, and guess I'll keep it up. I do try to keep you as posted as I can on what's happening, whether good or bad. I'm sure I simply record how it is with most young medical officers or soldiers away from home under the abnormal circumstances of war. The temporarily bad is replaced by the temporarily good, and our experiences for inexplicable reasons seem to have been common to each wartime generation before us. Try not to worry as I go on.

You will recall I wrote that I'd stuck my neck out with Colonel Carter some time back. I'd reached an all-time low, but my morale took the usual 180-degree upturn common to all of us here as soon as I got it off my chest. It was after that sleepless night of frustration a month back, and I've not been so griped at any time since. All of us are much less in the dark as to what is expected of us now, and things do run more smoothly. The chief and Dunlap allowed me to fix up my ward the way I wanted, although far from sold on my ideas at the time. It runs well enough now that they're satisfied with it. So am I.

Adams, Martinak, Small, Dunlap, Arnold, Bowyer, and I got a truck and took the seashore drive last night. That was a pleasant diversion made more interesting by four tipsy French naval officers whom we'd picked up along the way. Adams acted as interpreter and found they were only recently back from Boston, with which they were impressed. Adams told them we were Texas cowboys, and they thought that pretty fine, too. They definitely did not like American liquor that "scratched their throats." When we let them out, they sounded off with a lusty, "Vive la France—vive les Americaines!" That seems to more or less express the sentiments of most of the French we see around here.

An officer's club was opened up in Bizerte today for all Allied officers in the vicinity. Maybe we'll have a place to spend more than the usual one or two dollars per month we've been spending to date. I'll mosey around to see what it looks like the first chance I get. Also a big PX opened today, and I'll be able to buy much needed insignia. My caduceus looks like it might have lain in the lion's den at nearby Carthage since the time the Romans destroyed it, so many centuries ago.

THE TIME FLIES 7
End of Summer 1943

AUGUST 27, 1943. Your July 31 airmail came today, and another came from Dean Moursund who said he'd enjoyed seeing you in Dallas.

I thought Suzanne was pretty smart to drag a stool out to the stairway to use for a table. Maybe she's sort of like her mommy. I told you I'd sent her all I could find for her birthday, didn't I? I can't make any promises but will try to get back to Tunis for Christmas presents for the two of you, or for whoever's name I draw in the family drawing. Draw names soon, honey, and tell me who I drew. I'll let you know in time to get something in the States in case I can't find anything over here.

Maggie, I'm sorry about the candlesticks, but none seem available in this part of Tunisia. I'll get back to the city if work slacks up, but I made every brass shop in the local medina without finding any. Maybe I'll be in Europe in the near future and find something there. Nobody knows.

Had another busy night but finished by 10:30 P.M. That meant I'd have a busy one on the ward today, and I've just finished after putting in eleven hours at it. My forty-bed ward stays full most of the time. Most of the cases are what we diagnose as "North African mocus," and they usually clear up promptly with plenty of soap and water on a daily basis. The

British soldiers in the desert do not ordinarily have access to adequate supplies for regular bathing, and they develop all sorts of skin lesions from local infections—otherwise known as "mocus." Another form of mocus is that which the rabbis have prevented since the time of Abraham by their ritual performed on all male newborns the eighth day. We also find cases of hemorrhoids, hernias, sprains, fractures, and others, these latter not contracted from church benches. Rowe and Dunlap's ward is the same size as mine and they get all postoperative cases that come in, as well as the more seriously injured, and even some of the "mocus." I usually continue to treat my own postoperative cases on their ward, but do little else there. They are actually responsible for all cases on my ward and come around once or twice a week to check them over. The arrangement is practical and personally gratifying without reduplication of doctors' efforts.

AUGUST 28, 1943. Your July 30 letter came today telling me of Aunt Alice's death. I know my Aunt Phoebe will be lost without her, and I'm awfully sorry they have to be separated. I'd guess Aunt Alice's age at eighty-two, but I never thought of her as old. She was always so interested in people and things that one never noticed her age.

I didn't have much work to do today and balked at what little I did have. Did a herniorrhaphy this morning, and as Bussey was following me in the operating room, I stayed to watch him repair a femoral hernia. Having never seen one done before, I was quite interested, particularly as Bussey demonstrated each move as he went along. I believe I could do one now as easily as I can the much more common inguinal types. He is conscientious about his work, performing textbook surgery as Mayo-trained men always do, but I believe for the ordinary run of cases I'd prefer Dunlap as more versatile. Incidentally, Bussey is pleased to get Devereux for his captain, never failing to tell me so whenever our paths cross—usually at the latrine.

Tonight's war news told of the Japs withdrawing from New Georgia Island. The news continues to be very good on all fronts, and I'm anxious for later editions of *Time* to see how they interpret it.

AUGUST 29, 1943. Sunday again, and this time it seems like Sunday. My word, the weeks do speed by! It seems like a lifetime since we were together, but I can't imagine having been away from home over five months. It seems like we were beefing about Camp Don B. Passage no more than a couple of weeks back. If the time keeps moving so fast, maybe it won't seem like so long until I'll be with you again. I'm sure

Suzanne's growth in the interval will be a shock to me, though, as I'm only beginning to get used to her last pictures.

Not much work today. I got through by noon and have been at a loss for something to do. Too bad I don't have a batch of clothes to wash, but I did two weeks' accumulation yesterday and have nothing soiled. You did know we do our own laundry? And you know most of us don't do any ironing, and those who do smell like hot biscuits? None of the officers own an iron, but the nurses do and are liberal with them.

Ford came by last night for a long bull session. He hasn't had a drink since his tentmates tied him to the flagpole while he sobered up and quieted down. The sober state being almost pathological in his case, he explains that since Carol isn't here he has no one to drink with, no place to go, and nothing to do, so what the heck? He added that he did not intend to wash a sock, sleep without a sheet, eat a mouthful of powdered egg, fill out a government form, or draw a sober breath for a full month after getting back to the States. Also, like nearly everyone else over here, he says he doesn't intend to work as hard when he gets back home as he did before he left. Maybe nobody, especially doctors, will work very hard when they get out. It could very well be that those who stayed home will have everything sewed up so tight there won't be much for us to do. We may have to play second fiddle to them, at that. "Ain't it a funny world?" And a soldier's mind does harbor thoughts such as these at times.

AUGUST 30, 1943. Jones, Arnold, and Brown, all ex-students from Texas Med, are interested, but not atwitter, at your friend Margaret and their ex-dean's coming blessed event. They have very, very little use for Dr. Spock, as you know. I'll bet Mrs. Schoeffer is all pepped up over it. I was very surprised, what with Margaret's going to be a doctor. Maybe she is glad that's over with, or is it?

I don't know what to do about your allotment but guess I'll just have to let it slide until I learn whether the August check came in. I got a notice some time ago that your check in the amount of $1,252.73 would go to the Alvin State Bank. It was from the War Department Office of Dependency Benefits, 213 Washington Street, Newark, New Jersey, and by way of identification bore the initials MST. They tell me here that you were not entitled to a change in the amount for June. If things aren't straight by the time you receive this, do write to the Office of Dependency Benefits, referring them to your letter and those MST initials, and ask them what the heck? The letter I have states that you have been furnished a copy of it and that correspondence should not be necessary. Give all information if you write, and be as nasty as you like. You might also give your bank all of the information and get them to write, too. The principle of the thing provokes me to no end. To think I'm in a foreign country where communications take from two weeks to three months to reach the States, if indeed they ever do, and my wife and baby don't get the money they're dependent on to live when it's due. Tell them that, although they've probably heard it from so many sources they're calloused to it.

A British Lieutenant Kowlosy came in just now to see about one of his "blokes" who is a patient here. Merrick is out so I've been pumping the officer about this and that and finally got a good conversation out of him. I found that his great-grandfather from whom the name came was Hungarian. This Hungarian had a brother, and both of them were active on the wrong side of a revolution there a century ago. The grandfather fled to England while the brother went to America. The grandfather settled in Highgate simply because he did not have money to pay the required toll for proceeding toward London. Highgate is now a London suburb and is still the home of the Kowlosys.

More about Highgate from my source. A few centuries earlier, a thirteen-year-old boy named Richard Willingham or Whittington, or something like that, was trudging down the highway with his cat. By the time he had come within a mile or so of Highgate, he was so exhausted and so hungry he'd given up all hope of ever reaching his destination. He sat down upon a rock by the side of the road to either rest or die, not really caring which. That rock is still pointed out simply because the English never forget historical facts and never destroy landmarks that commemorate them. Anyway, as Richard sat there, Bow bells rang out, and he realized he could not be far from the city. He got up straightway and went on in, later becoming Lord Mayor of London. "He became Lord Mayor three times, actually," says Lieutenant Kowlosy. Most English statements of fact do end in "actually." Merrick came back about that time, actually.

Major Dunlap, Captains Hahn, Soper, La Due, Turnbow, E. Jones, Brown, and I played poker until 10:30 last night. Ours is called the "scrub team" to differentiate it from the "varsity squad," made up of our CO, Jones, Lebermann, Willis, and Sebastian. Sometimes our Dunlap, La Due, and White play. They play no-limit. We play a twenty-five cent limit. I won thirteen dollars that I can't spend. When we were premed classmates, that Sebastian was a mean poker player, and I'll bet he still is. He, Lebermann, and Willis were classmates in medical school where Lebermann and Willis should have learned better.

SEPTEMBER 1, 1943. I was busy last night and didn't get a chance to write. Am writing in the afternoon this time, lest the procedure be repeated.

I was moved to our musician's team along with Alessandra at noon yesterday. Bowyer went to the shock ward, Johnson to Small's team, White to Bussey's, Brown to Dunlap's, and Peterson to Sebastian's. This completes the scrambling of all the old teams. I hated to leave my ward when everything was running so smoothly, but the new ward seems to be running just as smoothly in every way. Maybe the organization will profit from all of this, as everyone will certainly get new ideas from their new associates.

Postman has been on a two-day strike again, and nothing over here happens that can be told. Fact is, nothing happens in these parts, period. We did have fried eggs—not powdered—for breakfast this morning, and of course that is news of the highest order. I believe we've had fresh eggs only once before, and that was the morning I slept through breakfast. No telling what our mess fund had to pay for those eggs, but probably plenty. On the last account, I heard Craven had tried to buy a few thousand. The best price he could find was more than a dime each. We all blasphemed the natives considerably for trying to hold us up on everything when we first arrived. It turns out that we weren't lily white either. They have paid soldiers four dollars per carton for cigarettes costing us only forty-five cents. They'll also pay twenty-five dollars for a pair of field shoes. Evidently, inflation is the culprit rather than the natives. That must go pretty hard on local laborers in these parts.

McCauley got hold of a pair of scales somewhere, calibrated in kilos, of course. Most of the officers have found they've lost considerable weight, while most of the nurses have gained moderately. Martinak has lost twenty pounds, and I, thirty. I weigh 148, my lowest since high school days. I don't see how that is possible since I do eat like a horse, and I don't doubt that I've even eaten a bit of horse itself, now and then.

SEPTEMBER 3, 1943. Maybe your postmaster is right about your airmails cluttering up the service, but I find it hard to believe. We're told V-mail always has priority, airmail only moves if there is available space, and regular mail comes in last. I doubt the postmaster's story, because most of your letters require more than a month to reach me, whether V-mail, air, or regular. You can tell him for me that being there at the post office in Alvin, he couldn't possibly understand what a long letter from a wife means to a soldier in North Africa. Tell him I'd be happy to settle for two or three letters per week if I had any assurance they'd get through, but no such assurance exists. Neither he, you, nor I knows which ones will make it through. And he might also be told that we've yet to run across comparable misery to that of no mail from home for four or more days. Of course we'll tolerate it if the mail actually becomes so heavy it has to be curtailed, but don't stop until you have to, please.

Bowyer and I had an interesting patient last night. He was not an American, although American aviators came to see him, bringing him candy, cigarettes, and chewing gum. His name is Fritz Luenger, and he has a thick neck that drops down vertically from the back of his head. His erstwhile adversaries tell us that if their respective positions had been reversed, Fritz would have brought them such things. Maybe so. Armies certainly are peculiar things in some ways, and I suppose their air corps are no different.

Bowyer and I worked on Fritz for over two hours, finding him an appreciative and cooperative patient. Some thief had relieved him of a fine watch before he reached us, and he was worried for fear of losing the three rings we'd taken from his fingers. He was particularly concerned about his wedding ring, which incidentally was worn on his right hand. We hope he'll be all right physically, mentally, and morally after the war is over. And I guess that is about all I may tell you about Fritz except that he is thirty-two years old.

Sorry I didn't get to write last night, but before Fritz came in, Uncle Harry had sent the chaplain to round up several of us away from Soper's radio to come to his quarters and eat up some turkey and hot dogs he'd acquired somewhere. We all had a very nice two hours with him, and there was not a drop of liquor in evidence.

Turnbow reports sadly that Marilyn's mother writes that little Marilyn was asking for him a lot that day. She'd been saying that if her daddy was home, he'd play with her. McCauley, who left his wife and child in Detroit when he came into the army a year before most of us, says it requires eighteen months for things at home to adjust to a soldier's absence.

SEPTEMBER 4, 1943. I was real glad to get Randolph's letter telling about your father's condition. The talk of X-ray treatments, collapsed vertebrae, etc., along with the history of urinary difficulty he'd given me last spring had me worried. Tell Randolph thanks. Tell him, too, that Brown was pleased to hear from him and glad he'd applied for a commission. I'm glad he offered to go but hope he doesn't get called in. If he is called up, tell him for me that in my experience it takes about sixteen months to adjust. What at first are likely interpreted as so many unjust inequalities, finally turn out to be inevitable army life situations, and are accepted as such. The situations don't change, but one's bitterness does, particularly when busy.

[My wife's brother-in-law, Randolph Jones of Houston, had graduated with Brown and Jabez Galt in 1941. He had finished his internship and started assisting a Houston neurosurgeon. Called into the army in 1943, he'd been sent to Walter Reed in Washington, D.C., for further training and, finally, to Belgium as a neurosurgeon. His unit was in the Battle of the Bulge and got back home before ours did.]

One of the local British officers is quartered on top of the highest hill in this area, which gives him a magnificent view. He invited McClung and me over for dinner last night, and we had a most interesting evening. He is quartered in an old castlelike structure at the very tip of North Africa, the hill rising up a bit less than a thousand feet over the Mediterranean, and we've been wanting to go up there ever since our arrival. Well, we had a fine evening, the three of us being served by the officer's enlisted man whom he referred to as his batman. We had roast beef, potatoes, and onions, all excellent—or at least made so by the inevitable Scotch whiskey. You know, England sends each officer a fifth of a gallon every month. Finished up with real English hot tea, cream and sugar, which was also good.

In addition to the excellent meal and wonderful view, we also had a bit of excitement. As I've probably told you before, the Germans are in the habit of sending a few bombers over to harass Bizerte Harbor from time to time. They have to come in low to escape our radars and ack-ack, which they frequently do. Last night after dinner, a single bomber came in from the Mediterranean flying so low we could look down on it and right into the eyes of one of its pilots. Incidentally, he got through the ack-ack, dropped his bombs, and came right by us again, unscratched.

Not much work today. Guess we're too far from the activity to expect much more here. I imagine that some day out of a clear sky, I'm going to take a bit of an interesting trip, but you'll know it if I do. We saw a clipping from the *Dallas News* today that referred to us as "the famous 56th." My, my, my! If we're ever famous, it will be because some general's press agents give us a big buildup. We've had personages and events around here that might do the trick, too. [Among other flamboyant personages who'd been around was Gen. George Patton, who'd been stealing the show from other English and American generals in the Sicilian campaign. He'd come over to check up on the cases of "battle fatigue" we'd been receiving from Sicily. He'd have no part of such a diagnosis, although the army pretty well proves the point that the average soldier has a breaking point, beyond which he cannot function effectively after a certain number of hours on the front line. It was in our receiving section that he'd slapped one of these enlisted men, calling him a g—d—coward. *The Stars and Stripes* got hold of this news and publicized it widely, probably not dismaying the general too much. His enlisted men weren't too perturbed by it, either, as my ward full of them said they'd rather serve under him, slapped or not, than under any other general in the field. He moved so fast they felt safer under him, although it was said to dismay his superiors.][1]

SEPTEMBER 5, 1943. Boy, I hit the jackpot today! Eleven letters from you, three from Mary, and one from Mama. All of these were either regular or airmails, their dates ranging from August 5 through 17. I'm sure they came over by convoy without knocking any soldiers out of their V-mails.

All eight pictures of you and Suzanne came through, and I was tickled to get them. McClung was impressed with the setting as well as the subjects. He thought your home the most comfortable looking place imaginable. I do hope you can keep getting film, for all of us enjoy pictures from home. Suzanne's hair looks cute all platted up, doesn't it? Her mommy looks pretty cute too, honey, and how I'd love to see you.

I also believe a bit of ignoring might be an excellent way to help a two-year-old out of tantrums. Boy, the little buggers develop minds of their own mighty early, don't they? Glad you told me about it.

I'm relieved that your August allotment came through okay. Hon, I enjoy hearing about your finances. And if you've saved up two hundred dollars on the insurance loan and a set of Compton's and a dress, you're surely doing fine. If you'd apply that two hundred on the insurance loan, you'd save six percent and could borrow it back any time you needed it. I just learned from today's letters that you'd sent Mama's and Jeanette's checks, too. They think it was mighty fine of you and so do I. I'm glad you bought the crystal and had the typewriter cleaned. [I'd had to borrow thirteen hundred dollars for uniforms and the like when I went into the army. I got what I could from insurance and the rest from members of my family.]

Another quiet day. Highlight was seeing a paratrooper who had injured a knee during a jump back in Fort Benning, Georgia, in July, 1942. He has shied clear of the medics ever since it happened for fear he'd be grounded. He'd made a good many jumps since his accident in spite of pain, the last one July 9th during the Sicilian landings. He stayed through the campaign but then turned in and got the first x-ray he's had. By golly, he has an old, ununited fracture of his kneecap! He must really have what it takes, and I guess the world doesn't produce any better soldier than that.

SEPTEMBER 6, 1943. The chaplain had quite an experience last night. Either that or he bribed a driver to tell one whale of an exaggerated story. Anyway, the enlisted men were having a dance. The Red Cross had somehow convinced the parents of two truckloads of French girls that they'd be properly chaperoned and have a good time if they attended. So the chaplain and the two drivers went to the appointed place to pick up the girls. While the girls were getting on the trucks, seven British sailors came by and became obnoxious. The final result was, according to the drivers, that the chaplain fought all seven of them. They were delighted to add he licked all seven of them. Boy! They think he is really something and he must be—all six feet, one inch, and two hundred pounds of him. I'd never join his Baptist church if I thought I'd irritated him in any way just before the baptism. (The sailors were intimidated by his rank, I'd bet.)

I've again arrived at a point where I'm not earning my salt. My ward is full of the North African mocus, which requires very little of my time and even less of whatever medical intelligence remains. It's funny how we work our heads off for a few days and then loaf for a week or so. If everyone in the army could do whatever he had to in one stretch and get it over with, a ten-year war could probably be fought to its conclusion in thirty days.

SEPTEMBER 7, 1943. The week is still quiet. Fritz Luenger, about whom I wrote, parachuted to safety from his falling bomber, or he'd not have lived to be our patient. We have to talk mostly through an interpreter, but we get along that way. He seems a lot like anybody else we treat. I believe I told you some American airmen brought him gifts as soon as they learned he was here. They wanted to make sure he was treated well and could write home to tell about it, for they tell us American airmen falling into German hands are well treated. For all I know, these two Americans may have been the very ones who shot Fritz down. Some funny war!

Our CO volunteered the information last night that my captaincy would probably come within the next ten days. I mention this in spite of the fact it may very well get snarled up in red tape somewhere. I know you can stand the suspense as well as I can.

SEPTEMBER 8, 1943. Two fried eggs for breakfast make this a red-letter day. Also, be advised that I've vacillated to the point of recognizing several things that reflect credit on our commanding officer.

Martinak is on Small's surgical team. He still doesn't have much to do but is happier than when he was on the shock ward with even less to occupy his time. He says Macy and Jean are moving to Henderson about the 15th.

SEPTEMBER 9, 1943. Soper, Brown, Arnold, Lebermann, Dunlap, Devereux, Turnbow, Adams, and I have just come back from the beach after a swim. That is the finest beach one can imagine, and we always have a big time when we go down there. Each time we go we vow to return every day for more of the same. Why don't we? Because we're simply too lazy for any use, I suppose.

Turnbow is exactly like a little kid. He plays as naturally as a child and with as much imagination. Tonight after everyone else had walked up on the beach, Turnbow was still swimming slowly. Of course, he was in no more than a foot of water as he chugged along. He yelled out that he was playing like he was an LST fixing to "beach." In case you've forgotten, an LST is one of several types of landing craft the navy has for beach landings. It is the type that made landings in Sicily possible. It is also what we crossed the Atlantic in, Turnbow being as inhuman as the captain of the vessel and never getting seasick.

A book could be written about Turnbow, and while I'm at it, I may as well expose a bit more of his unique insides. He was the first inebriate I ever heard excuse himself for a night's intemperance by waking up those of his running mates who were asleep when he came in, to ask if they'd noticed how drunk it was outside. I heard the question used by entertainers afterward, but conceivably, Turnbow may have originated it that night.

We're all doing less and less, day by day. One or two have reservations on the first army plane with the space to spare to take them to Cairo. I'm going to try to get a pass, too. Undoubtedly, we're going to move before long, but I surely can't tell where or when.

Colonel Carter got a swell trip to England and hasn't come back yet. He had to accompany a British general whom he'd cared for here for some weeks. The old gentleman, the general that is, pulled what he calls a "goofer" during one of the bigger air raids a few weeks back. He stood outside and watched it in great glee until taking a fair-sized chunk of flak in his right shoulder. Evidently the metal was falling straight down and with the force of a bullet. It entered his shoulder, tore down through his lung, diaphragm, liver, and colon to lodge in his pelvis. Nobody knows why it didn't kill him except he had one blamed good surgeon to patch him and practically nurse him ever since. He'll get well, I think.

Our war news continues mighty good. I hope it never gets bad again.

SEPTEMBER 10, 1943. I wonder how folks at home are taking the war news. All that we get is extremely good. McCleary remarks that when Italy fell, he almost did, too, with his celebrating. I smelled some of his so-called cognac. It smelled about like kerosene and likely tasted worse. I decided at the time that I was happy enough without it.

Today we heard that the Italian fleet has come over to the Allies intact, and that's really news. There has been a rumor all day that the Allies have landed at four French ports, but none of us believe it.

Last night Jabez Galt, La Due, an English officer, and I went into town to see Bob Hope in *Ghost Chasers*, or some such title. We never saw it. About halfway through the first short feature, all sound effects stopped. After thirty minutes of catcalls and worse, it was announced that the projection machine was on the blink. The show was cancelled, as it frequently is. Our sound equipment over here must be holdovers from the middle twenties, well worn and well bombed. In disgust, we walked about halfway back to the hospital before an ambulance picked us up.

I have been reminded again of those days at Fort Sam Houston when all of us attempted to get quickly off the post at the end of each day so we'd not be caught there during retreat. I could never overcome an embarrassing self-consciousness at the ritual of getting out of my car to face the flag, stand at attention, and salute. We have the same ceremony here at 6:00 P.M. We still try to escape the ritual by scurrying inside at the bugler's first note. Today, however, Arnold, Jones, McClung, Merrick, and I turned to face the flag, came to attention, and saluted smartly, holding the salute throughout the entire ritual of retreat. It all happened because along with mischievous Martinak, we'd been sitting outside our quarters talking and waiting for the bugle's first note. It came, and we all jumped for the door as usual. But unnoticed, Martinak had sneaked inside a minute sooner and locked the door. His giggling reached our ears above the bugle notes throughout the ceremony. We'll extract retribution as soon as all agree on what is appropriate.

SEPTEMBER 13, 1943. Many medical students around 1935 were assigned to write a paper on the topic of sulfanilamide. The drug had only recently been released and was the first antibacterial agent available that really worked. Research for their paper invariably carried the students through a score of articles by Long and Bliss, America's leading authorities on the drug. Well, what do you know? Colonel Winans' friend who has spent a good deal of time with us this summer, Col. Perrin Long of Johns Hopkins, is that same Long of sulfanilamide fame. He is presently consultant in internal medicine for our North African theater. When I researched my paper on the topic, I'd no idea of ever meeting either Long or Bliss. Equally famous is the area's consultant in surgery, Colonel Churchill of Harvard, who is also a frequent visitor. War does throw celebrities and lowly lieutenants together sometimes.

I finished my work on the ward in about forty-five minutes this morning and have spent the rest of the day reading Sinclair Lewis's *Arrowsmith*. The characters are all so typical of those found around teaching hospitals that I was amazed a medical layman could have such understanding of them. Where else but in the latrine could I ever have had the matter explained? Voicing my amazement to all who happened to be present at the time I was there, who should speak up but Colonel Perrin Long? He volunteered the information that Sinclair Lewis had collaborated with Paul de Kruif, Ph.D. in bacteriology and a former professor in Johns Hopkins. That's interesting. I believe it, and nowhere except in a latrine would I have been chitchatting with anyone who could have explained it.

My centigrade thermometer reached 32 degrees today. That is by far the hottest day we've seen this summer, 89.6 degrees F.

Willis has just brought me my binoculars. He borrows them quite regularly to go out and watch Mediterranean traffic. He attempts to evaluate our war effort by counting the ships from day to day. His estimate tonight is that the European war will be over in six months and the Pacific war six months after that. I hope he's more infallible in that area than in some others. My sour note here is not to be interpreted as unfavorable criticism of musical or surgical ability.

---

[1]Editor's note: Most of the statement in brackets appears to be incorrect. I doubt that *Stars and Stripes* ever publicized the slapping incidents in Sicily by Patton. At Eisenhower's request, the war correspondents did not file stories on the two incidents, and it did not become public knowledge until November 1943 when Drew Pearson first revealed it on his weekly radio show. Collins's statement that it would not have dismayed Patton too much is probably incorrect. Also, his statement that the incidents took place in North Africa is wrong, as both incidents took place in Sicily in the 15th and 93d Evacuation Hospitals. …Carlo D'Este

THE LAST DAYS AT BIZERTE 8

Early September 1943

SEPTEMBER 12, 1943. The Tulane Medical College unit has moved in on us and is bivouacked in our backyard. We've heard nothing official as yet, but we believe they will eventually take over our buildings. Their Methodist chaplain conducted services here today, and Dunlap and I went over to hear him. We sat so far back that we couldn't really hear what he was saying, and we had not been to a service since the Sunday in Orleansville, on the way out from Casablanca. Still, Dunlap claims we did get a mighty sermon from an ant we were watching beneath our feet. The ant had his heart set on carrying a beetle many times his size across a ten-foot strip of grass. He finally made it, but it took him twenty minutes by Dunlap's watch. He claims the sermon we got was "Tackle the big things." Who'd believe Dunlap is to be forty on his next birthday?

SEPTEMBER 15, 1943. Dunlap, Johnson, Craven, Bowyer, and I went into Bizerte last night to take in the officer's club, so I didn't write you. The club is largely just an upstairs terrace overlooking Lake Bizerte and the harbor. The lake isn't really a lake, being more correctly a gut. It is an outpouching of deep tidewater from the Mediterranean, and the two are connected by a narrow neck of deep water through which ships pass readily. British, French, and

American officers sit up here at the club and drink vin rouge for lack of anything better to do. Just the same, we all enjoyed the evening and have decided to go back.

We have to give up our utopia of fine buildings and move across the fence into tents but not for two more days. The arrangement will last until we reopen a hospital elsewhere. The Tulane unit will move into the buildings and operate a station hospital. They've been getting in our hair for the past ten days or so, and now we'll turn the tables on them.

Your August 27 and 29 V-mails came yesterday. I'm glad to learn that Pvt. Goldstein's letter survived censorship. Of course, he was not the only British soldier to survive the Dunkirk disaster and escape back to England, but he's probably the only one you or I will ever communicate with. He didn't even get time off for a furlough home before shipping out to Tobruk. He spent days writing that letter for you and I'm sure would have told you more about the French underground girl if he'd felt he could. He is afraid Blanche is still active in the underground and he might blow her cover. He's been back to visit us once since leaving the hospital.

I'd really love to take you and Suzanne to some of the beaches around here. They're no better than the ones at Galveston, but some of them are just as good. Mediterranean water is less salty than that in the Gulf of Mexico and is very clear. Some beaches do become cluttered with seaweed from time to time, but not usually. I suppose we'll be spending a lot of time in the water from now on, and maybe I'll get tanned again. I've lost all the tan acquired in San Antonio, having made no effort to maintain it here.

As to the books I'd like you to send me, any of the pocket book editions of best-seller novels or biographies would be fine, and any books you may run across on medical history, also. And I wish you'd subscribe to the *Reader's Digest* for me. Maybe I'll be too busy to read them when they first arrive, but I can always save them for slack periods.

SEPTEMBER 16, 1943. The young fathers in the outfit look forward to those letters from home that relate the everyday things engaged in by mothers and little ones. These are the matters that keep us posted not only on our wives' activities but also on the development of the little ones. Snapshots of wives and children are in great demand, notwithstanding the pain they may cause. It is the rapid development of the children that causes the shock.

Having been reduced to smoking either English cigarettes or corn silk for some days, a package from home containing two flat fifties of Camels and six packages of Philip Morrises was most welcome.

I told you the Tulane unit had been getting in our hair for some time. They're in bivouac, and we're doing practically nothing. We might as well be bivouacked, too. Now such a situation presents both groups with a problem. Ours is a problem in management. How do we get all of that fresh New Orleans currency out of their pockets and into ours in a legitimate manner? Their problem is how to prevent this. Our solution seems clear enough, as all we'd have to do is teach them the evils of gambling. Their solution is none of our business. Whether they originated the idea in a moment of avarice, or whether we did it from our sense of duty, I'm not sure, but dice games seem to have solved our problem instead of theirs. We do seem to have done our duty by them, teaching them how evil such "three dimensional vice" can become for some people. We're flush while they're so broke I doubt we'll have the opportunity to teach them about the evil of "two dimensional vice," that type played with cards rather than dice. Ha.

SEPTEMBER 18, 1943. Well, we had quite a party last night. It's the first one I've attended since you and I went to the New Year's hop at Charlie's Place in Oak Cliff. All in all, it was pretty flat without the wives to help us celebrate. Sobriety wasn't one of its weak points, and probably the chaplain is the only officer around who isn't ready to sign the pledge. I had a good time I guess, but alcohol seems to increase my homesickness above the chronic level constant with all of us who have wives and babies at home. I surely do miss you, Margaret, every day of the world, more than I can possibly tell you. The party broke up at 11:00 P.M., and our heads after that, although mine isn't too bad since I ate breakfast.

I'm ready to crucify Dunlap again. Still, he's so meek and humble with his cussedness, making no defense of his orneriness. Would-be crucifiers get little satisfaction from their plans. Anyway, a string of six or seven of us noticed that visiting officers were giving our younger nurses a grand rush while ignoring our oldest. She was a lady in her fifties with whom we agreed to dance, tagging each other at reasonable intervals. I was next to last in the line with Dunlap following me. After too many dances with the lady, I caught Dunlap just as he was sneaking out. He admitted that he was pretty terrible, confessing without bitterness and without repentance. So what can you do with a guy like that? Maybe I can frame him some time.

Still, my luck held out pretty well. On leading him home, we found one of the psychiatrists from the Tulane group in the tent, drunker than

Dunlap. I left the neighbor psychoanalyzing him. This morning, witnesses tell me the shrink made out to test reflexes by hitting Dunlap on the head with a shoe. The diagnosis became obvious at once—the patient was suffering from juvenile regression characterized by blind fury. Salutary, indeed, the results of good psychoanalysis.

SEPTEMBER 20, 1943. Stated simply, I'm going to report a squabble between the Baylor and Tulane units. And rather than harboring a delusion that units are led by highly educated physicians whose maturity should insure against such squabbles, I take the position that esprit de corps implies a readiness to display hostility. Of course the word "unit" implies an esprit de corps.

As I "come clean" on the squabble, I do so in the belief that with so many individuals involved, both units are fairly representative of the human species. Admittedly both organizations have been conditioned by war. And war is an inexplicably tolerated and recurrent human experience!

The squabble's opening foray was a scream of anguish let out by our replacement when we moved our own stuff out of the hospital. I guess there'll be no more dice games, either. Having been under our feet for about two weeks, the Tulaners had noticed the equipment and conveniences we had installed. They must have thought we'd just walk out and leave it all with them, but no such thing ever crossed our minds.

In defense of anybody's adolescent attitude, it probably should be made clear that our supply section had offered on several occasions to trade them our functioning PA system, telephone system, plumbing system, installed wiring, installed water pipes, and the like for theirs. Ours was functioning and theirs was packed, but ours had been used since June and theirs was new and shiny. They procrastinated and refused to trade.

Of course, we had accomplished a great deal here without any outside help, but they were green and couldn't appreciate that. We had gathered up and disposed of unbelievable quantities of refuse from French, Italian, and German occupations of the buildings. How could they know about that? We'd also deloused the place, scrubbed walls, ceilings, and floors and spread many a gallon of whitewash where it did the most good. Of course, they couldn't know about any of that, either, but we did. So all the screams of anguish were cool cloths to our figuratively fevered brows. We could hardly bear to abandon the fruits of our own labor to those whose brows had not sweat. And to anyone who believes he hears a growl somewhat like a dog in someone's manger, I can only point out that McGuffey would never have immortalized that particular dog in the first place, had he not acted in so human a manner.

Finally, capping the climax and adding the coolest of all cloths to our brows, the base section declined our invitation to come out and inspect our equipment when the Tulane unit reported us for stripping the buildings. Our innocence is so appalling, and it's all been great fun. Now we're all going to reread *How to Win Friends and Influence People*. We'll begin just as soon as we finish savoring our report from the British major across the road. He says his outfit has been replaced at least a dozen times in the past three years. Each time, his replacement's attitude has been the same as the Tulane unit's.

We moved and settled down into our tents yesterday. We're so unified by the row with Tulane—so filled with a new esprit de corps—that we like tents. You know the Germans yielded their place as our number-one enemy sometime ago. They retain second place on a permanent basis while first place shifts from one superior officer to another, one branch of the service to another, one military unit to another, or one segment of society to another. Sometimes it's all civilians, sometimes labor, but always somebody. Once it was even lovely voiced Kate Smith singing "God Bless America," but you know about that.

SEPTEMBER 21, 1943. I'm always running out of paper and can't buy any around here. I frequently connive with supply for typewriter second sheets, which serve very well. Unless I can connive, I'll just have to use Merrick's V-mails while they last.

Still funny business is the mail service. One or two of us may get a letter ten days faster than anyone else in the outfit, then wait two weeks to a month for fill-ins. Mail to the States is just as capricious, for some wife is always writing, "Why does Dorothy La Due get a letter dated August 29 when my latest is dated the 17?" The next week Dorothy will ask La Due why he can't write a letter every day if Brown can. Also, "Why don't you tell me interesting things like Ben tells Mattie?" or, "If Martinak can tell where he is and write the details of an air raid, why can't you?" At the time Martinak wrote about the air raid, he shook in his boots wondering if the censor would catch it and file a complaint against him. Then some husband will sit down to write, others watching him like a hawk, clamoring after his first paragraph to stop so that their wives won't fuss.

Did I tell you we listen to Lord Haw-Haw broadcasting lies from Berlin in his perfect Oxford accent? We hear him many evenings as he puts out one after another. Many of them are so obvious that a schoolboy would detect them, while others may be detectable only because we're on the particular ground he's speaking about. He'll tell how a few hundred German bombers devastated our area on such-and-such a date when we know the area has hardly been touched.

Daily life in our present medina may approach that of Riley, but only if Riley can be imagined to live in idleness in a wonderful climate, in a country "that looks like Texas with Arabs on it," and only if he can be imagined to have a wife and child or children in the good old U.S.A. Riley would undoubtedly get bored if it continued much longer. And if this letter is censored, we're bound to be moving on.

SEPTEMBER 22, 1943. Colonel Carter is still not back from flying his British general to London. The old general made us a present of his Mercedes sedan, which is quite an automobile when our motor pool can keep it functioning. It had belonged to General Von Arnim of the Afrika Korps, and possibly to Rommel for all I know.

SEPTEMBER 23, 1943. A bunch of us went to Tunis and Carthage yesterday and got back at 10:30 P.M. to learn that our boredom might not last another day. We found half of our stuff already on trucks and ready to move out. I'm sad this couldn't have waited another couple of days, for I had passage on an army plane for Cairo tomorrow morning and now can't go.

SEPTEMBER 24, 1943. We spent this day getting our personal belongings ready for the move and at 6:00 P.M. were divided into three groups. The nurses are to go on one of three ships, a group of officers and enlisted men on each of the other two. At 7:00 P.M. my group boarded trucks, but "snafu" (GI acronym for "situation normal—all fouled up") overtook us. We had to wait on the road for an hour and a half until our orders had been cleared somewhere up the line of command. After another two-hour wait while our equipment was being loaded, we finally got on board ship at 10:00 P.M. Do remember, we'd been up since 5:00 A.M. in wool—heavy army wool—on the hottest day we'd had in Bizerte.

SEPTEMBER 28, 1943 [written after landing at Paestum, Italy]. Our ship was an LST, identical to the bucking torment we'd crossed on in the Atlantic. This landing ship tank is an ingenious, flat-bottomed prodigy of necessity, designed for landing armored tanks and troops.

ITALY
CAPITULATES   9
September–October 1943

SEPTEMBER 29, 1943. Paestum.[1] Writing has not been possible for a few days due to the complete change in our living quarters. We're more settled at the moment, but I can't tell you much more than that just yet.

I am living in a large tent with more tentmates than I've ever had before. And it isn't every lieutenant who gets to share quarters with six majors, either. Rippy, Dunlap, Sebastian, Lebermann, M. Jones, Willis, along with the usual hoi polloi like Martinak, Merrick, McCauley, Hahn, Rowe, and I share this one.

We had a typical Gulf Coast country downpour last night accompanied by high winds, both elements anathema to tent dwellers. And it's been so long since we've seen rain, we weren't prepared for it. We had to spend a couple of hours securing our own tents and then helping others with theirs. One of the tents housing the nurses blew down, and they were like a bunch of drowned rats, as you may well imagine. We all pitched in and did what we could for them, which wasn't just a heck of a lot. As usual my luck held, and mine was one of the few beds in our tent that did not get wet. Also as usual, Dunlap's bed was in a poorly chosen area and nearly floated off, everything he had getting soaked.

The soil here, for all the world, is like that at Alvin and grows Bermuda grass and nut grass just as

A visit to Greek temples at Paestum, Italy. Collins is on the right.

luxuriantly. I believe the nut grass has grown three inches since last night, and everything is green and clean. That was some rain, some wind, and some tent living!

SEPTEMBER 30, 1943. I believe my last letter written from North Africa had us bedded down for our voyage. We didn't move until about dusk next day!

Most of the following afternoon we were in sight of mountains, some on Sicily and others on the many small islands of the Tyrrhenian Sea. It was a pretty trip, and although some of our group who had not crossed the Atlantic in an LST thought it a rough one, we knew better.

On Monday morning, after having been on our craft since Friday evening, we were offshore between Salerno and Paestum. Two weeks earlier the 36th Division of Texas had made its landings there, the first Allied troops on European soil since the Dunkirk debacle.

Since there were no docks at our landing site and since heavy equipment had to be unloaded, our ship's captain had to wait for a smooth sea before grounding on the beach. So we waited. Not until late afternoon would the captain risk it. The upshot of the long wait was that not only did the navy have to feed us a noon meal in the form of a hasty lunch, but they also had to feed us a fine supper of real steaks, potatoes, and fresh light bread prepared for themselves. We'd not had such a meal in months and entertained paranoid thoughts that we may well have had them if the navy hadn't always beat us to the ingredients originally destined for army distribution.

At last the captain was satisfied he could come into smooth and shallow water. He headed toward the shore with sufficient speed to ground his vessel with a hard jolt and much muddying of the water. The nose ramp was let down onto pontoon bridges sent out from shore, and many of our trucks reached the sandy beach without a problem. However, night came on and darkness was a problem in the total blackout.

Soon after dark a "janfu" order (GI acronym for "joint army/navy foul-up") came for everyone to shoulder his gear and cross the pontoons that stretched for a hundred yards or so toward the beach. We tried, but by the time we were halfway out, word came back that the tide had risen and water at the end of the pontoons was already waist deep. We had to lug our packs back up the ramp, spending the rest of the night in our bunks. Being too lazy to undo my pack at that hour, I just slept in my clothes with a life preserver for a pillow and no blankets. So did everyone else.

Next morning we had to get up at 6:00 A.M. and pass right by the ship's galley, where about a thousand fresh eggs were already fried, but the navy wouldn't give us breakfast. They'd given us powdered eggs for the breakfasts before, but this time we went to shore for C-rations cold. The water was no more than a foot deep at the end of the pontoons. As that did not get above our leggings, most of the Baylor unit reached Italy with pants dry and feet but slightly damp.

After a short truck ride we found ourselves in a country not unlike the Texas coast. Such things as the high mountains to the east and an ancient Roman wall across the road from us constituted differences, of course. We sat for hours in the shade of our trucks before proceeding with the six-mile trip to the muddy corn field that is our present bivouac area.

It should be pointed out at this point that while we'd spent several days and nights getting from North Africa to Italy, we'd missed no meals and no sleep. This truly remarkable feat was occurring simultaneously in other outfits, so that several thousand troops and their equipment moved safely. We all landed upon hostile territory without port facilities, thanks to landing ship tanks and landing craft infantry developed by our country [LSTs and LCIs].

We were lucky we got to wait before going on to our bivouac area. It gave us a chance to look around a bit. Within a radius of two hundred yards or so we could see five Greek temples, all built before the time of Christ and dedicated to various Greek pagan gods by colonists in the area at the time. The particular temple dedicated to Neptune is said to be the best preserved Greek temple in the world, and I don't doubt it a bit. Archeologists and geologists tell us that local, comparatively tiny adjustments in sea levels partly submersion these temples for centuries. I wonder if possibly this submersion helped the preservation. At any rate, the temple to Neptune is much better preserved than the Parthenon in Athens.

In studying exposed structure materials in the Neptune temple, the stone is obviously some sort of conglomerate, and from its looks could just as easily be a processed concrete as a natural stone. What if all ancient stone structures such as Stonehenge and Jerusalem's Wailing Wall and the Easter Islands' statuary were carried to their present locations by the bucketful? But I wander.

Stone steps clear across the front lead up to the temple's floor. This floor supports six huge, perfectly rounded, symmetrically fluted twenty-foot stone columns in the front and back, plus eleven more on each side. They look to be about five feet in diameter at their bases and smaller at their tops to make them graceful. Longitudinal grooves, rounded in their depths of about two inches, are spaced evenly about every two inches around each column. If hand-done art produced these columns rather than turning lathes, nobody can equal the ancient Greeks in art. If they had lathes, they were smarter mechanically than the world knows. Crowning the columns are flat stones about a foot thick and six feet square. Resting upon the crowns are rectangular girders about four feet square and eight feet long that connect adjacent columns all around. Upon these girders a gently sloped roof of stone rests, still in place and in marvelous condition. (You know a similar roof over the Parthenon was lost a few centuries back when ammunition stored in the place exploded.)

I suppose the impressive thing about this old temple is the absence of visible arches and the beauty and symmetry of plain, straight lines. An altar three feet above the floor occupies the entire temple except for a three-foot aisle all around.

I still can't see how in the world the ancient Greeks built the Paestum Temple of Neptune with no more sophistication in mathematics and machinery than we were taught they had. Adams, Arnold, Lebermann, the two Galts, and I went the hundred yards or so from our trucks to see the temples and tried to persuade others to go over there when we got back, but only a few went. Martinak said if they'd already been there for two thousand years, he'd have plenty of time to see them, and I guess he will.

Well, we finally moved on, reaching our bivouac area about noon. The six-mile trip was made on good blacktop highway, lined on either side by sycamores and surrounded by fields of the same crops we raise at home. The country is as prosperous looking as our Midwest farming area and is well fenced with barbed wire. The farmhouses are neat and fairly large.

Honey, these things are a sight for sore eyes after the barrenness of eastern Tunisia. It all does look like civilization. There is considerable dairying in evidence, and the barns, like the houses, are of stone and stucco with red tile roofs. Good silos, also of stone and bearing German trademarks, are by each barn, and German machinery is out in the weather everywhere as at home. Except for a few destroyed German tanks, a very few damaged buildings, and some shot-up trees here and there, one would never suspect that a hard fight had taken place anywhere around here.

The livestock looks good and includes sheep, pigs, cattle, horses, and water buffalo. The dairy cows are the mothers, surely, of those large white oxen we saw in Tunisia. The water buffalo are large, black and muddy, and look mean, wild and African, but are fat. As their buffalo cows are all bobtailed, I suspect they're used for milk as well as meat.

The people look more undernourished than those in North Africa and wear a more dejected expression than did our Italian prisoner detachment in Bizerte. At any time we look up, this main road is lined by unarmed Italian soldiers walking in two's and three's, carrying packs and apparently going someplace—probably home. From a neighbor boy who looks about age eight but declares he's fourteen, we learn that Italian schools have been closed for three years.

By way of conclusion, let me say that our life in bivouac is characterized by:

· reunion with the nurses, who had spent one night in pup tents with another hospital and were glad to get back to large ward tents;

· one hectic night of high winds and rains, when it looked like every tent in the area would go down, and several did including one occupied by nurses;

· chow lines serving C-rations three times daily with only a rare K-ration, no bread;

· officers, nurses, and enlisted men drying some articles and washing others wet by the storm;

· no lights at night, so that most of the outfit goes to bed with the chickens and wakes up next morning a good three hours before chow time;

· incessant crap games engaged in by most of the officers and watched by those not engaged;

· high morale—we're a good outfit;

· rain, mud, rain, mud—however sometimes it's sunshiny and hot.

OCTOBER 1, 1943. Borrowing the chaplain's typewriter for this letter could prove to be a booby trap, tempting me to say too much. However, having no table anywhere makes writing by hand practically impossible.

Living in tents this way is not really so bad. Indeed, in lots of ways it is fun. We're much more closely associated than ever before, and the wit of such men as M. Jones, Sebastian, Lebermann, Willis, Rowe, and Alessandra and others is available to all rather than just to their tentmates. There is no moon. Darkness sets in at 6:00 P.M., and we operate the bivouac in total blackout. These facts have altered our way of life, but it has all been funny so far. We go to bed about 7:30. This makes us wake up about 5:00 A.M., and we can't eat until 8:00 A.M. Result is we just lie in the blankets until 7:00 every morning listening to the clowns listed above baiting Hudson Dunlap. Dunlap, of course, retorts with his usual witticisms that never seem to get old. No telling how long it can last, but for the present those two hours each morning are worth whatever inconvenience is incurred in getting them. We were accustomed to sleeping through a couple of the warmest hours in Africa each day, but our nights are so long here we'll have to devise some other diversion.

Our way of life has had to undergo another change also. We're all so close that we've had to express ourselves without those careless and frequently obscene expletives so common with soldiers of every rank. I wonder if the nurses are having the same trouble. But if their language has coarsened any, I'm not aware of it. Anyway, we're within fifty feet of their tent and are avoiding many frequently used, ugly expressions.

Last night, to the accompaniment of Willis's fine accordion, both officers and nurses joined in a couple of hours of community singing. Dunlap says he heard a few "cheese notes" scattered here and there, but it all sounded fine to me. For my part, that organization activity beats dances all hollow.

Maybe it's true that men are only boys grown tall, but for whatever underlying psychological reason, crap games start out early in the morning and last until darkness obscures spots on the dice. The players alternate with the "sweaters" for a good many hours each day, and nobody seems to care too much about the outcome. It's really the only way to kill time with all reading material packed up and positively no setting foot out of the area at present.

OCTOBER 2, 1943. Among the minor highlights of our present life, I suppose the sunburn of one of our vitriolic majors deserves special mention. The major is of a practical mind, which would not tolerate such encumbrances as undershirts but which didn't prevent his pulling off his outer shirt on occasion. Also, those of us who were classmates with him in either premed or medical school days remember he did hate to lose and was prone to yield to superstitions in an effort to change his luck whenever he had a losing streak—which was really blamed seldom as I recall. If sitting, he might stand to change his luck, and if standing, he might sit. If wearing a cap, he'd put it on backward, etc.

Now in the absence of an undershirt, pulling off his outer shirt would expose the major's torso, whose integument is as pale and tender as a baby's, the major being quite blond. Such skin, of course, is quite vulnerable to burning when exposed to the sun, and bright sun is all we've been having since the big rain. So our daily dice games, held around a cot out in the warm sunshine, are enough to stimulate the major to take off his wool shirt in the heat of the game, particularly in view of the unbelievably bad run of luck he has been having.

Being one of the participants in yesterday's dice game, I'm quite naturally happy to relate that the major shot dice practically from breakfast time until the sun went down, losing consistently. He was so angry he took off his shirt early in the morning and didn't put it back on until the game ended at dark. He just kept fading and shooting for hours with the following itemizable results:

1. The major ended the day a heavy loser.
2. The major has a lulu of a blistered torso.
3. The major is unhappy, in contradistinction to some subordinates.
4. As night fell, the major grabbed the dice and thew them away.
5. There is no dice game this morning.
6. One of the dice was found this morning on the latrine box.

7. A detail of five to ten officers, among them the major, has stayed on the job most of today searching for the other cube.

8. A rumor is being spread that officers aren't very mature people.

9. I managed a rare accomplishment and won a little gambling.

OCTOBER 3, 1943. We had another big rain, but it did no damage—no wind. Rains come up suddenly and with no warning, but the water runs off quickly. Today is warm and bright and everybody is happy.

Those of us who got our fatigues and leggings wet yesterday found an ideal spot for doing our laundry today. A nearby abandoned farm has a concrete watering trough still intact and with running water still available. At one end of the trough is a built-in washtub and a scrub board, also of concrete. I never saw such a fine place to wash clothes—not even at home. Of course, I didn't look with a seeing eye at home, having not even a slight interest in washing clothes. Now if things dry out, I'll be all ready to move again.

There being no "sin of the third dimension" going on yesterday nor today, Martinak, Arons, Small, and I played bridge most of yesterday. With Marshall Jones taking my place today, it's still going on. Many a man-hour went into searching for dice yesterday—only the one ever showing up.

OCTOBER 4, 1943. We had the first real meal in more than a week today. Supply had found a yearling steer and butchered it. They also scared up local flour for biscuits and potatoes.

We are to move into buildings about a hundred miles from here tomorrow. Will go by way of Naples, which we're all anxious to see. In fact, we'd hoped to set up there, but no such luck. Still, we'll be in the area but about forty miles east of Naples. We're told the city we're to be in has a population of about 25,000 but is in sad shape at present.

While we have such a good place for washing at the neighborhood farmhouse, I washed my mattress cover and all of my khakis today. I noticed nearby peasants plowing with two oxen hitched to a plow of Rumanian manufacture. I'd like to have gotten a feel of the operation by moving closer, but an intervening creek cut me off. I could see that the oxen moved about as fast as a team of mules would under similar circumstances. They seem to move pretty slow at first glance.

Our tent living has been simplified a great deal by the past two days of sunshine. Also, another pair of dice has appeared from somewhere, and our sunburned major is rattling them in his hand trying to get up another dice game. I'm sure it won't take him more than five minutes at most.

We have a new major named William Boles who caught up with us yesterday. He'd come to Bizerte with the Tulane unit but had sort of taken up with us in the dice games, and our CO got him transferred at his request. He trained in eye, ears, nose, and throat at Johns Hopkins and says he had a lot of trouble finding us. We're listed as present location unknown, he says.

OCTOBER 7, 1943. Avellino. We're back at work at last and living in buildings again. They were new and beautiful, a military academy before the bombs came, but are now without any glass and have a few extra holes in the walls here and there. Still, they are terrazzo floored, which beats the cow pasture we bivouacked in for more than a week after landing in Italy.

Our city is Avellino, which lies in the midst of a beautiful and bountiful area up in the mountains. We get plenty of locally grown figs, apples, oranges, and grapes as a welcome supplement to our C-rations. We'll also be able to get all the fresh vegetables we need as soon as we're settled.

Martinak and I have a twelve by twenty-foot room with a twelve-foot ceiling and plastered walls and a floor of terrazzo blocks. Two large French doors at one end lead on to a small, iron-railed balcony that overlooks a narrow courtyard. The room needs no windows and has none. Looking beyond our courtyard, we see a wide city street completely canopied by either sycamore or eucalyptus trees, I'm not sure which.

I'd think this building no more than ten years old, and it was likely a dormitory for the academy. Being on the second floor, our room is reached by a marble stairway. Leading up from a marble-tiled and wainscoted hall, we enter through double doors in the end opposite our balcony. None of the utilities are functional since the bombing, so our usual eight-holer is set up outside, and we will soon have outside showers.

Our mess hall, about the swankiest thing you ever saw, is downstairs. We still eat C-rations from a mess kit but are seated at large, white cloth-covered tables and sit in chairs instead of benches. It sure beats having to sit on the wet ground in a muddy cornfield. Quite a haven.

Our wards are similar buildings. [We were told the entire complex had housed the "scuola allievo ufficiale," a military school under the Mussolini regime.] One wing of the building housing the wards is unusable, but we do have enough well-roofed space to house as many patients as we'll be able to handle. Too bad all of the glass is gone from the windows, but that does seem to beat tents, even so.

We had to set up the hospital immediately upon our arrival, and what with debris everywhere, we certainly had a job. All of the officers and nurses pitched in to scrubbing floors, carting off trash, and setting up cots. We were able to care for patients within three hours after our arrival and did so. That must be a record of some sort for a 750-bed hospital. All of this was yesterday. Today we've expanded to eleven hundred beds, and at 6:00 P.M. officers and nurses are still helping the enlisted men with the manual labor.

The bulk of our patients so far has been Americans who had been in enemy hospitals, some since the invasion of Sicily. As our armies advance and overtake these hospitals, the enemy abandons his own and our sick. The speed with which this is happening certainly creates problems for our medical corps. These American prisoners all tell us they received the same treatment from both Italians and Germans as their own soldiers did. They also say their mail came uncensored through the Red Cross. They're all glad to get back on American food even if it is C-rations. I ask again, who cares to contest my previous statement that everyone in an army is insane? These enemies try their best to kill each other, but when they only maim each other, both sides bend over backward to be nice to the other. We bend over backward being nice to our captured patients, too, and they seem to reciprocate with a great deal of appreciation—we're really pretty friendly! And so goes the war. [We were to learn at Anzio that the mutual hatred did not stop with hospitalization. We had to set up separate wards for wounded Germans.]

OCTOBER 8, 1943. Oh boy, no mail 'til yet and we're going on our third week! We're too busy to miss it during the day—but not so at night.

Our haven with dry floors, lights from our own generators at night, and tables with chairs and white cloths is still so novel we thrill over it. Six of the nurses on the third floor of this building aren't faring quite as well yet, as their roof leaks. I'm sure it will be fixed at once since it rains every day.

The medical service is so busy that Bowyer and White were transferred over there today. I guess we'll all have a turn at it, but it's been so long since I've taken a medical history, I'd as soon not. I was busy in the operating room from 1:00 P.M. until 5:00 today, so maybe I won't be transferred.

Honey, I finished *For Whom The Bell Tolls* and you'd enjoy it, even if we did hear it reviewed that time. I'm now reading a book by Upton Sinclair called *Oil!* He sounds like a radical, and he sure doesn't like the oil companies.

OCTOBER 10, 1943. Some of the outfit got a few letters today. Not old Pappy; not the CO either, and it gave him the blues like I'd never seen before. Martinak got two from Macy describing Jean's cuteness and he got the blues. You can't win I guess.

Golly, but we've been busy, the busiest we've ever been. The rush started within three hours after our arrival and has not abated one bit. We've been too busy to even think about getting settled, and still they come. All of our cots are full. The enlisted men have given up theirs, and still our halls and other available spots are filled with patients lying on litters. Well, I asked for it rather than to be idle.

I saw John Talley, an old Baylor classmate, yesterday. He is Helen Fisher's brother, you know, and he came by to see James Fisher. Of course, he ran into at least a dozen doctors whom he knew. He had been practicing at Hamilton, Texas, for years before coming into the army and is now a battalion surgeon. He came in at Salerno with the 36th Division and was pinned down by enemy fire for several days. Tell Helen that he is okay and has lost thirty-five pounds like the rest of us. He has good yarns to tell about his experience at Salerno.

OCTOBER 12, 1943. Just a note 'cause I'm too busy to write more. I'm well and just busy enough not to have idle time on my hands.

OCTOBER 13, 1943. Your letter of September 20 came yesterday, the long philosophical one, just before I went entirely berserk not hearing from you. The postman still owes me all of those from August 20 through September 20, except for one dated September 6. I keep hoping for a jackpot of letters.

It's funny, but even before your letter came, I'd also been thinking about the changes folks might undergo during separations in wartime. I don't have any idea that I'll see any changes in you, honey, and if I do, I'm convinced you'll still be my idea of perfection. I'd not really thought of your changing any, but I have worried that I might present you with a new set of my own prejudices and shortcomings that would require adjustments on your part. Actually, we here at the hospital don't go through much that would change us, but we do gripe to no end, mostly about being separated from our folks at home. We all settle down to the routine when we're busy, but that rest period we had was sure hard on morale and tough on nostalgia.

We hear that Walter Winchell has been barred from the air for asking why so few divisions are on the Italian front while so many are on the USO front at home. Anything to that? We also hear that Jack Pepper, the Dallas comedian who visited us with the Bob Hope show, has been jailed for talking too much. Is there anything to that? The Dallas wives threw a party for him, and maybe they pumped him dry about the Baylor unit and North Africa, too, but I don't give much credence to the rumor that he'd be locked up.

I think your idea of coming to meet me whenever the day of my homecoming rolls around is keen. Maybe we could meet in New Orleans or someplace. I wish that was going to be tomorrow, or next month, or even next year for sure.

I had a busy night as OD and am tired. Please forgive this short note.

OCTOBER 14, 1943. The fellows who coined the phrase "sunny Italy" were either satirical humorists or had never visited this section in October. I guess it may be about as sunny as California and probably has about the same climate. Both last night and tonight have been as clear as a bell with full moons rising over the mountains, but days are cloudy, cold, and damp. The thermometer here on my table is registering 14 degrees C (59 degrees F) at the moment and probably hasn't been above that all day. Still, the natives tell us it rarely freezes even in the coldest of winter.

Another banner day, with apple salad complete with locally grown hazel nuts and celery. The apples are also locally grown, as are the water buffalo from which locally purchased steaks were cut for our supper. Such breaks are most welcome after a few days on either C-, K-, or U-rations.

And speaking of eating, I hope the chocolates you sent in September come through all right. That's one thing we never get, although cheap hard candies are usually available and will likely catch up with us in a few days. Sweet milk, chocolate malts, ice cream, and good chocolate candy will be on the menus of nearly everyone here for their first meal when they get home. They'll also probably order a steak, fried chicken, three eggs sunny side up, along with American whiskey. Light bread with fresh butter will also be in demand as well as crisp bacon. My mouth waters. [Twenty-four months after that was written, I landed at Newport News where a shipload of returning soldiers were shown a huge dining hall. Each of us was served a quart of milk, a loaf of bread, and a one-pound T-bone steak.]

Now about Italian wine. That which was brought to us at Paestum tasted just like it had salt and pepper added to it. Four swallows of that stuff on any one day was my limit, although a few, notably Dunlap, got higher than a kite on it once. He was pretty funny walking around in the mud barefooted. The wine here is different and as good as the very best I ever tasted at home. The next time our unit has a rest period, I'm sure a good bit of it will be consumed. It seems to be abundantly available, and we have a large carboy full of it in the hall complete with spigot, siphon tubes, and cups for drawing it. We also have one cup for a kitty to receive whatever one thinks he owes, at eighty cents per quart. I've been much too busy so far to feed that kitty or ever owe it anything.

Surgery has been the busiest in our history at this location, but so has medicine. Three surgical service lieutenants have now been assigned to medicine, with others expecting to follow at any time. I wouldn't mind too much, but neither of my superiors on the team are interested in ward work and that may prevent my being transferred. One or both of them will certainly have to do a lot more on the ward than they are accustomed to if I'm moved. All three of us work alone in the operating room— McCauley, our receiving officer, being very careful not to assign the more complicated cases to our team. He is wise that way.

Would you see if you can find me a seven-jeweled Elgin watch, please. I've cleaned so many "fine" watches for the nurses and doctors over here that I'm sick of them. None will stand the gaff like a seven-jeweled Elgin. I had to clean and oil my own yesterday and found that the case is about gone. I'm afraid I can't get more than a few more months' wear out of it so I'd like a plain wrist watch with second hand, but not a sweep second. Please get whomever you buy it from to: 1) re-oil all pinions, particularly the balance staff jewels; 2) remove the balance wheel assembly and leave it out of the case for shipping; 3) enclose one extra mainspring and three extra crystals. But don't worry if you can't find such a watch. I'll keep mine going if I have to.

OCTOBER 15, 1943. We can see the big white monastery near the top of our closest mountain for the first time, unobscured by the usual clouds. The day has been warm and clear for a change.

I got back some laundry today, the first I've had a washwoman do since we left the States. Boy, the stuff is the cleanest it's ever been, and it's ironed as well. I'm so tickled that I won't fuss at its being too wet to wear. I wasn't even annoyed at having to spread it out on our upstairs patio floor to dry. I'm only sorry that I didn't send all of my dirty clothes, but I kept most of them in reserve until I saw they would come back. You may be interested to know that in addition to a pillow case and laundry bag, the batch I sent out included four pairs of socks, two handkerchiefs, four T-shirts and four shorts, a pair of khaki pants and one khaki shirt—all for thirty-eight cents. I will now trust sending her twice that amount of cotton plus the wool pants I've been wearing for the past month. Well, yes, the collar of a wool shirt gets pretty dirty when worn by a medical officer for thirty consecutive days. This is particularly true when said officer gets very few neck washes and even fewer baths. We smell pretty "gamey," too, as the pioneers used to say. But then, we're invited to very few debutante parties and no afternoon teas at all.

I slept from 7:00 until 11:00 this morning, and that four hours is all the sleep I've had since night before last. Such hours don't particularly lend themselves to fastidiousness, but I feel pretty fresh, at that. I don't know how many cases I did last night, but it was plenty. I could have done more if it were possible to get our system to functioning better. We just can't get the operating rooms set up quickly enough between cases.

There were three German prisoners in the batch I operated on last night. Their attitudes seem less supermannish than those at Bizerte. However, they still think they will win the war.

In last night's bull sessions between cases, my major said he used to be provoked at war veterans for sitting around so much, but now he intends to "sit as much as I d— please whenever I get home." He has not decided just what sort of practice he'll set up, but it sure won't be traumatic surgery. Colonel Carter rejoins that he'll sit, too, and he believes we all will. I doubt that any of them will be able to take more than a week of loafing. I'm sure I won't.

My captain got into a jam last night—probably from being too tired to think straight, I guess. He removed a shell fragment from its position out of a rather large artery in a man's leg. The fragment had been acting as an effective plug in the hole it had made, and its removal released a formidable hemorrhage that got away from him. He yelled for help, but our major couldn't drop his own operation at that point so I went to help. The two of us managed without too much spilling of the man's blood. The captain wishes the war would end so that he could get back to delivering other people's babies and fondling his own.

Honey, your August 24 and 26 airmails came yesterday, which make three I've had in the past month. I do think it cute of Suzanne to like little fellows so much. And yes, I'm probably about one lap ahead of Charles Seton and will keep my eyes open for him. We are also a lap ahead of Peyton but expect him around in a day or two. Glad you enjoyed *Rabble In Arms*, and I'm sure you'll enjoy *Oliver Wiswell*.

Martinak's had a cold for several days that is better today. Merrick and several others have also had them. Nobody has really been on the sick list.

OCTOBER 16, 1943. I wrote you an airmail this afternoon and will mail this with it, to see how they check on travel time.

All cases in the house requiring surgery have been attended to for the first time in over a week. There must be other hospitals in the area now helping us with the load. We've certainly broken all of our previous records and have already seen a fourth as many patients as we did all summer and early fall in Bizerte.

I enjoyed Suzanne's little monologue about the bingo. Her pop thinks he has a pretty smart little gal to say all of that before she is two years old.

I told Adams I'd asked you for a watch and specified a seven-jeweled Elgin. He had written Dotty that same day and asked her to send him an Ingersoll, promising to send it right back to her if she paid over two dollars for it. Swiss watches are now plentiful around here for twelve dollars and up, so don't worry if you can't find me an Elgin. I'll buy a Swiss if I ever have to have one.

OCTOBER 17, 1943. Your V-mails of September 7, 9, and 10 came today, and also Mama's of the 10, breaking a long "dry spell." They are welcome, I can tell you, and so will be the "jackpot" when it arrives.

I haven't received a letter yet telling of Suzanne's sore throat and am glad the one telling me she's well reached me first. And no, I didn't think your remark about little Jimmy was catty. Anyway, he's older than Suzanne.

I did tell you we're only thirty-five miles from Naples, didn't I? And we're only a little farther from Pompeii. We've been too busy to visit either place but are looking forward to doing so in the near future.

We're still not busy, and the relief is sure welcome. I believe I never in my life put in nine such days. I'm sure we'll remember this experience all of our lives.

Where is Tilton General Hospital? I supposed Randolph was in the army by now but didn't know it for sure until arrival of today's mail. Tell him to buy an air mattress, a pair of pliers, and a canvas bucket if he gets into a field outfit, but not to load himself with much else. He'll need no clothes over here other than three suits of khaki and two of wool, with six pairs of socks and six sets of underwear. No need to stock up on toilet goods or cigarettes, as they're always available. His watch should not be fancy and should be cleaned and oiled just before leaving the States. Two suits of woolen underwear is a good investment, but I've always been able to buy underwear, shoes, and shirts over here. A valpac is essential, and lots of little zippered gadgets of canvas are nice to have. Duffel bags are also a must as they may serve as his only available chair or table at times. You might also tell him that army inefficiencies and injustices are unavoidable and after eighteen months in the service will amuse rather than irritate. And maybe he'll be lucky enough to get into an outfit that doesn't have a fixed table of organization that freezes everyone in rank. Boy, oh boy!

OCTOBER 18, 1943. Well, I walked out our gateway for the first time since we've been here. The street outside is a pretty busy one, so Johnson and I stepped out and watched folks pass by as we waited for supper. They aren't a bad looking bunch, and most of them nodded and smiled as they passed, although we understand the majority of the locals are bitter about their city being bombed when they thought it unnecessary. Anyway, we enjoyed a half hour of seeing them pass the gates. And we talked to a few who spoke English and even to some who had been to America.

I've had hardly anything to do today, still a welcome change from those first nine hectic ones. Martinak confessed that he'd hated to go to his ward of late. I've had the same feeling but not so acutely since we're quieter. I did two minor elective cases today, a benign chestwall tumor and an ingrown toenail. Pretty tame.

Martinak and I expect to visit the nearby city in a day or two. When we go, I'm hoping the stores have merchandise to sell.

But now my borrowed iron is hot and I must press my OD pants.

OCTOBER 19, 1943. Your two V-mails arrived today in a single envelope, so the day sure isn't a total loss. I had one minor case, and except for routine dressing, had nothing else. Since such routines never take more than an hour or so, I'm pretty idle. I'll have even less tomorrow since my German lieutenant and three enlisted men will go to a general hospital.

My starch and the other things still have not come. Whenever it does, I'll have all of my khakis starched for the first time since leaving home and will put them away until spring. Martinak got eight boxes of starch the other day and hid them in his duffel bag at once. Since we're into wool, he was afraid everyone would razz him about his supply.

You just might get this on our anniversary, so let me tell you again how glad I am that we have one. I love you very much, miss you more than you'll ever know, think about you constantly, and am very happy that you're "the rest of me." I sent you a vase I'd picked up in Tunis some time ago, sending it via Mama. I hope it reaches you on November 9. Boy! When I get home I'll never consent to let you out of my sight for more than a few hours, so prepare for it. Kiss Suzy.

OCTOBER 20, 1943. I'm now allowed to tell you I'm in Italy in case you didn't already know it. And in view of the more lenient censor, I also sent you two long airmail letters in separate envelopes. One told of the trip from Bizerte to Italy and the other told of a trip to Naples. We also went to Pompeii. Nine officers and twenty nurses about filled two personnel carriers. Brown and Devereux and I stayed together to shop, but we are sorry at it. On the other hand, the nurses usually find worthwhile things, it seems. They all found silk stockings, gloves, and the like, and Ruth Hungerford found a real nice cameo for fifty dollars. Frances Raymond found a keen doll for fifteen, while I've yet to see one of any size or price anywhere.

Merrick and Martinak went up to visit our mountain top monastery, and they report a wonderful trip. It looks to be no more than a couple of miles from here but is really twelve miles east of us and a half a mile above us. I'll try to go tomorrow or next day.

OCTOBER 21, 1943. Four airmails and a V-mail yesterday, and you'd seen brother Bill. I know Mama is pleased he was able to lease out her mineral rights on the Sampson place. I've not yet received her letter with the details.

Well, I've been to Naples and Pompeii and hope to get back there again before we leave the area. I understand the Naples harbor is the most beautiful in the world, but I didn't get to see it this time. I did see the Isle of Capri from a distance and saw the king's palace in Naples. It is the most elaborate building I've ever been in, but I didn't really see much of the inside. We can go in again if I get back and have the time. In the two hours I was in Naples, most of what I saw was pretty ugly. The Via Roma is the main shopping street, but like those of Casablanca and Tunis, is disappointing.

The stores are small and poorly stocked, the merchants going to some lengths to explain that the Germans beat us to all of their merchandise. I saw no fine jewelry but did manage to buy some cheap, locally produced pieces. I had a hundred dollars with me, expecting to spend all of it, but I got out after spending only thirty. I did buy you a gold-plated silver bag and bracelet that I hope you will like, and also two pairs of silk hose, and a pair of gloves whose quality I'd certainly not vouch for.

Your letter telling me I'd drawn Wilma Jean's name was waiting for me when I got back to the hospital. I'm enclosing a silver bag for her that I found in a curio shop at the gates of Pompeii. I hope she'll like it. I did not find anything suitable for Suzanne, but somewhere there are dolls and I do hope to find the place sometime.

Pompeii! By George, Pompeii is something! I don't know when it was built, but I do know it was built by clever, clever, wine-drinking, sensuous, and evil-minded people. Clever they were because they laid out a beautiful city with straight, narrow streets, pavement, plumbing, sewage, gardens, public baths, fountains, and a public amphitheater. And clever they were because they could work with iron, lead, bronze, copper, gold, and silver, as well as with stone, marble, bricks, mortar, tile, and wood. Clever were some with paint and brush, because the walls of some homes and buildings have lifelike murals on them. One building, the house of two brothers, is adorned by murals of Cupid riding the waves in a chariot drawn by two dolphins. You've seen copies of this many times, and its colors are still as bright as you please.

Wine drinking must have been the favorite daylight diversion of the Pompeiians. On both main and side streets, every other shop was a wine bar. They look not unlike our soda fountains or ice cream cabinets, having six to twelve large stone jars of about twenty-gallon capacity set down in mortar to form the bar. In some of the nicer places the mortar was then covered with either marble or multicolored tile. Tiled shelves arranged in stair steps back of the bar evidently held their wine glasses, or whatever they drank from.

At least by present day standards, these people were evil minded. By anybody's standards they were sensuous voluptuaries. The degree of sensuality would be almost unbelievable except for the fact of the excellent, that is realistic, paintings and sculpture work left. This holds true not only in the easily recognized brothels but in many homes. Many are adorned by technically fine paintings of subjects that, today, are typically favored by the naughtier of small American boys who mark up the walls of public school rest rooms. Italian officials have hidden these behind lattice covers to be opened to the view of male tourists only. But the Pompeiians didn't hide them. Rather they brought in masters to paint them all over their homes, on the walls of entry halls and living and dining rooms, and bedrooms. Sodom and Gomorrah just might have occupied second and third place to early Pompeii. On the wall of one of the brothels is some odd looking graffiti scratched into the wall and identified as ancient Hebrew script that translates into two words: Sodom and Gomorrah.

The streets of Pompeii were narrow so that chariot traffic had to be limited to one way on each street. The streets had been used long enough to cut rather deep ruts into the paving stones. These ruts reveal the exact width of the vehicles. At the street intersections these clever people placed stepping stones that the wheeled vehicles had to straddle, so that pedestrians could cross a wet or muddy street above the mess.

The main street, wider than most, is lined by round columns that evidently once supported something or other. It is this street and these columns that we see in most pictures of Pompeii. It looks out toward Mount Vesuvius, which is five miles away and still smoking after its eruption in 70 A.D. Its ashes and pumice covered a two-story town of 25,000 people so suddenly that the inhabitants could not escape.

When the city was excavated centuries later, many of the people were found. The remains could be carefully filled with liquid plaster of Paris and allowed to harden. This hardened plaster was then dug out as a carefully molded reproduction of whatever had occupied the cavity. Many pet animals as well as many human bodies were cast in this way, in the exact attitudes of their last moments.

Two such casts are there on display. One is of a woman holding some sort of brass vessel against her abdomen. I couldn't imagine what she was doing in that position, but our guide suggested that she might have been overcome by fumes and could have assumed a meaningless position before ashes covered her.

A second plaster figure is that of a slave, his status revealed by the belt he was wearing. Freemen wore tunics without belts. The slave must have died peacefully, his head pillowed upon his arm. His features are like a man of forty-five and are perfectly preserved. He has a modern Roman nose, a good forehead, medium-spaced eyes, but a weak chin. Maybe that chin explains why he was a slave.

We didn't spend as much time in the forum and the baths as I would have liked. Most of the floor and roof of the baths are preserved. Unlike Greek architecture, its roof was arched. The floors were of marble, and the ceilings and walls were decorated with intricate plaster moldings. There were three large baths in the structure, each about twelve square feet. The guide said one was for hot water, one for warm, and the other for cold. I'm sorry I don't carry a better picture of it in my mind.

The forum was a large, Greek-type building, with many of its columns and girders still standing. Part of it was two-story, but my memory is again hazy and that second story may simply have been a balcony. Within or in front of the forum, chariot races or gladiator combats were held until later years, when an amphitheater was constructed. Maybe I need to go back and see these things without the shock of all of those pornographic paintings beforehand.

Much, much more should be written of Pompeii: the stone olive oil press; the lead pipe joints that are "wiped" just like modern plumbers wipe a joint; the stove in one house with copper vessels still on it; the large-headed bronze pegs that served for nails; the iron lattice work over a window; the marble fountains in the gardens; the deep grooves on either side of a large public fountain, worn by centuries of drinkers resting their hands as they drank; the election bills printed on street walls; the serpents painted on the fronts of pharmacies; the many paintings depicting Greek mythology; the pornographic figures over many doorways, much as we might nail good luck horseshoes. And much more.

OCTOBER 22, 1943. I don't recall one day's mail ever spanning three different months before, but today one of August 30 and another of October 2 came. Also a September 1 and 5 arrived in the same mail.

I hope you find the collie puppy for Suzanne and do hope it will still be a pup when I get back home. I'd probably play with it more than she would. Her pictures and the one of her mommy came ages ago, and I'm aching for more of both parties. Sorry, but I can't get the films for you here.

Today was some day and I'm getting to be quite a gadabout. James Galt, Bowyer, E. Jones, Alessandra, and I got a weapons carrier and driver and drove up to the Benedictine monastery, over four thousand feet elevation, so you can imagine the sort of road we had.

Soon after we'd arrived, here came our CO, Sid Galt, Rowe, and two of our nurses in the command car. The group of us decided this was the most interesting trip any of us had made since leaving the U.S.A. Alessandra acted as interpreter and did very well, in spite of all of his denials that he remembered any Italian. One of the monks did kid him about his accent being like those in Naples, and he erred in translation one time, giving us the age of a statue of the Virgin Mary as "more than two thousand years old."

The original monastery was built in the eleventh century, and many of the original articles are still about. There were about ten monks up there, all young, all lonesome, all with excellent personalities, and they showed us quite a good time.

We were first taken into the main chapel, and old impressionable me, I nearly had a fit. Golly, it was so beautiful, you had to fight back the tears. The domed ceiling was very high, and its paintings were in their original 300-year-old state (unlike those in the Saint Louis Cathedral in New Orleans), and it all made you realize that Christianity was pretty old and pretty fine. The altar, too, was a thing of elaborate beauty, inlaid with lapis lazuli, mother-of-pearl, and other semiprecious stones and must have required years to finish. Of course, years don't mean much in a thing that has been alive eight hundred years and more. The handiwork around the place shows it.

Back of the altar, through a hand-carved ebony door was the choir loft. High above was a pipe organ with 1,022 pipes. Brother Raphael, whom we'd nicknamed Junior due to his boyish appearance, was induced to play the organ. Now maybe Junior is a master, or maybe that organ is a masterpiece, or possibly it was just the atmosphere of the place, I just don't know. But I know I never heard music like that before. Even our CO, whose one remark about the altar had been that "it would make a nice bar," was impressed and said so.

And that choir room merits more comment than I can give it. It was perhaps fifty feet long and twenty wide with a center aisle, and three rows of seats on either side of the aisle curving across the ends of the loft. Maybe calling them "built-in" sounds too much like the fixtures of a bank, but they were far from that sort of thing. These seats were of hand-carved walnut. And when I say carved, I do mean carved—carved over every square centimeter of their surfaces. Ends, braces, arm rests, and all were carved in intricate designs of people, animals, and scenes. Whether the carving job consumed fifty, seventy-five, or two hundred years is practically nothing in the minds of these people.

I don't know the name of the next thing we saw, but it was one of those shrines off to the side of the main chapel as in every Catholic church. The dominant thing in this particular shrine was a huge, gold-crowned Madonna and child. This Madonna is ever so old, but we never did find out just how old as Alessandra's translation wasn't equal to the problem. This figure is probably fifteen feet tall and lavishly bedecked in gold, as you'll see from the picture. There were excellent murals on the walls, too, and those portions of the wall not covered by the paintings were covered by gold and silver figurines donated by the diocese through the years. Figurines cover the walls clear up to the ceiling, twenty or more feet above.

We were taken to their observatory, in which are housed both ancient and modern meteorological instruments. The monks seem to work up there a great deal and told us that pilots in the present war come up there to use their observatory and get their weather predictions. The view from this promontory three thousand or so feet above the heavily wooded valley below was what you can imagine it to be. Just don't be afraid to let your imagination run riot, or you'll not do the scene justice. Our eyes will never be disappointed if we get to come back here later. Sure, nothing can really be more beautiful than that valley I wrote you about back in Algeria, but the view from up here is its equal.

Although we started out with a single monk, Junior, guiding us, by now all of the monks were in our party and were old buddies. They were quiet and reserved at first but were now kidding Alessandra about his lingo, smoking our cigarettes, laughing, and having a big time. Even the father superior came along, entering in on our discussion as to the best brand of American cigarettes. He promptly gave his opinion and said the very best brand was whichever one he had access to at the moment.

They next took us to their library, which would do credit to any library or museum, either. They showed us volume after volume printed on parchment and bound in calfskin, with dates back as far as 1510. The order won't allow them to become doctors, but ancient and modern books are there if they want to learn medicine.

Finally, our buddies the monks took us into their living quarters. We went into a big living room where the furniture was both antique and beautiful. After seating us around, Junior, who had slipped away somewhat earlier, came in with a steaming hot drink in little tiny cups and saucers that had raised gold figures on them and were 250 years old. He explained that the drink had only the face of coffee but was made from chestnuts—they'd had no coffee in years. He was also carrying an interesting square glass bottle filled with a clear liquid. After we'd drunk some of our black drink, he poured about a jiggerful from the square bottle into each of our cups. Whereas the original had been tasty and warming, this was now better and even more warming. The name sounded like "kemmel" and was made with caraway seed. Finishing our "coffee," we all had another jigger of kemmel and then just sat and talked for a while. Maybe we couldn't handle our feet, I don't know.

We eventually had to leave, of course, but not until after we'd spent more than three hours up there. On the way out, I asked for a folder of the place. Junior took me to a counter where there were all sorts of rosaries, figurines, pamphlets, and the like. We all got a copy of the one I'm sending you, and I was to pay for all of them. They asked so little for them that I had no change small enough. I handed him what I thought was a hundred lire note, but he saw that it was a thousand lire. Quick as a flash he put the note on the counter and motioned for me to take everything in the case. He's about the first native we've encountered since leaving home who would not take the thousand with profuse but oily thanks.

Oh, if I don't hurry, you'll tire of reading this, and I won't get us back to the hospital in time for supper. So we left after much handshaking and backslapping, and all the way down the mountain we could look back and see those lonesome monks waving their white flannel hoods high above their heads at us. Boy! I sure want to go back. We all decided that we'd been to our Christmas celebration just two months and three days early and would not likely see another until after the end of the war.

OCTOBER 23, 1943. From the three V-mails that came today, I learn that Suzanne's birthday gifts arrived in time for her party on September 28. I also learned of her keen interest in natural phenomena as they pertain to cows. Martinak and I both enjoyed that.

I'm writing this on one of the airmail sheets you sent. I'll not need any more, as the various members of the unit probably have enough hoarded up by this time to last all of us about ten years.

Nothing to relate today except that I'm loafing and thoroughly enjoying it. Spent most of the morning working on Dick Young's sorry watch that is now running. Baby, don't ever buy a Swiss watch, please. And if there's a chance of your having to live away from good watchmakers, don't buy one with sweep second hands or other fancy gadgets. My hobby of keeping the unit's watches running works out fine on American watches, but I've seen lots of trash wrapped up in fancy cases over here that I'm sure I can't do anything for.

Have I told you we've all been issued a stick of gum, a package of Lifesavers, and a pack of cigarettes each night at supper since we've been here? A good thing, too, because we have no PX since leaving Africa. Still, you and Suzanne are welcome to my share of gum, Lifesavers, hard candy, Mars bars, and Spam forevermore.

Turnbow, the lucky stiff, found some real cute dolls in Naples! Wouldn't you know it? I must get back there and find one for Suzanne.

OCTOBER 24, 1943. Boy, it's nice to get a handful of letters every day again. They still owe us lots more, but they do come through every day.

My conscience did hurt me now to have to send my two-year-old daughter a cloisonne vase instead of a doll or something for her birthday. I'm glad the letter was all right. I found that vase in Tunis. I found no doll.

Taking advantage of the first opportunity I've had in some weeks, I went to church this morning. I really missed the red ant Hudson Dunlap and I watched at the last service as I didn't get much out of the chaplain's sermon on "Light."

I have visited Naples, Pompeii, Paestum, Battipaglia, Salerno, Avellino, and a few other small towns in Italy. The two-hour trip to Naples was far too short for satisfaction. It will have to be supplemented by further visits, for there is much to see. The trips to Pompeii and the monastery I've described in another letter, but I'll tell you a bit more about the monks.

All of the monks are noticeably pink cheeked. Living at the altitude they do, human blood is unable to absorb the necessary amount of oxygen in each blood cell as it does under the greater atmospheric pressure at sea level. Consequently, the blood-forming bone marrow is stimulated to produce more red blood cells, thus more pink in the cheeks.

In answer to your question about the hand-sized fragment of bark from a cork tree, I did cut it from the living tree myself. Not from a tree under which I'd slept but from one under which I'd sat to eat my lunch our first day out of Casablanca—one under which I'd sat and "smelled the flowers."

Honey, two pictures of you and Suzanne came today. Both are good, but I thought you'd had your hair cut and it's still long. Our daughter is cute as pie and I'd give a million to see her—being led by her mother, that is.

I was sure *Oliver Wiswell* would make you mad, but isn't it good reading? I think you're right about just as soon not knowing some truths. Maybe you'd just as well not read Upton Sinclair's *Oil!* You married a guy, though, who doesn't seem to have sense enough to avoid even those truths that detract from happiness, so I guess I'll have to learn to keep my mouth shut. Honey, it killed my soul to learn in college that the Kaiser and the Germans may not have been solely to blame for World War I. It always kills my soul to learn that our country, state, town, or people are not the paragons of perfection that childish, childish idealism might picture them. Those things hurt like the dickens, and yet it seems I go out of my way to find them out. I do seem to be waxing philosophical, but before I stop I'll mention another big hurt. That is the bitter one that came with the realization before I ever studied medicine that doctors were not minor gods and not always motivated by altruism.

OCTOBER 27, 1943. I've been asked to tell what a medical officer might read during those frequent intervals when his duties were minimal to nil. In our hospital, a right good library has been maintained since we left San Antonio. A couple of weeks before we left, Colonel Winans handed me a few hundred dollars someone in Dallas had given him for the purpose, and he told me to go buy whatever seemed appropriate for a foundation. I bought what I could find, including *Encyclopedia Britannica, Webster's Unabridged Dictionary, Harvard Classics, King James Bible, The Decline and Fall of the Roman Empire, War and Peace*, and others, until the money ran out. Literally hundreds of current popular novels, detective stories, and the like have been added since. Any member of the Baylor unit can read just about anything he likes. Current issues of the slick paper periodicals and popular pulps also find their way over here. We are short of civilian professional journals, but the military furnishes current material pertinent to our needs. A pretty good batch of reading material.

I hadn't time to read a novel in fifteen years until I got into the army. Now I've read many of the recent best sellers and those of the past fifteen years, too. Have even read *The Decline and Fall of the Roman Empire* by Gibbon, *War and Peace* by Tolstoy, H. G. Wells' *Outline of History*, and other classics, in addition to Kenneth Roberts and Lloyd Douglas novels.

Current rumors have us moving soon and all signs say yes.

OCTOBER 28, 1943. Four pictures of Suzanne, two of them wearing Mommy's hat and gloves came today, much to my own and Martinak's delight. We thought they were awfully good, honey, but I wish you'd manage to get into more of them with her.

Honey, don't worry about our family being so spread out. I'll bet there won't be more than four years between Suzy and our next, and that isn't too much. We can get an early start just as soon as I get back.

Boy, would our older nurse be flattered if she could read your remark about jealousy! She is not far from sixty, I expect. And since you took advantage of that opportunity to tell me how "very jealous you are," let me take this one to reassure you that you'll never have legitimate cause to be.

I finally got around to washing out some socks and underwear that have been soaking for a few days. I'd send them to the washwoman, but we are now in wool, so I've no shirts or trousers I'd trust out. And socks and underwear aren't enough to justify the trouble. I don't mind washing them, anyway. I just hate getting started at it. When I think about what a convenient place to wash that would have been in San Antonio, and I didn't even appreciate it! Here we carry cold water upstairs in a helmet, have no soap chips and no scrub board and no line to hang them on.

Martinak, McClung, and I went into town this morning hoping to rent bicycles. We only found two, so I just decided to walk instead. I had not been downtown before and I did enjoy the trip. By and large, Avellino is in pretty good shape, although some of the streets are blocked by debris eight or more feet high. We bought a dozen fresh eggs—oh, boy!—and some clothespins, but couldn't find anything else.

OCTOBER 29, 1943. Sixteen days travel time is about the best a letter from you has ever made, but your October 13 V-mail and September 13 airmail came today.

Glad that Johne D and Randolph's baby boy arrived safely, and so hope he's theirs for keeps. Too bad Randolph couldn't have seen him, but he probably will before he goes overseas.

I sent my last five patients back to duty today and don't even have the usual one hour's work to do. It sure would be swell if the thirty or sixty days of actual work that will be required of me during this war could be done in a single stretch and have it over with.

I've read all but about fifty pages of *The Robe* today and have really enjoyed it. I'm glad you picked that one, as much of the country described in it is the same Italian country I'm in now. Also, the descriptions of Palestine sound exactly like Tunisia, so I can follow easily and with interest.

OCTOBER 30, 1943. I don't believe I ever told you that I always look at your messages in the upper left hand corner of the V-mail first. Wish that I had some blank space there.

Today's October 17 V-mail says your last letter from me was dated September 23. I guess that was the last one written from Bizerte, which we now refer to as "the resort." There was no chance to write for several days after that, and you probably did go for twenty-four days without a letter. I went a whole month, too.

Funny that we both thought of meeting in New Orleans after the war—or is it? Guess we both look forward to that meeting as a sort of second honeymoon, and what better place for it than the site of our first?

Brown, Bowyer, Devereux, and I had planned to go to a good restaurant tonight, but we've been rained out. We'll probably go tomorrow, hoping that they serve on Sunday. Devereux and I prepared ourselves for a good meal by bike riding after lunch. We nearly pulled our leg muscles. These hills are nice to coast down but tough to pull up.

OCTOBER 31, 1943. After about ten days of pretty weather, the cold drizzles set in again yesterday. This is the sort of day designed for making those who are at home with their families proud that they have a family and happy to be with them. But it is the sort of day to make those away from home wish more than ever that they weren't away. In other words, honey, I sure do miss you every day, but particularly today. She's a blue Sunday—blue as can be—but morale holds up well, even so.

Martinak and I started the day off at breakfast with two of those eggs we got yesterday. Boy, they've tasted good these past two days. My appetite has returned for the first time since we've been in Italy. And speaking of food, here's one of Rose Craig's poems written soon after we reached Bizerte:

> The bugler blew—we donned our jeans
> And sallied forth to meat and beans.
> Then noon came round, we stopped to eat.
> What did we have? 'Twas beans and meat.
> The sun went down, the moon came up
> And we on meat and beans did sup.
> We traveled long, we're tired and dirty
> From Casablanca to bombed Bizerte.
> It's ended, but the memory lingers
> Kept alive by bandaged fingers
> Result of keys and cans of tin—
> (Some we never did get in)
> If I live through this damn war
> I will not spend my money for
> A bite of hash, a hunk of stew
> Or any bean that ever grew.
> Here's hoping there will never be
> Another week of Ration C.

In case I never did tell you, there are three types of C-ration. The first is meat and beans, which tastes about like our familiar pork and beans and is the only one I can eat. The second is meat and vegetable stew and tastes about like it. I can eat a bit of it if I just have to—a little of it. The third type is meat and vegetable hash, and only those on the verge of starvation or those with perverted appetites and tastes can eat it. I've never been able to get down more than a couple of mouthfuls of it. Soldiers are issued the cans with a key for opening, and many cut fingers result. One also gets a can of biscuits that always taste like the stick of spearmint gum enclosed with them. The biscuit tin also contains a powdered beverage of either coffee, chocolate, or lemonade and five pieces of hard candy. This hard candy was the bon bon that children in North Africa begged for and is also the caramella Italian children now ask for. Kids of both continents soon tire of the stuff, though.

Have you ever heard anything from my paper? Did the Dean ever get a copy from the surgeon general? Did you ever give him the new copy with the changes Mike DeBakey had demanded? Don't worry if JAMA rejects it, as it may be a bit out of date in the light of subsequent events. There is a bill to be presented to the coming congress that I'd think might really pass, and if so, the surgeon general of the U.S. Public Health Service will control medical education. He might also control medical practice, which would certainly be a calamity for private practice.

There are three or four tons of hard coal down in the basement here, and I built a fire in our stove with some of it. Talk about heat! We've never had so much from our usual soft coal, but even with all dampers closed and all room doors open, it's still too hot. This is the first time we've had no trouble boiling out our underwear and getting it clean. How about that housewifely talk?

We're still not only out of patients, but our equipment has been dismantled and loaded for a move. Mallory and McCauley are back after a reconnoitering trip someplace, I don't know where.

Here's another poem by Rose Craig:

WISHFUL THINKING
If a fairy, good, would grant one wish
And I could have no more,
I'd have a bathroom built for one
And I'd close and lock the door.

---

[1]Editor's note: Paestum was the site of one of the fierce battles fought several weeks earlier in September 1943, in the Salerno beachhead, which was invaded by Mark Clark's U.S. Fifth Army on September 9. Another Texas unit, the U.S. 36th Division, landed at Paestum. ...Carlo W. D'Este

DRAGONI AUTUMN   10
November 1943

NOVEMBER 3, 1943. We're completely set up in tents for the first time, and all of the medical officers are in the little 8 x 10 foot side wall tents that have six-foot end poles and four-foot side walls. This gives room for two cots, one set up lengthwise on either side just inside the front flaps. All of the majors are just one to a tent, but below the rank of major there are two to a tent.

Martinak and I are back together again. A filled barracks bag at the foot of each cot serves as the only table in the tent, and the tent poles can be used to hang valpacs on. There is still room for my folding canvas chair, and that is a comfort.

We're in the flat and narrow valley of the Volturno River with foothills of the rugged Apennines hemming us in on all sides. It is really a very picturesque spot and not too far from the front lines.

Honey, I have to tell you some disappointing news but don't let it disturb you unduly. The fact is our CO turned in recommendations for all lieutenants to be promoted to captain just like he told us, but some mix-up has delayed the promotions for Peterson, Arnold, and me. It is a bit hard to take, but the CO assures us his recommendations have gone back today and should be heard from within a matter of a week or so. Now that we know promotions can go through for men on foreign duty, I have more hopes of getting one than I ever did before. I just hope it won't be too long delayed. In any case, don't let it upset you.

I've been pretty busy today and have a busy night ahead. I'll be OD and will earn my pay for a change.

NOVEMBER 4, 1943. We can't use lights at night, but the supply tent has been so blackout-treated that they're permitted in there. We can write there sometimes. The officers' tents can't be made lightproof, so remain dark. We have plenty of wood, and our tents all have wood-burning stoves in them. They do very well, and we do need them. The officers' tents are not floored, but most scrounge enough scrap lumber to get their duffel bags and cots off the ground.

The field outfits believe our unit a bunch of mollycoddled sissies for having tents and cots. Wounded men come in here and report our cots are the first they've slept on in a year. They also frequently report that our issue of clean clothes to them are their first changes in weeks or months.

Apparently the organization will be as busy here as it was at our last location. My major had the good grace to send me to bed at 1:30 this morning so I'd be able to take care of the ward this morning. I've tried for the past seven hours to get two minor cases into the operating room, but more serious ones keep mine bumped off the schedule.

NOVEMBER 5, 1943. We've been busy today, finally reaching a stopping place about 6:00. We probably won't have much to do tonight as our ward is now full, but we never can be certain about that. Today's wounded were less seriously hurt than yesterday's—a blessing.

We all seem to enjoy anything edible these days, and the chow is improving again. We had fresh GI hamburger for the first time in two months today, a big improvement over water buffalo. Another modern miracle in our kitchen—today our cooks learned how to prepare the powdered eggs so that they really do taste like fresh scrambled. May our mess sergeants never lose the secret!

Ma Nature still smiles on us these days. Rain would just about do us in, what with our living in tents and in a recently plowed field, but we've had no rain. This, the natives tell us, is some sort of record for this time of year. We'll see.

NOVEMBER 6, 1943. I've been in for a lot of razzing since most of the other lieutenants got promotions and I didn't. The razzing is easy to take—the asinine sympathy extended by some isn't. Chaplain claims we three nonpromoted ones are memorizing the book of Job to fortify ourselves with ready quotes.

Colonel Carter addresses me as "captain" when he's feeling good—
the nurses and wardmen, when they think I am. Alessandra sarcastically
stresses the eternal justice of the army, but Brown claims it still backs
every train into the stations. The CO compliments me for being a good
sport on coming to the promotion party when the news broke. I sure
didn't correct that worthy one, but actually I tore out to the party
thinking my promotion had arrived with all of the others. It was a matter
of some minutes before I was aware of the true situation. Oh well, all of
our promotions will eventually come through.

Our surgical service has been reorganized in a way that I'm sure will
improve our effectiveness. I'd love to know whose idea it was, but I'm
too remote from the decision-making area for that. At any rate, surgical
teams will now operate for eight hours and then stay out for sixteen. The
operating rooms can't be kept ready for more than two teams at a time,
anyway, and the new system will allow for eight hours' sleep after eight
hours' work. The old system caused each team to loaf between cases, of
course, while the rooms were being equipped with sterile equipment and
new patients brought in and made ready for surgery. Now a preoperative
tent has been set up to do many tasks formerly done in the operating
room. It can be run entirely by nurses and wardmen, with minimal direct
supervision by the surgeons once the patient has been evaluated and
preoperative orders written. It has taken an unbelievable amount of trial
and error in the field to finally work this out, but at this point I'm sure
we are a fine organization.

NOVEMBER 7, 1943. The front is moving north at a fast rate,
and we've already been leapfrogged by two other outfits. We've done
very little for two days now and surely won't be here long unless the
advance of troops hits a snag.

We heard the BBC today for the first time in a couple of weeks. The
announcer was more optimistic about things than he's ever been before.

We were mighty close to the front when we arrived here a few days
ago. We could hear enemy artillery fire as well as our own, and for the
first time were able to feel the ground shake. All of that has moved away
from us now, but we're hearing the bombs dropped by our own bombers
for the first time. We watched great numbers of American bombers fly
over today, and twelve minutes after each wave passed, we'd hear the
rumbling of their dropped bombs. We also saw our first German fighter
planes—four of them. They flew over our hospital looking for our
bombers, and we watched them a bit. They soon left our area without
finding anything to shoot at.

It has been raining all afternoon and is real nasty outside in our plowed ground. Our tents have stayed dry.

Kiev fell two days ago according to our British announcer. He believes this a major setback for the German armies in Russia.

NOVEMBER 8, 1943. A goodly number of Christmas packages arrived today. They have all been opened and contained quite a wide variety of loot. Fruitcakes came but were mostly molded. Chocolate box candy arrived in excellent condition. A good many received welcomed cigarettes—we're presently rationed to a single package per day. One of the momentous decisions that we all have to make is whether to gorge on candy or hoard it. It is unbelievably good tasting to those who've done without chocolate for seven months.

It has rained for twenty-four hours and is very messy outside. Footing is insecure, and our most fastidious dresser fell flat on his face and stomach just outside the mess hall tonight. Down into the mud he went, dress gloves—of all things—new combat jacket, pinks, and new combat boots! It tickled everybody's mean streak to pieces, but the victim was unabashed as always. This victim is the same young administrative officer who was sent to Tunis to pick up a troupe of French entertainers and bring them to our hospital in Bizerte. I wrote you about his arrival at meal time when he sat down at the nearest table, pointed a finger at the bread, and called out loudly, "Passez vous moi le pain!" ("Pass me the bread!"), swearing by all that was holy that he'd forgotten the English phrase for it.

In spite of the rain, the day provided two unusual bits of beauty in the way of Italian landscapes that we all enjoyed. The range of mountains to our immediate east has been snow covered all afternoon. Few of us had ever seen snow-capped mountains before, and this in itself was spectacular. Then there was a temporary break in a small section of the cloud cover. The sun came out to shine over no more than a square mile of the mountainside, and that, too, was spectacular. Right in the center of the bright area was a small village surrounded by a green wheat field. This was all perhaps a thousand or so feet above us on a gentle slope, and everything except that village and the green wheat was under a canopy of dark clouds. It was most picturesque—most!

NOVEMBER 10, 1943. If further comment on the weather is appropriate, let it be recorded that yesterday and today have been clear and cold, and our mud has gone, at least temporarily.

A medical officer wrote his wife on the 21st of October telling her of a number of Italian cities and towns that he had visited. The base censor returned it to him today. The censor warned that although our location as "somewhere in Italy" was permissible, no towns could be mentioned by name. I'm sure many have inadvertently made the same error, instructions having not arrived to make no mention of cities.

NOVEMBER 11, 1943. Oh, my! The chocolate candy is all gone tonight, but making it last for two days was a triumph. That was more of a treat than you'll ever know. Please send me two more boxes of chocolates, and thanks.

So what did I tell you? You're a captain's wife, at last! I'm hoping the "emergency military cable" advising you of this gets to you before my letters do telling of its delay. I'm just as relieved that it came as I was disgusted when it failed to show up with the others. Still, tickled as I am, I need to go on record with you as being humbled by the undeniable fact that there are plenty of officers and enlisted men around who deserved promotions fully as much and even more than those of us who received them. I can't escape a guilty feeling with my rank now the same as Sid Galt's and Devereux's, when both are so much better qualified for the responsibilities of surgery than I'll ever be. Most of the men whose promotions came ahead of the three of ours, whose were delayed, say they now feel better about their own. I'm all puffed up with the congratulations.

I've a new pair of OD pants and they fit. Since I've lost so much weight, my figure is more like what army pants were designed for. So, my clothes are right comfortable for a change.

NOVEMBER 12, 1943. Well, okay. I'll fuss at you, if you like, for not working at the Red Cross and donating that pint of blood. We sure use a lot of it over here, and it has saved many a life. Soldiers themselves, those not at the front, donate a great many pints.

A defunct German tank has been sitting across the road from us ever since we arrived, and many of our personnel have gone over to inspect it out of curiosity. It still contained ammunition just as the Germans left it, and this afternoon when the engineers started to dismantle the thing, it blew up with a terrible bang. Nobody got killed for a wonder, but two men were peppered with shrapnel. One of the men was sent to me, and I dug fragments out of him for an hour. Lesson: I'm not about to mess with anything that even looks a little like a German might have been around it.

NOVEMBER 13, 1943. Seems to me that after honeymooning in New Orleans just three years ago, our money ran out after four days.

Instead of baked Alaska at Antoine's or oysters Rockefeller at the Roosevelt, we were eating hamburgers at the Toddle House. I'd settle again for those hamburgers, right now! And I believe New Orleans is more foreign looking than any large city I've seen since. Of course, some of the ones in North Africa and Italy are more foreign looking, but they aren't as large. Maybe we can see all of this together some day and delight in it.

NOVEMBER 14, 1943. It has been warm today and has rained and rained and rained. This soil has just enough clay mixed in to be very slick when wet. I thought I was a goner several times on the way to my ward. I haven't seen anybody go down yet but hope to (sure, I hope to) tomorrow. One of our captains, dressed in brand new wool pants, caught a solid footing just in time to save himself this morning.

NOVEMBER 15, 1943. More weather—we had a cloudburst lasting for fifteen minutes this afternoon. Great fun it was, too! Martinak's and my tent fared better than most. Nothing got wet in spite of a small river running through the center for a short time. We'd certainly have had much more if we'd not ditched and dammed the flood away from our tent. As usual, a solid sheet of water ran right through Dunlap's tent in a depth of four or five inches, but his was not the only one this time. A lighter rain has lasted all day, and the real downpour was actually fun while it lasted. Martinak just now remarked that he liked our present quarters better than any we've had overseas. Our stove does make it cozy and has already dried most of the floor as well as our wet shoes, socks, and leggings.

We're hearing artillery fire again tonight for the first time in several days. Imagine those soldiers up at the front on a night like this after two such days as we've had. They have no tents and very few raincoats. I know, because most of my patients today came in soaking wet and seemed to think nothing of it.

NOVEMBER 18, 1943. Anyone doubting that weather is a fit subject for conversation has simply never been in a war and never lived in a tent. At least they've certainly not been to war in Italy, or they'd know that no conversation, genteel or otherwise, can be carried on without mentioning the weather. So today has poured rain as usual, and we're in one big loblolly of mud, as you might imagine.

The loblolly, as though a great big egg beater had been run over the area, is easily explained. Vehicles running through churn up a batter six inches deep everywhere, as thick as hot cake batter. Personnel and patients concentrate a population of twelve to fifteen hundred people in an area no bigger than two blocks' square. Frequent incoming and outgoing ambulances and scattered latrines insure a great mobility in the population. And supplies for this many guarantee many a truck trip in and out each day. So all in all, something is churning practically every square foot of ground in this plowed potato field every few minutes, day and night.

Soldiers at the front live in the same loblolly, in the same downpour of rain, but in freezing weather in the higher altitudes. They do this without stoves, without tents, without cots, and many without raincoats, and all with only one army blanket each. It is from these conditions that our patients come, ill and wet to be sure, but with high morale. Kenneth Roberts wrote that nothing so depresses the human spirit as long, continued rain. I'm sure he is right, but our soldiers are taking it all in stride.

In contrast to the life of the fighting soldier, our daily temperatures here in the valley never get down to freezing. We live in dry tents with warm stoves, plenty of blankets, hot food three times a day, good raincoats, electric lights, hot showers, and reading material. You'd think we'd not have the gall to gripe, but not so.

56th Evac Hospital at Dragoni, Italy, a site synonymous with rain, mud, and cold.

Brown, White, and Johnson were transferred to the medical service for a week while we were at Avellino. I am starting on that service today. Internal medicine is, of course, my real love and the thing my formal training was qualifying me for, so I'm glad to be back with the type cases I'll do when the war is over. The work isn't hard and we aren't complaining, but it has been quite a spell since I've reasoned along medical lines. Naturally, I'd draw the ward farthest from my tent, and with all that mud to wade through five or six times a day.

Sergeant Liggett came by today. It was the first time I'd seen him since we nearly dropped our truck over the precipice in the mountains last summer. I'll never forget the look on his face when he spun the steering wheel on the approach to that hairpin turn, and our truck kept moving straight ahead. He thinks that story will stand some stretching when we get home, and he hopes our listeners won't ever get together and compare notes. If they should happen to, they might think they've heard accounts of two separate events.

Now I do wish I could limit myself to reporting only the pleasant happenings within our Baylor unit, but of course that would distort the true picture of any unit that ever went to war. I have not escaped involvement in traumatic interpersonal relationships, but I must say they have been infrequent and resolved with no damage to the U.S. Army, the medical corps, or the Baylor unit.

It seems to me that the very natures of an army and the 5,000-year-old medical profession present incompatibilities that must inevitably lead to clashes. If these are not between the institutions themselves, they'll crop up between the individuals in the unit.

Traditionally, the medical man has been an individualist. He has set up and readily joined organizations designed to increase and disseminate the profession's knowledge. He has even subordinated his individual freedom to their regulation. He will just as readily subordinate himself to the military in times of national need, but not in the capacity of a physician unless he can maintain the management of his patients. He has resisted all efforts, including those of the military, that might remove patient management from his control. Indeed, it was successful resistance in this area that resulted in the formation of the medical corps in the first place. Being so ingrained in these traditions, medical officers really can't function without maintaining control. They mustn't.

Getting down to unpleasant cases, I was on a major's team once when he thoughtlessly opened the door to a misinterpretation by our subordinates. The man is a good surgeon, and a definite plus to the morale of patients and personnel alike, but a definite minus in rendering postoperative care.

Typically, after each move nurses and medical officers, including the majors, all pitch in to help set up cots and other equipment on the new locations. This time as we finished our task, our major looked at one of our overworked young nurses and forgot all about military chain of command. Unused to giving orders anyway, he said to her, "Now, you run it any way you like," never realizing that it might not be taken as anything other than a fatherly affability.

Unfortunately, the young nurse he'd spoken to was not from Baylor and, instead, was a product of some accelerated wartime training program. She probably received as much education as the usual nurse of these days but had missed some essential indoctrination that usually goes along with that education. Even more unfortunate from my point of view, she was the nurse for the ward to which I'd recently been assigned.

Oh, my! The young lady's personality underwent immediate change, as did her attitude toward me. There was really no actual insubordination for the first week, but the atmosphere around the nurse's station on my ward was pretty strained at times. Finally, a soldier was admitted with a fractured skull and blood-tinged spinal fluid leaking from one ear. He would need head surgery but not until he had been evacuated back to a general hospital. Such patients were in considerable danger of a fatal meningitis unless the leakage of fluid was allowed to continue, its flow blocking bacterial passage from the ear canal into the brain. I examined the soldier and wrote an order that his ear was not to be syringed out nor plugged with cotton. Ah, but when I returned two hours later the man's ear was as clean as a hound's tooth and neatly plugged with cotton.

Well, I was completely nonplused for the moment, having never before had any but the most pleasant relationships with every nurse I'd worked with. Of course, I recovered and did what I had to, as also did a scandalized major and a highly irritated CO. Things worked out, all of us no doubt cowed but wiser, when the nurse was reprimanded and a set of unified rules laid down for every ward in the hospital to follow.

One rule was that each ward should be ready for an inspection by the CO each morning. And that gentleman actually made such rounds for the first time ever. We became more formally military for a few weeks, and overt personality clashes never surfaced again during the war.

Incidentally, our chief nurse told me her duties had been simplified a lot by the blowup.

NOVEMBER 21, 1943. I had a letter from Dean Moursund telling me the *Journal of American Medical Colleges* is going to publish my article. He adds, "You'd better be prepared for some bombardment by the diehard medical politicos. They may not agree with you in all of your presentation. It is a good paper, and if it creates argument, good and well." The article was accepted by the journal promptly. I appreciated his submitting it for me and hope somebody proofreads it for me.

Johnson and I had barely gotten acquainted with our wards after being transferred to the medical service, when he got sick. I've had all of the work that was assigned to the two of us. Medicine is just naturally more interesting than surgery, and I've enjoyed the work a lot. Johnson had a bad cold and will be okay in a few days. I'd like to be over here on a permanent basis but probably should stay on surgery as long as I'm in the army.

Martinak is pleased to have been put on Dunlap's team in this last scramble. Small never would let him do anything on his own and Dunlap probably will. I hope he will get as much out of the association with Dunlap as I did, for the "little red man" can teach him plenty.

I must tell you of another of Dunlap's mishaps. I can't understand why he keeps himself in so much hot water nor why it is so amusing. He's done everything from losing his billfold to losing his knife, his mess kit, his helmet, and even his gas mask. Today he spent an hour trying to start his fire with wet wood, everyone around kidding him while he finally got it lit. He then went over to his ward for a bit. Meanwhile, the back of his tent caught and burned quite a hole before anyone noticed it. Happily, none of his stuff burned. Tomorrow, he'll probably fall down in the mud, and the day after lose his raincoat. For all of this, he is highly intelligent, deeply committed to his patients, and amply qualified to care for them. And if that be a personal judgment, who is better qualified to render it than one with six months' experience as the lowest man on his team?

NOVEMBER 23, 1943. Every night about this time, the nostalgic and sentimental music of "Ev'ry Night about This Time" comes over the PA system. It wreaks havoc on many a resolve to express only cheerfulness and high morale in letters home. Young men with younger wives and much younger children four or five thousand miles away, and faced with the many uncertainties inherent in war, probably need very few reminders such as this song exudes. So, damn the war, anyway!

As of this date, we've had nine days of rain to one when the sun shined for short periods. With our high mountains on both east and west, there'd be no more than six hours of sunshine even on a clear day. Both the mud and the muddy shoes are becoming jokes, like my promotion arriving eight days late. I still get a good deal of kidding about that.

The best part of the mud joke has been the recent attempt of the engineers to drag the driveways and footpaths around here. This resulted in our loblolly becoming evenly spread over the entire area, including into the ruts cut by trucks and ambulances. Now, every time a vehicle goes through, and this means often, a muddy sheet flies out for several feet on either side. So most of us have stopped compromising with the mud. We no longer try to step around it but just walk straight through to wherever we're headed, and to heck with the mud.

Martinak just came in after another very busy day on Dunlap's team. He's very happy with his change to a new team. Most of the surgery has been minor, but there's lots of it. I've missed the last two surgical rushes, this time by being on the medical service that isn't busy, last time by being on our musician's team.

My one pneumonia patient is squawking to get out of bed after only a few days of treatment with the recently released Triple Sulfas drug. I told him he was flattering his doctor, but I should have admitted he was not indebted to me but to the German dye industry. Their chemists synthesized sulfanilamide prior to World War I but failed to develop it, their socialized system providing no incentive. The army has sure removed any lingering ideas I may have had that a socialized system of medicine might be good. I sure hope America never embraces any such ideas.

NOVEMBER 24, 1943. Two highlights in today's events—first, we had good American steak for supper, good steak and good gravy and plenty of both. We've been wondering for some weeks where all of that good beef and those good hams were going. They'd not been coming to the Italian front, for sure.

The second highlight was really the first, as it came in the early morning hours. Martinak had made his usual successful effort lighting our fire with wet fuel. Almost immediately, though, the tent filled with smoke so acrid and so dense that we had to tear outside into the cold, scantily dressed as we were. Our loudly protested cries over the empty tin can covering our stove pipe were ignored, although some of our clean livin', innocent, and fun lovin' neighbors peeked out to watch the fun.

The guilty party could have been Turnbow, Merrick, or the chaplain but was more likely all three. We're again faced with the necessity to devise something appropriate for getting even sometime. I'll tell you what—smoke from burning wet cedar together with wet diesel fuel and wet charcoal is nothing like smoke from a good cigarette, particularly when inhaled in dense concentrations while lying down in a very small tent!

NOVEMBER 25, 1943. Thanksgiving day, and none of our neighbors—nor we—realized a holiday was near until noon chow today. We had good baked turkey, cranberry sauce, mashed potatoes, gravy, and I don't know what else. All of our patients had the same dinner, and we hear all installations in Italy did, too. That must surely have presented an "economy-sized" logistic problem capably solved. It sure was good.

The weather again! We had a hard wind accompanied by the hardest rain I ever saw today. Our living quarters were not messed up, but the center of Martinak and Dunlap's ward caved in, right in the middle of the storm. So also did the mess hall and most of the latrines. Some rain! Some blow! Some luck we stayed dry!

Aside from a dry place to sleep, a medical officer's greatest comfort is undoubtedly the type folding canvas chair several of us brought all the way from San Antonio. There is absolutely no place else in this entire hospital where I can sit down and lean back. Who at home would ever have realized such a thing? Next most important item is a pair of those high-off-the-ground, wooden-soled bath sandals. Not only do I wear them in the shower, but I also keep them at the door of my tent where I can reach them each time I come in. I get out of my always wet and muddy leggings and shoes and slip them on. In a very few minutes, our stove dries out the wool socks on my feet and I'm warm and comfortable. My hatchet, duffel bag, and leather shaving kit are the next most important things. Indeed, except for the clothes on our backs and our reading and writing materials, just about all else is so much excess baggage.

Johnson and I will go back to surgery tomorrow. One or two of the majors are squalling their heads off about having only two men per team. The ones howling the loudest are those who've worked the least since we've been overseas. Oddly enough, or typically enough according to some views, two of these are the only ones ever singled out for personnel commendations. I don't know.

NOVEMBER 26, 1943. More of the soldier's comforts: imagine a bedroom furnished with only a canvas cot, a stove, and a chair. No shelves, no dresser, no hooks or nails on a wall. No bed table, no reading table, no cabinets. No floor except a muddy, wet one. Where does he empty out his pockets at night? Where does he hang his hat? His coat? His dress clothes, if he has any? Where do his dirty clothes go? His shaving material, towels, soap, toothbrush? His clean handkerchiefs or his writing material? Having no footlocker and no wardrobe, the answer to all these "where's" is the barracks bag or the valpac. But his comforts can be expanded unbelievably if he can scrounge for boxes, used lumber, and the like, provided he has a hatchet as a substitute for both saw and hammer. Only the barracks bag and valpac are available for the first few days after a move, but if the soldier belongs to semistationary units such as ours, he can expand his comforts very quickly after each move. Of course, the limitations of logistics demands he dispose of all accumulated paraphernalia prior to the next move.

So, three weeks after setting up in this location, I've had time and weather to expand my comforts. Martinak has had to work and will be jealous when he sees what a swell platform I built to raise my bunk up four inches out of the mud. It is two feet longer than the bunk, thus providing a dry spot at the head of my bed for the upright duffel bag, substitute for a bed table. Of course, my platform provides all the dry space beneath my cot for dirty clothes, shoes, and the like. I owe Martinak so many considerations, I'll have to duplicate this improvement to go under his cot if I get the chance before he does.

Johnson and I go back on surgery tomorrow. He goes on Sebastian's service with Alessandra, and I go on Bussey's with Rowe. Both of my new teammates are hard workers and do excellent work, so I'm fortunate.

Getting off our musician's team may preserve my sanity, and I do welcome the change. Alessandra was worried I'd lose it before the blowup over the skull fracture took a big weight off my shoulders. I'll sure not have that sort of mess to contend with on Bussey's team.

I'm sure nobody can ever figure out why rumors run riot in an army, but they do. All I know is we're more vulnerable to them now than we were while at home. We nearly all swallowed a rumor that multiple landings had been made on the French coast at the same time Sicily was invaded. And there's a new, red-hot one today that more landings have been made on the French west coast. We just don't know. Our vulnerability is bound to be enhanced by our lack of knowledge, but for some reason we pay little attention to the news, whether by broadcast or in print. I'm sure that the closer soldiers get to the front, the less they pay attention to legitimate news. Maybe it's all because the rumors sound so much more dramatic and better than the actual truth.

Dunlap's folks have sent him so much stuff he has no use for, that he and Small can barely get into their tent. He got twenty packages one day, which contents included such things as nose drops, vitamins, blades, sharpeners, and even a civilian necktie. Everyone who can, gathers around to watch him open his packages at every opportunity. He has an old bachelor uncle in Tulsa who sends him lots of packages that are priceless.

DECEMBER 1, 1943. Well, I'm back at work after laying off for a couple of days with a cold. Mostly though, I'm goldbricking as there's practically no work, and our tent is cozy and warm in a cold, wet world and is decidedly more inviting than a practically empty ward.

Our stove has not been drawing properly for several days, smoking too much and heating too little. So Martinak and I took the stovepipe down this morning. The one horizontal joint in the line was almost entirely filled up with soot. I'd never seen anything like it, even through a boyhood when such stoves were our only means of heat in the winter. Anyway, we cleaned it out and resisted a temptation to leave it clogged up and substitute it for Turnbow's horizontal joint. Come to think of it, some of our neighbors just might have made such a substitution on us— tantalizing thought! Even heroes at war, I notice, aren't above such innocent diversions.

There is a real innocent and simple looking clock puzzle here in the tent that I finally worked out yesterday while alone. I saddled Martinak with it yesterday, and he gave it up after an hour or two, disgusted. Johnson is here to sit in my chair and read, so I'll spoil his morning pretty soon by giving him a try at it.

Brown pulled the prize boo-boo of an entire army career last night and is entertaining all of us with an embellished account of his discomfiture. A second lieutenant, sent in from his battalion aid station, irritated Brown by admitting that he had only a slight backache. He explained that General So-and-So had ordered him to be evacuated back to the United States. Of course, backache is the classical complaint of the seasoned army goldbrick, so Brown bristled and pooh-poohed the idea of sending such a case back to the States. He didn't get really irritated until he noticed a medal pinned on the soldier's jacket.

"What's that?" asks Brown, sarcastically. "A good conduct medal?"

"No, sir," answers the lieutenant. "It's a Medal of Honor."

The news failed to reach Brown's conscious level until he told the story to Alessandra, who identified its description as the Congressional Medal of Honor. All officers right up to the general staff salute it. Every soldier who receives it, regardless of rank, is returned stateside to receive the President's congratulations. Recipients escape army red tape and expedite their journey by being returned through medical corps echelons. Ha! Brown will be in for lots of kidding.

DECEMBER 2, 1943. We had ice for the first time inside the tent this morning, and it is rumored we're going to lose our stoves to conserve fuel. Could be, but I sure hope not.

The only time Dunlap was able to keep a fire going in his tent was the time he burned the back end out of it. So he came over here last night to visit and stay warm. I threw the clock puzzle into his lap, and he worked on it for more than an hour before throwing it back to me in disgust. Having already worked it, I was able to do it again in front of him in a couple of minutes. That riled him so, he fought it again for another hour and a half. He then ordered that it be held for him as he was coming right back and work it even if it took all night. I really thought he might, but he hasn't been back.

The work is so light that one man could easily do what Bussey, Rowe, and I stumble over each other doing every day. Ordinarily I'd expect to be moving, but I've a feeling we'll be right here until after Christmas.

Sebastian came by and talked for a couple of hours last night. He's decided he won't mess with any teaching at the new medical school unless they make him an associate professor. We enjoyed his visit, as always.

DECEMBER 3, 1943. I sent you a hundred-dollar money order yesterday and also sent all the letters I received since the last batch I returned. Also sent a pair of hose I'd bought for Jeanette's Christmas.

Not so chilly today, since it has been raining all day. This is Martinak's morning to get the fire going, and he's had a time of it. We've been disgusted with our present batch of coal, which leaves an unbelievable amount of soot everywhere. We're now burning wet wood, but it's hard to start, of course. Honey, somewhere in our home we just must have a wood-burning stove. They're not really a great deal of trouble and smell so good. Also, wood cutting would furnish a good excuse for spending a day in the woods now and then.

We barely keep enough work on the wards these days to necessitate going over once a day. We're functioning as a station hospital again, meaning we now may keep patients three weeks instead of three days if it requires that much time to get them back to duty. We aren't earning our salt, even so.

Groups of officers and nurses are being sent on three-day rest periods to a very beautiful and famous island whose name I can't reveal. I look forward to my turn as the army has taken over a very swanky hotel [Hotel Quisisana on Capri] that puts us up for a dollar per day, meals and all. The civilian employees have been retained, and elaborate dinners are served by waiters in evening clothes while a fine orchestra plays. Real beds, clean sheets, and hot baths are bragged on by all who have returned so far. That will be something after our long sojourn here at "Camp Chaos," so named by our hospital announcers. McCauley, Hahn, Bowyer, Devereux, White, and Ken Roberts all go tomorrow, along with four of the nurses. Everyone has been much impressed.

Can you read my V-mails? It seems to me my handwriting gets worse by the day. I've never had any trouble reading your letters, but I've seen V-mails from overseas that could hardly be made out.

DECEMBER 5, 1943. Pretty day, today. No rain. No mail. Usual quantity of mud. Took a case to the operating room tonight for the first time in about three weeks. An Italian civilian had walked into a land mine, which didn't really mess him up a great deal. I was able to dig out the few pieces of scrap metal from his back, chest, arms, hands, and legs in a few minutes under local anesthetic. He was lucky, at that.

I'm taking Devereux's place while he's on leave, and I work in the pre-op ward. Practically nothing of a professional nature is going on, but there are other diversions. One of our enlisted men, a character for sure, has a guitar and is singing holy roller and tear-jerker songs to his own accompaniment. Typical songs are "The Rosewood Casket," "Cheer Up My Brother," "Great Speckled Bird," and "Eastbound Express." He volunteers the information that "he has writ down a whole bookful, from which he played for years," but he says he can only remember them now after two bottles of vino. Then he can see every page of that book in his mind's eye "and can turn through it, page by page, singing every song in it." White gets a big kick out of those songs.

DECEMBER 6, 1943. It won't be long until Christmas, will it? We all naturally wonder if we'll miss the next one, too, although nearly everyone feels like we'll get home long before that. I noticed in *Stars and Stripes* that more than five million packages have already arrived over here. Sure is fun to receive them, but that does seem like a whale of a lot of packages. When the time comes, do wish all of your folks a merry Christmas from me and a merry one to your husband's wife and daughter.

Ha! Do I sometimes mention the weather? I've a feeling that as the years pass, the depth of mud here in Camp Chaos will increase with each repetition of the tale. Maybe I'd better set the record straight by actual measurement. On inspection at the moment, my shoes show wet mud from the soles up about an inch, but dry mud covers the toes of my right shoe up to the third lacing grommet all around. The left shoe has mud all around to within an inch of the six-inch top—I stepped off into a deeper puddle today. Actually, this mud is no deeper than that in many a barnyard of Brazoria County, Texas, each winter, but this is sunny Italy. Half the outfit wears boots, Martinak included, but I find the tops of GI shoes high enough. And by keeping my trouser legs rolled well above them, I manage well enough. I do wear leggings when out in actual rain, but even that is not nearly as heavy as GI boots.

The engineers keep our roadways scraped with bulldozers, pushing loose mud to either side. That helps the roads a lot. But we're getting higher and higher levies of mud built up that we have to wade through when getting to and from the roads.

The chief nurse of the Mediterranean sector is a lieutenant colonel. She has been here conferring with our nurses and gave them a pep talk that they appreciated. She assured them that if they didn't like the mud or their quarters, she'd move them to a fixed hospital somewhere any time they requested it. I'm sure the knowledge reassured them, but nobody took her up on the offer. Captain Rea, our chief nurse, has been sent back to the States, and Miss Meadors has been promoted to take her place. All of our nurses, except Rose Craig and one other, have been promoted to first lieutenant. These two older ones refused to accept theirs, as acceptance would bind them to the Articles of War, thus suspending their constitutional rights. I understand that by not accepting the promotions, they remain civilian employees and can quit any time they choose.

We aren't earning our salt. Bussey, who can't stand to loaf, remarked that he wished we'd either fold up or get back to work. I'm for that. He, Rowe, and I stumble all over each other on the ward without enough to do. On the other hand, I'd like to be on this team through one rush period. Bussey, for all of his old maidishness, is conscientious and was always one of the better students in our premed days. I'm sure I'd learn a lot from him.

I've read some more books that I don't believe I've told you about. Finished *Arundel* a week or two ago and have read *Stars On The Sea* and Wendell Willkie's *One World*. If you haven't read the latter, you should. Don't tell your dad, but I'm sold on Mr. Willkie since reading his report from his world trip. I guess he can afford to talk big plans since he is a private citizen and wouldn't have to implement any of them, but he seems to talk much like I believe. I sure don't see how either party could tolerate him for a leader, though.

Well, well, well. We're going to do an appendectomy and I must go.

DECEMBER 7, 1943. Can you remember two years ago when they stopped the show we were watching to announce that the Japs were bombing Pearl Harbor? By golly, I thought they'd lost their minds and would capitulate within a couple of months. It's remarkable how uninformed all of us were.

Your November 9 letter came today. Sure, I remember spending our anniversary last year driving from Jasper and maneuvers back to Alvin. Sure do wish I could have spent it the same way this year. I don't remember your fussing about having to spend it that way—as a matter of fact I can't seem to remember your ever fussing about anything. All I'm able to recall about you at this point is what a swell disposition you had and how pleasant you were to be around.

I still have the binoculars and won't trade them for anything else. I wish I could send them home but am too afraid the censor would confiscate them, even if they are a fine souvenir. You know all captured enemy material belongs to the army unless one's CO feels that it is of more value as a souvenir than as war material. I wouldn't like to trust those through the mail, even with the CO's blessings.

I got a Christmas box from Joe and Mardi tonight. They sent a carton of cigarettes, two decks of bridge cards, four awfully nice handkerchiefs, Hervey Allen's *Forest and the Fort*, and Victor Robinson's *The Story of Medicine*. All were very welcome, and I'm looking forward to brushing up on the history. There are lots of presents tonight, but I always seem to get the best ones. Martinak got a pound of Sir Walter Raleigh pipe tobacco from Dr. Newsom, his old chief, and Dunlap got a pound of good salted peanuts. I'll help each of them out on those items until my Edgeworth tobacco gets here.

I'm all atwitter about your trip to Washington. I'll bet I don't get anything but old letters for the next two weeks and won't know what you've decided. I'll also bet it was my promotion's failing to come through that made you decide you needed a change. I can tell you I felt like I needed one when three of my former students received theirs, and for those eight days mine still had not come through. Say, how can you manage gasoline for such a trip, and will your tires stand it?

We've had a most unusual event here at Camp Chaos today. One of our newer nurses, whose name I've not yet learned, got married to an infantry lieutenant today. It seems they had to apply through the army to get the license and the army's consent. He is located in Egypt, and she didn't know he was in Italy until he breezed in this afternoon.

Well, they got five days' leave right away. The chaplain married them in the chapel at 2:00 P.M. with half of the nurses and officers as witnesses. Chaplain allowed that anyone who would wade through the necessary mud to get to the chapel was really anxious to get married. I "allowed" to myself that it was a mighty romantic way to get married. The guy picked up a ring in Cairo on the way over. The bride wore officer's "pinks and blouse," as did the groom. There were no flowers and no wedding cake. Wilson played the wedding march on our portable organ. Ma Reagan gave the bride away, and to tell the truth, I felt weepy as a mother of six girls.

Bussey let Rowe do the appendectomy that called me away from your letter last night. Rowe had spent considerable time in the operating room at Methodist in Oak Cliff during his internship and did a nice job in record time. I second-assisted and heckled Rowe, which was acceptable. The patient is doing fine, but if he'd known how out of practice his doctors were, he'd probably have been scared.

The bunch returned from the beautiful island today. They all enjoyed it very much, but Bowyer and Devereux missed the Blue Grotto, visiting Tiberius' villa instead. It is too bad we can't get to see the many things of interest in Italy, but of course we didn't come here to tour the country.

Oh, have I ever told you it rained here? Today, same as Monday! We've had ice one time, but most of the time it's pretty warm. I never have gotten my heavy coat out and doubt it will ever be needed in Italy. I hope not.

Martinak and I get mutual kicks out of the antics of our daughters. I told him about Suzanne's dressing up in your unmentionables.

DECEMBER 8, 1943. There goes "Every Night About This Time" on the loudspeaker again. Somebody really likes to listen to that one, as well as many other old ones designed to turn one's thoughts back a bit. I guess the enlisted men and nurses get as homesick as the officers—they're the ones who play the records.

Same as Monday—rain and no work to speak of. Our ward is full, but most of the men aren't sick and are just boarding with us until the general hospital in Naples can take them in for elective surgery. I'm sure I could do all of the work on the entire service at this point and never be overworked. I'm enjoying the book Joe sent, *The Story of Medicine*, and have also read all the copies of *Reader's Digest* in the past few days. Martinak has read twenty-seven novels and countless who-dunnits since leaving the States.

I'm scheduled to make the island trip on either the 13th or 17th. I sure hope nothing prevents it. I can remember reading Axel Munthe's *Story of San Michele* years ago and would love to see its setting. That's good reading, too, in case you missed it. I guess I should consult the encyclopedia before I go over there, but I won't have time to see more than a few things, anyway.

I still manage to get about three showers a week. Compare that with what one of my itching patients told me tonight. He said it had been four weeks since he'd had a bath and wondered if that might be why he itches. He's looking forward to ten o'clock tomorrow when the showers are reserved for patients.

DECEMBER 9, 1943. Hahn's brother, an air pilot, was forced down on Russian soil after a raid on Japanese territory. Russia, an ally against Germany, is neutral on Japan. Therefore, Russia interned the plane and all the personnel in it. Johnson can't understand this. It sure is a peculiar situation.

Eating is becoming a problem again but for different reasons than before. Christmas packages have brought in so much fruitcake and other sweets that we all keep our appetites ruined. Meals at 8:00 A.M., 11:30 A.M., and 4:30 P.M. are too close to permit nibbling in between, so the only real chow we tolerate is breakfast. Nausea seems to overtake us as we approach the mess hall, but that did not keep us from eating an entire batch of real good peanuts Bussey got at eleven o'clock this morning.

DECEMBER 10, 1943 [to Mama]. I would have very much liked being in Waco when you were and going to Harris' East Terrace and Uncle Rush's farms. When I get back, I don't see how Margaret and I can be anything but small town dwellers if I'm to be around those things that I miss so much now.

I'm glad I could write you of the nice things I heard about brother Charles E. that time in Casablanca. I probably didn't tell you, but I ran into Dr. Leslie Sadler of Waco while there. He and my Colonel Carter had been classmates in medical school, and Dr. Sadler invited the two of us to his hospital for dinner. He told us of Charley's versatility, saying that he could do more things well than any doctor he, Dr. Sadler, had ever seen. Such versatility is certainly a prime asset at present, but probably as medicine becomes more sophisticated and specialized, it may well cease to be so. I just hope the sophistication doesn't result in a mandatory shuffling of patients from one specialist to another. The pitfall could be that the system becomes so expensive, it converts large segments of the population into medical indigents. Should that ever be the case, the quantity of human suffering created by new discoveries and new treatments might very well exceed the quantity relieved.

Merry Christmas to all.

DRAGON NEW YEAR   11

December 1943–January 1944

DECEMBER 10, 1943. Lots of rain, but your letter of November 8th and Mama's of the 23d came today to make things better. They make a world of difference in our outlook, even when it's raining.

Hey, I wouldn't try to educate Faye about doctors. People have had their own ideas about what was good doctoring and what wasn't since before the time of Christ. As to canned milk formulas, many good doctors believe them as good as the commercially prepared infant formulas. Since her doctor prescribed Similac, which is certainly good, I wouldn't plant doubts in her mind. Of course, Suzanne was raised on whatever samples I could scrounge from the detail men who called on me at the clinic. Such samples may have been Similac one week and Carnation the next. If you remember, her diet ran the gamut and was probably not the same on any consecutive week, but she never had colic.

Now as to taking Suzanne to Faye's specialist, I'm sure your doctor would advise you to should problems arise to indicate it. You might tell him you'll always abide by his instructions, including a visit to a pediatrician if he ever deems it necessary—then forget it. I remember an article ten years ago by Morris Fishbein, editor of *JAMA*, advocating that ninety percent of all medical practice should be done by general practitioners, letting them decide when the specialist was needed.

I wish I could share your problems with Suzanne. Not that I feel I could do any better than you but simply to back up your judgment. That's a monkey on your back, but it can't be helped. Just remember that she can be reasoned with at age twenty, if not twenty months, and perhaps by age eighteen. I'm glad you didn't paddle the little shaver the second time she crawled out of bed that night. Maybe it's asking too much of a little bitty feller to go off to bed by herself, all lonesome and all—I don't know.

Rowe and I worry Bussey by our administering medical treatment instead of calling someone from the medical service to do it. We wouldn't if anything serious came up, but as a rule the receiving section recognizes those. I enjoy medical cases more than surgical but do need to learn all of the surgery I can as long as I'm in the army.

Martinak, Turnbow, and I hope to spend a few days at Capri next week. Had asked some time ago that arrangements be made, but yesterday when I asked Colonel Carter for an exact date, I couldn't pin him down. Martinak was mad at him for asking, "Oh, do you want to go?" We understand that the army has conscripted the finest hotel on the island for our use. Clean sheets, tablecloths, napkins, and waiters will be some novelties!

DECEMBER 15, 1943. Jabez Galt, Martinak, Turnbow, and I returned last night from a very fine trip out of our mud. I'm sorry I can't tell you where we've been, but we now learn censorship forbids it. Anyway, we had two nights and a day on a very picturesque island, which is no longer indigenous to those goats from which it took its name in ancient times.

Our group also included several from the nurses' section. Any misgivings we may have had about having the nurses on our hands were completely wasted. We were no sooner on our boat than they were taken over by the air corps. We saw no more of them until a trip to the Blue Grotto, where the air corps officers declined to take them.

The island lies in the entrance to what is reputed to be the most beautiful harbor in the world. I believe it lives up to its reputation. It is situated at the upper end of a shepherd's crook of Italian coastline, several miles in length, and is well sheltered.

The entire panorama—Bay of Naples, Capri, Naples Harbor, the city, and the coastline down to Sorrento—can all be taken in by the naked eye from the ferry in the bay. It is most impressive. Vesuvius rises up about a mile from the center point of the shepherd's crook, smoke from its peak rising another mile or so. From Vesuvius to Naples the shoreline is a string of buildings, which from a ferry out in the harbor all look clean, white, and undamaged. Land and buildings rise up from the shoreline like a huge amphitheater. Naples itself extends back for several miles, rising perhaps one thousand feet above it, so that the streets look like terraces. Miles back of all this are the mountains. Only the center one, taller than the rest, is snow covered. This panorama is even more impressive when viewed from the cliff at the east end of the island.

Now Capri with its 5 1/2-square mile area lies only two or three miles off the shoreline, down near Sorrento. It is 4 1/2 miles long and has two harbors, Marina Grande and Marina Piccola, each with a village of the same name. Then there are the villages of Capri, about five hundred feet above Marina Grande, and Anacapri at the thousand-foot level. The long axis of the island is oblique to the shoreline, and its topography is rough, of course. It has been a playground since before the time of Christ. The Emperor Tiberius who appointed Pontius Pilate was living there at the time of the crucifixion. While less restful than Bermuda and no more beautiful, Capri certainly is more picturesque. The east end is a steep cliff nine hundred feet high, while Monte Solaro rises nineteen hundred feet at the west end. Tiberius spent the last ten years of his life on the island and built twelve villas there.

We landed at Marina Grande, a village whose main street serves as its quay. Literally scores of gaily painted rowboats were tied up there when we came in. A funicular with a single cable car runs up to Capri where most of the shops are. The fare on this car is one lira. Lots of flowers were in bloom, and all citrus fruits were nearly ripe and loading the trees.

There was no evidence of a war going on. No mud, no artillery fire, no tents, no flies, no tanks, no trucks, no sick, no wounded. Neither were there clouds, and all rank was forgotten. It was truly a paradise for all of us.

We stayed at the Grande Hotel Quisisana, certainly one of Europe's best. To those of us who had not slept in a real bed with linen sheets and good mattresses for eight months, our rooms were luxurious. They would have been luxurious even if we'd been sleeping in our usual home surroundings. As a matter of fact, the Quisisana is just swanky as all get out and could not have been afforded on a captain's allowance in ordinary times. It cost us a dollar per day, meals included and no tipping allowed.

The regular civilian hotel staff still operated it as in more affluent times for more affluent people. Tablecloths and napkins are of exquisite linen, of course, and silverware is ostentatious and in lavish quantities, including silver dishes. Meals are elaborately served by immaculately and formally dressed waiters under the direction of a headwaiter in full dress including tails. The waiters, one to dish up the food and the other to serve it, wore short white jackets, but they had on formal dress trousers, stiff-bosomed shirts with studs, and white ties. The headwaiter had a cheery greeting in perfect English for all as we entered and as we left. The hotel was even willing to serve water with the meals, a novelty over here.

The food was actually from military sources, but one could hardly believe it. It was excellent. The chefs in French North Africa could do pretty well with GI food but could not equal Italians in this regard. Even the macaroni called for second servings.

The dining room was very spacious with high ceilings, large columns, white walls, and enormous glass windows all along one wall. These windows overlooked a meticulously groomed formal garden, with a blue background of Mediterranean beyond. The woodwork was hand carved, but not elaborately so. A two-foot border of mosaic in bright colors was around the tops of the walls. The chairs were of mahogany, cane bottomed, simple, and comfortable. Each table had either a potted plant or cut flowers as a part of the decoration. These were always fresh.

The real high spot of the hotel was the lounge. May as well confess that most of its occupants were also pretty high as a rule, coming as they did from similar or worse surroundings than our own. The bar was all along one side, and it opened at 9:00 A.M. and closed at midnight. You might say it opened with a bang each morning to the amazement of many of us, who were learning for the first time that morning drinking can be tolerated with the same end results as evening. Young air corps officers all seemed to be trying to do a heap of living while there, but the bar was patronized by everyone. I'd never before heard of drinks as "Stingers," "Zombies," and "Sidecars." The usual wines, champagnes, cognacs, and Tom Collins' were also available. The new ones seemed appropriately named, I might add.

The wall opposite the bar was all glazed like the dining room and overlooked the same garden with the blue sea in the background. The floor of the lounge was of tile mosaic in greens, tans, browns, and black. Italian artisans must certainly be the world's very best with tile, as were the Romans. There were many white columns in the room, each with potted poinsettias blooming anemically. There must have been a hundred comfortable chairs, all in heavy linen or silk and figured in colors harmonizing with the floor. All very gay—all very exquisite in my unreliable opinion.

All Baylor unit personnel went in a group to see the Blue Grotto. This trip taught us the reason for all of the gaily painted rowboats at the Marina Grande. No other conveyance can make it into the grotto. Its one opening is so low that the occupants of each boat have to lie down in the bottom. The boatman then has to time his dash inside at the low point of the swells of the sea, lest his gunwales be slammed against the top of the entrance. Our boatman wasn't such a skilled timer, and we got splashed with seawater as our gunwales slammed against the rock opening.

We forgave our boatman as soon as we got inside the Blue Grotto. It is beautiful. The domed ceiling must be thirty feet above the water. There are no stalactites from the ceiling, as Capri has no groundwater but depends upon catching rainwater, or shipping in what fresh water is needed. The grotto must be about 150 feet long. Such natural light as comes in through the tiny opening gives the water a unique blue color seen nowhere else, and that provides its name. This blue is somewhere between an aquamarine and the medium blue of the Mediterranean and is eerie but beautiful. At the suggestion of the other boatmen we all struck matches so we could see the smooth, translucent walls, which look like wax. Of course, the boatmen also suggested that we give each of them a cigarette while we had lights in order to save our matches. Finally our considerate guides pointed out where Claudius Tiberius had started construction of a stairway that was to go up through a thousand feet of rock to a villa above. This was in the back of the grotto and had been abandoned after being dug a couple of hundred feet or so. I couldn't learn why they stopped.

Now the highlight of the trip, at least for those of us who had come across the North Atlantic with him, was when Turnbow got seasick and vomited in the Blue Grotto, remarking that nothing was too good for him. You recall he was the only man on the LST who did not get sick when we came over. Maybe he's simply abandoned all of that "clean living" he used to brag about. He stayed plenty sick in that little boat to the delight of all of us, his friends. In token of our sympathy, we each offered to stick our fingers down his throat whenever he stopped heaving.

In the afternoon we took a taxi up to Anacapri where the elevation is just under a thousand feet. I've already described the view of the Bay of Naples from the ferry that brought us over. It was as beautiful as I said, but now imagine the same panorama viewed from the elevation on Anacapri. It was breathtaking, and even an aviator would have to be impressed, I'm sure.

Aside from the splendid view, there are two other things of interest at Anacapri. First, there is an interesting sixteenth century church with an interesting tile floor. Then, there is Axel Munthe's San Michele, which he described so well in his novel, *The Story of San Michele*.

Inlays of the many-colored floor of the church depict a large scene of Eden and its inhabitants. This was put together four hundred years ago by an artist who evidently believed paradise was inhabited by many fat trees, fat animals, and a fat, innocent looking Adam. He pictured Eve as fat, scared, sophisticated and running away from the Lord's fat, angry angel. Adam's expression of complete innocence and assurance in the presence of that angry angel was hilarious. His face and eyes had the same expression of contentment worn by one or two of the cows. I'd think it safe to bet good money that sixteenth century artist thanked his Lord daily that he was "not as woman" and then got up off his knees and slapped his wife.

Now if you haven't read Axel Munthe's novel, it sure would be worth your time. He designed and built the pretty villa called San Michele and described it in *The Story of San Michele*. He filled it during his lifetime spent on the island with many interesting Roman relics picked up hereabouts. He also made room for a great many Egyptian relics, as well. In the garden, he uncovered a black and white tile mosaic floor just as it had been laid down by ancient Roman artisans, in what was then one of the twelve villas of Tiberius on Capri. It is still in perfect condition. A 4,000-year-old Egyptian idol carved from black stone is also interesting and so is a granite replica of the sphinx. The idol is shaped like an eagle with a man's head, a reverse of many pictures in Egyptian tombs.

An old monastery built in the thirteenth century on a cliff above Marina Piccola looked interesting, so we went over. All of the monks we've seen are pleased to have visitors and show people about. Like the others, this one fills you with awe at the antiquity of its furnishings and artwork. Their chapel has a high ceiling completely covered with fifteenth century paintings, all bright and fresh looking.

Anything else I might have to say about Capri must wait until I see you. That I could say this much should be ample evidence of my sobriety on the trip. Anyway, I had a swell trip that raised my morale as much as a letter from home. Also, when we got back we found there'd been no rain in four days and all of the mud had dried up. It's a fine world.

DECEMBER 16, 1943. I was tickled to get your Alabama and Virginia V-mails with all their news of the babes. Sounds like they are good little travelers. I hope your change of scenery does as much for you as my trip to Capri did for me.

No rain again today. I cleaned and shined my shoes this morning, and they're still presentably shined and don't have a bit of mud on them. Almost too good to be true, but our mud really dries in a hurry whenever the rain lets up.

Colonel Winans asked me if I'd like to transfer to his service permanently, and I told him I would. I wasn't really surprised, as both he and Rippy have hinted at it since before we left the States. Of course, I never wanted to leave internal medicine in the first place and would probably like it as much as ever. I'll almost certainly like it better than a setup where there are three men to do the work of one or one to do the work of three, and that with no authority at all. I've had it both ways on surgery and am still on Bussey's team, but all teams will change Sunday.

Sorry you had to pay so much for my watch. I'd figured on about $23.50 but didn't know anything about a tax. Also sorry you went to the trouble of sending me your financial statement. I would urge you to keep the books, honey, and total them every month. I'll send the insurance company fifty dollars each month from here.

DECEMBER 17, 1943. You bugger, you didn't give me your Washington address. If it comes tomorrow, I'll send your mail there for two weeks and then back to Alvin. I had been dubious about your tires, as they sure have lots of miles on them. I was glad to learn Randolph was along and sure am glad the trip is over and you made it okay.

There is so much back mail stacked up somewhere that I've been getting a letter or two every day since I got back from Capri. I'm not sure I'll recognize any lull caused by your trip.

I've not heard it officially but expect to go on the medical service tomorrow. The surgical service will be holding an election tomorrow to see if the men would prefer forming permanent teams. Each man is also supposed to set down his preference as to which team he'd rather be on. I hope that little popularity contest will involve me only as an onlooker.

DECEMBER 18, 1943. This organization has received no mail for the past two days. It might be interesting for you to know what goes on, to explain such omissions from time to time. It is generally known that soldiers' mail does receive high priority in the logistics of war, but key personnel who must use the same mode of transportation naturally "bump" the mail bags if space is critical. Did I ever mention Ford's prize statement on this situation? It was a day of no mail but of an inspection visit of our activities by Clair Boothe Luce and Senator Margaret Chase Smith. Ford's remark: "If they're going to send old bags over here, they ought to send mail bags!" Actually, the ladies were right nice looking.

Among the prized Christmas presents is a book, *As I Remember Him*, the autobiography of Hans Zinsser. He was the author of the textbook of bacteriology we used in medical school, and he wrote this new book when he knew he was dying of leukemia. His outlook under the circumstances was unbelievably detached and tranquil.

As the tactical situations of our army vary from fixed positions to rapid advance, the demands on our two services vary from primarily medical to primarily surgical. Surgery takes the brunt of our load with each advance, but medicine is overworked during fixed fronts. But sooner or later we fall back from the front and neither service has anything to do, doctors falling over each other on practically empty wards and morale plunging. We're presently in the "sooner or later" period. Dunlap's ward is going to be closed, and his team is coming over to ours. That will make about twice as many doctors on the ward as there are new patients each day. A single doctor could do everything necessary in about an hour. A recent order from the CO that all medical officers remain on their wards from 8:00 A.M. to 4:00 P.M. has been rescinded as impractical, most patients arriving after 5:00 P.M., anyway. Obviously the CO has recognized that idle officers create a morale problem but hasn't seemed to realize that "sewing buttons on eggs" is even worse. I'd certainly not like his job and am willing to believe in his sober moments he'd love to be relieved of it. Merry Christmas to all at home!

DECEMBER 19, 1943. What do you know? Dunlap's team didn't move in with us after all, as he and Charley Bussey never could get together on how to arrange the equipment. Colonel Carter threw up his hands and had both Dunlap and Willis move in with him. I'm real glad nobody thinks they can get along with us, as three of us are already too many.

Colonel Winans told me today that Carter balked at giving me up to the medical service. Looks like I can't make the change at this time. I don't know what's up, but I'm sure I'll manage in either place.

Congratulate Johne D and Randolph for me on John's arrival. The announcement came today. Also tell Randolph that if his organization has a fixed table of organization that freezes him in grade, he'll get an automatic promotion when he gets overseas. The increase in pay will support little John.

I don't understand why it took three weeks for you to learn of my promotion. I sent you a cablegram on the day I got it, but I'll bet the message had to go to London by air and be cabled from there. All of our promotions were supposed to have come through in May or June but were delayed by the usual red tape.

The Baylor unit received forty-seven large mail sacks of packages today! Can you imagine? I got lemon drops, Edgeworth tobacco, starch, and a fruit cake from Mama. It all begins to look very Christmasy.

Yesterday the pre-op ward put up a Christmas tree and started decorating it. Before the X-ray section knew what they were up to, pre-op conned them out of all of the extra tinfoil and red paper that films come in—all they had on hand—and cut them up into various tree decorations. The enlisted men from X-ray hit the ceiling when they saw what fine decorations they'd given away. It was all very funny and also very infectious, practically every ward now competing with every other one for the best decorations. We received some equipment recently that had been packed in spun glass, which looked just like commercial angel's hair. Pre-op confiscated it before anyone else had the idea, and their tree is as nicely decorated as any I ever saw. And it looks quite conventional, too, which it certainly isn't.

Everyone has been cutting out strips of red bells, Santas, and the like from magazine pictures, and the patients have pitched in like fourth graders wanting to help. Rowe brought over some unpopped corn that promptly went into mess kits and was popped. Half a dozen soldiers have made chains from the popcorn and Lifesavers, and they look very fine. Bussey started the whole thing off, and he and I have worked on that tree most of the day, everyone having a fine time. For all of his reserve, Bussey is as human as the next and is a nice guy, as well as a good surgeon.

I sure was relieved when I found out you'd gone to Washington in Randolph's car instead of ours. I sure didn't see how our tires could have made that trip, and I knew rationing would prevent your replacing them.

DECEMBER 20, 1943 [to Mama]. Your airmails of November 3, 12, and 22 came today, along with a V-mail of the 24th. Also your fruit cake arrived, and I'm saving it until Christmas. Christmas would have had a very hard time making itself felt without fruitcake. This in spite of the fact that all of the folks who have sent presents have been unusually bountiful in their thoughtfulness.

Was glad to learn that Bill and Lucille were enjoying the work in Washington. I got a December 1 letter from Margaret today, and she had talked to them but hadn't seen them yet. I, too, thought the government used good judgment in getting Bill up there and am hoping he gets to use his judgment about things. Regimentation becomes very monotonous when your judgment is not needed, I can tell you.

Your not understanding our lulls in work is understandable, so I'll try to explain it for you. In the first place, an army must plan all personnel and all material based upon anticipated maximum demand. Therefore, there is always too much material and too many men for ordinary times. So we have too many hospitals and too many doctors most of the time. But every time a hospital moves, it goes ahead of all of the others and just as close to the front as it can. This results in its doctors and nurses and other personnel being very much overworked for a few weeks after each move. By that time, all personnel are worn out and thankfully the front moves up, other hospitals are brought forward, and almost overnight people rest. Thus, most of the time we do practically nothing, but whenever we do much, we do too much. Whenever the front moves forward there aren't enough of us, but when the front becomes static long enough for us to empty our beds, there are too many of us. The war is really going better for our side when we're overworked.

It isn't the most efficient institution tolerated by erring mankind; and for all of that, a functioning army may well be the most wonderful (literally), most fascinating, and most gigantic device yet.

DECEMBER 21, 1943. Heard from Mama today, but not from you. Three copies of the *Alvin Sun* came, too, but they still have my APO number 3784. Mom says both Bill and Lucille stay busy in Washington and both enjoy their work. I hope all of you get to see a lot of each other while you're there.

Our Christmas tree is looking better each day. Today there are even a few presents around it. I expect it to be pretty well loaded by the 25th. Some of the patients whom we should discharge have worked so hard on it that we haven't the heart to send them out before Christmas. Some way to fight a war!

Our drought broke yesterday but not enough to put us back into much mud. The rains nearly always come at night, relieving us of much need for raincoats. The engineers finally gravelled our streets and walks, adding just no end to our comforts.

Martinak stays in stitches reading H. Allen Smith's *Life in a Putty Knife Factory*. He's also read *Low Man on a Totem Pole* by the same author, and it was also a scream. Me, I don't get to read as much as I did, because as little as there is on the ward, it takes up more of my time than surgery did.

DECEMBER 23, 1943. Your December 2 V-mail came today. You needn't ever worry about my ego rising above ability to take disappointment. When my promotion failed to come through on maneuvers, I was pretty low, if you recall. When it failed to come through with the others this time, I was too low to even think about it, or at least I would have been if they hadn't all kidded me so. I sure was disgusted.

Martinak, Fisher, and Turnbow framed me today. You know I got a duplicate copy of *Arundel* a day or so ago? Well, I did and had loaned the duplicate to Fisher to read. The three of them sneaked the wrapper it came in out of my trash and carefully rewrapped the book and put it with today's mail. When I opened the package, I naturally thought for sure I'd received a third copy. The truth finally dawned on me when I opened it and found my signature on the flyleaf.

Whenever you realize America's very existence has to depend, in part at least, on an army that grants commissions to such "boys grown tall," it could make you shudder, but I'd not have them any other way. From *Arundel* comes this from one of the characters: "Nothing so depresses the human spirit as long, continued rain." Everyone in Camp Chaos would surely endorse that statement, doubled and in spades, yet.

We're still doing very little work, and there are still no rumors of a move. We'll qualify as staid citizens of this particular mud-bound community before much longer. Our outpatient department is doing a fair practice on the local paisanos, and they're picking up English much faster than we're learning Italian. They now greet Americans with the usual "Hi, Joe . . . Mussolini," followed by a Bronx cheer.

CHRISTMAS DAY, 1943. Man, I hope this is the last Christmas I'll ever spend away from you and home! But it would be lots worse if, for example, I wasn't with a good many old friends, although they're all sort of low at being away from home, too.

That was a mighty fine surprise at breakfast this morning—two fried eggs each, the first in more than two months. I don't know where they came from, most likely from the black market, but mighty welcome just the same.

And speaking of eggs, someone gave the chaplain two yesterday, which he was hoarding carefully. About 11:30 last night one of my majors had sobered up enough to walk without help, so he went alone into the chaplain's tent and swiped one of the eggs. Our fire was still going, an invitation for bringing it over here to cook. As we had neither bread nor butter and the major never has anything but the clothes on his back, he went over to Bowyer and Devereux's and swiped theirs along with some cheese he found. He needed Martinak's mess kit to cook in and helped himself while I was chiding him for stealing the chaplain's hoard. This was before we knew we'd have eggs for breakfast, but chiding never accomplishes a thing with the major, anyway. He'll never deny any charge, whether hurled in anger or just in kidding, but always has a ready rationalization thereby protecting his ego. His reasoning this time was such a classic, I'll just pass it on to you. "Wal yes," he said. "A man ought not to steal from his friends ordinarily, but the devil's after the chaplain tonight and has about got him, so it's all right." The chaplain's only sin was that he went over and sang with the group. We do have quite a mess of egg shell, crumbs, grease, and dirty mess kit to take care of this morning, but nobody ever stays mad at the major for long, whatever the mess.

The party last night must have been quite a success judging from the noise it generated. I had planned to go, but my cold and diarrhea had reappeared earlier, so I went to bed instead. The only party I know of that was noisier was the one I wrote you of in Bermuda. You remember it was at the USO club where soldiers and sailors from three nations were pitching their last drunk before leaving for Europe or North Africa. Anyway, our party was a loud one, and I'm sure nobody within a half a mile got any sleep until it was over. Guests were in and out of my tent from around noon until the major left after frying his egg. All were trying to convince me that what I really needed in my condition was a good, big shot of whatever they were drinking. Since I resisted all offers, I'm undoubtedly the "wellest" man in camp except for a few teetotalers.

We didn't get any mail yesterday, but several packages came in. I got a pound of aromatic tobacco mailed from Walgreen's in Houston, but by whom I don't know—possibly from the Dean of Baylor Med. Martinak got a couple of packages of stuff he has no use for, to add to a boxful of other things he has no use for. The pitiful thing is he's so sentimental about each gift, he can hardly bear to part with it. He has I don't know how many pounds of aromatic tobacco, which he doesn't like anymore after smoking my Edgeworth for a week or so. He also has box after box of tooth powder, shaving lotion, and talc, which are always available in our PX and not selling well there, either. He has a flashlight not as good as the one already issued him, jewel boxes, and even a package of Curtis mints, not as good as Lifesavers but served to us at every meal, anyway. I'm sure it's a problem to pick presents for a soldier on foreign duty, as there is so very little he has the slightest use for. However, all of my folks are to be complimented. None of you have sent anything that doesn't either fit in with my needs or add entertainment to the life we lead.

I wonder if you got back to Alvin by today. Wish I could have seen Suzanne at her second tree, but she couldn't have been any cuter than last year. Probably I'll get to see her next year at her cutest—I hope.

CHRISTMAS DAY, 1943 [to Mama]. A November 30 letter came today, the first to address me with my new rank. So it only took nineteen days for you to get the news.

I'm sure any remark to the effect that this has been a most unusual Christmas would be the height of something or other. I shan't make the remark but will say a good many factors combine to keep it from being as bad as it might have been. In the first place, we're most of us among friends, and in many instances friends of long-standing. And that sure beats being surrounded by strangers.

Then, for breakfast we had the first fried eggs we've seen in two or three months, and they were accompanied by crisp bacon and toast. At noon, every outfit over here had just about the sort of Christmas dinner the people would have had at home. Our cooks are excellent and took their time—dinner was an hour late—and everything on the menu tasted like home cooking. We had excellent turkey, creamed potatoes, sage dressing, gravy, cranberry sauce, English peas, pickled beets, both white and raisin bread, two kinds of fruitcake, and both mince and pumpkin pie. Nothing missing except home folks and a green salad.

I skipped the party last night, having got up about noon with a pretty bad cold and a little fever. I just took to my bed until today and seem to have recovered completely. The crowd spent most of the evening singing carols. Dunlap's comment after it ended was, "Forced gaiety, nothing but forced gaiety!"

DECEMBER 26, 1943. Still no work and still no transfer to the medical service, even though they receive two patients to our one and have only a third as many doctors as we do. Maybe I'll say something to Colonel Winans, but one never knows just what to do. We're bound to move shortly, and I'm expecting to transfer when we do.

DECEMBER 27, 1943. We've really had a beautiful day, the sort that provides opportunity to look around and reconsider this valley of the Volturno River. As I told Carter tonight on our way to eat, this is a beautiful spot if a man would give up griping long enough to take it in and appreciate it. He agreed, but I gathered he thought such a price would be too much to pay. The mountain range northeast of us slopes very gently into our valley and is heavily populated. The sun seems to shine on its upper slopes much of the time when the valley is in shadows. And even on a clear day, the valley is in shadows after 3:00 P.M. due to the steeper slopes southwest of us. Of course those upper slopes to our east are in sunshine a couple of hours later than we, and it is strikingly picturesque. There are two fair-sized villages up there, and from here their buildings look like expensive doll houses.

There is a large mountain north of us, which seems to block that end of the valley completely. It is high enough to remain snow capped and certainly glistens from here in today's sun. Incidentally, this is the same mountain seen back of Naples, and I erred a lot in my distances when I described it from Anacapri. So, we've a beautiful location, mud or not.

DECEMBER 28, 1943. Well, all of our mountains are covered with snow to give us an entirely new view. Also, we've had two days in a row without rain.

Our ward is full again tonight for the first time in weeks. Most of the cases are minor, but there are many of them; I don't know why. I went to the operating room for the first time in weeks and did one debridement.

Christmas packages stopped arriving today. I'll bet two full truck-loads came to this one organization, and most of them will have to be discarded when we move.

I'm reading Zinsser's *As I Remember Him* and enjoying it. It is the third book I've read since a Kenneth Roberts' novel, and it is much less spellbinding than the novels. Somebody around here said Roberts makes his characters suffer too much. But he was writing about mighty rough times, and the people involved did suffer a lot. Anyway, it is something of a relief not to be so spellbound, and this autobiography is a pleasure.

Maybe this is a good time to make an observation on the comparative merits of reading over drinking. Everyone has had to make adjustments since leaving home, some making it one way and some in another. A good many men, myself included, are reading more than ever before, and it can prove to be a lifesaver. However, quite a few do make their adjustment with alcohol exclusively, and most of us do to a limited extent. Christmas went much harder with the heavy drinkers than with the heavy readers, and the difference was very obvious. And so goes the Baylor unit.

[While considerable editing of the letters has left little evidence of the fact, the unit's first Christmas season overseas was an emotionally traumatic experience for most of us. Morale among officers was at an all time low never again approached during our months overseas. It gave rise to such major breaks in discipline as one drunken brawl in which a previously complete abstainer, as his position demanded, yielded to an order given in jest by a superior. The order was that he take a particularly long drink from a bottle being passed by him at the moment. He did so, passing out in short order and falling face down in the Dragoni mud, where he'd certainly have met his Maker had not someone turned him over so he could breathe.

[On another sad day, a major walked up to a regular army lieutenant colonel and without provocation announced that he had simply never liked the man, struck him on the chin with his fist, and knocked him down. Our CO placed the major in isolation under armed guard for the day or so it took him to make up his mind whether to release the offender or instigate court martial proceedings against him. The major was released, but his humiliation was great, as it should have been. I have deleted names here as in other transcriptions of letters where judgmental statements uncomplimentary to some were made. For who am I, or anyone else, to judge the actors in such dramas under such circumstances as we were all living? Should the unnamed parties be recognized, I simply plead that the reader never forget the circumstances, according any recognized shortcomings with the tolerance they deserve—a tolerance equal to that accorded to me so many times.]

DECEMBER 29, 1943. Another day without rain. Our tent floor is so dry, it has cracks in it. We could get along very well in low-quartered shoes, my own high-tops being practically free of mud tonight. We hear January is Italy's wettest month, but we're set for it with all of our gravel walks and with adequate ditching around our tents.

I'm still on surgery and busy again with minor cases.

We frequently wonder how the morale of our wives is holding up. I feel sure you seldom level with us on that score, being anxious to shield us from anything unpleasant. On the contrary, I suppose most of us ventilate our gripes as they arise—I'm sure I do, though I feel guilty about it often enough. But in spite of our gripes, my comrades and I maintain an overall, generally high morale. Even with such provocations as come to all from time to time—and some of them, like promotion failures, are great—we seem to bounce back in a matter of hours, at most. In the first place, all feel that our country is completely justified in the war it's fighting. With that justification, all would be pretty miserable as civilians when we've been called on for military service.

Then, in spite of its shortcomings, our army is a good, functioning fighting force. It is the result of planning and testing by a good many, highly intelligent men for more than 160 years, and we never lose sight of that for very long. Many of those things that irk us most were long since proved necessary for function. We don't forget that. Even on the infrequent occasions when our superiors seem less capable than we might wish, we know that somewhere along the chain of command such incapabilities will be recognized and compensated for—and are better tolerated than used as a pretext for insubordination. We don't forget our superiors are possessed of facts and responsibilities that we do not have, facts that might alter our judgments if we had them. No, we won't forget these things, and that will prevent army matters from getting us down. All of which is not to say we won't gripe—we certainly will—but it won't be a serious matter.

But enough. What a love letter! Please do remember you asked how my morale was and how interpersonal relations were in the Baylor unit. Both are okay. Kiss Suzanne.

DECEMBER 30, 1943. Yours of December 6 came today. I'm glad the cablegram I sent in November finally came through, even if it did take twenty-five days.

Well, I do hope you and Johne D get to watch a session of congress, but I sure hope they don't pass the Wagner-Murray-Dingell bill, either while you watch or after you get home. We sure will be lucky if some modification of it isn't passed in the next congress, even so. This bill, if passed, would radically change the nation's medical care.

Too bad little Johnny is having such a tough time getting started off. Weren't we lucky little Suzanne tolerated just about anything we had access to all through her babyhood? That surely wouldn't be why she sucks her thumb now. I can remember one of my sister Jeanette's beaus teasing me for sucking mine when I was at least four or five years old.

Colonel Carter asked me today if I'd rather be on the medical service. I hope my evasive answer didn't hurt his feelings. I'd not want to do that. He's been too nice to me, although I'm sure I must have tried his patience to the limit more times than once. I told him I'd be more satisfied if I had more work to do and that I thought I'd probably have more to do on medicine. He said he'd arrange it for me, and I sure hope he does.

Mattie sent Merrick some prints of pictures he'd taken inside our quarters at Bizerte. There is one of me that I'm sure she will send you if you ask. He also got a good color print of our hospital with the city of Bizerte and the Mediterranean in the background. Unfortunately, camera shots don't put the relative elevations in proper perspective.

DECEMBER 31, 1943. Your December 2, 3, and 4 airmails and your 13 V-mails came today. 'Twas a nice jackpot.

I know how frantic you were when Suzanne went visiting without your knowledge. I had the same experience with her one time in San Antonio when I suddenly realized she'd wandered out of the backyard where I'd been keeping an eye on her. I tore around to the front yard just as a passerby lady was leading her off the street. Suzy had walked right out into it, and that lady muttered something about "army people" and gave me a look that would sizzle bacon.

I hope you've told me what you're going to do. I don't believe Suzanne should take even a six-hour train ride to Waterbury at this time of year unless she has to. I wish I could help you with her problems, honey, and I do wish you success in mastering the tantrum difficulty. I also hope I don't alarm you about them. Be sure and keep me posted on all of the problems.

Well, I was finally transferred to the medical service today, both Colonel Winans and Colonel Carter keeping their word and evidently with the CO's blessings. The boys on medicine jeered me with, "You'll be sorry," the same jeering welcome we all got in North Africa and Italy when we arrived, and, "Your eyes were wide open." Somebody wanted to know did I just want to let my bedsores heal up. They do work, while those on surgery lie around in their tents most of the time. But the morale here is thriving, while on surgery at least four of the junior officers try to adjust on whiskey or grain alcohol. I'll probably work ten hours a day here in contrast to the two or three on surgery, but that sure suits me fine. I'd never have asked for a transfer but am glad it was suggested. Every officer on medicine has his own ward, but competent help is available on request. It is very close to medical practice in civilian life, while military surgery certainly isn't.

THE LAST NIGHT OF 1943! Darling, your husband loves you very much and wishes he could be with you by March, just as you heard, but he doesn't believe such rumors. Please don't wait in Washington on the strength of any such hope.

JANUARY 12, 1944 [to Mama]. Three letters from Ruth and one from you recently. They seldom arrive in chronological order, but are enjoyed. This may arrive by your birthday, and if so, let it wish you a happy one.

Am enjoying my work on the medical service more than that on surgery and feel like a doctor again. Wish I might have transferred sooner.

Thanks for sending Margaret's vase. I've not heard that she got it but do know she spent Christmas day in Washington with Johne D and Randolph, and that they wouldn't let her open another box I'd sent from Capri until then.

Our weather permits wool shirt-sleeves and no jacket most of the time, but it still rains about like at Alvin. Love to all.

COVERUP OF ANZIO 12
January–April 1944

J **ANUARY 21, 1944** [to Mama]. After reading your December 20 letter I'm afraid I've over-sensationalized some of our experiences for you. I can't for the life of me recall any bridge incident. The checkpoint I referred to was at a highway crossing, not a bridge. That must have thrown you off. Our convoy transporting hospital equipment and personnel did get lost once and was turned back at the last checkpoint before the German lines. The MPs were bug-eyed at an outfit the size of ours—and with nurse personnel—being so close to the front. The Germans do respect the red cross, and we're too big an outfit to be risked in any dangerous spots. Our experiences will have to be colored a bit to ever make breathtaking reading, I'm sure.

We closed down the hospital on short notice last week and moved to this staging area three days ago. We aren't going to set up and are living twenty officers to a tent near Naples. We have no idea where we're going nor how long we'll be right here, either. Being out of the last narrow valley, we're no longer so hemmed in and we get about two more daylight hours each day now.

Our life here is about like it's been in our other bivouac areas—loafing through the days and sleeping about twelve hours at night. You see we have no

155

lights, usually have no fires, and it gets cold as soon as the sun goes down; so there's really nothing to do but go to bed.

Morale always seems to go up while we're bivouacked. Any shortcomings of the organization or of its individual members are quickly forgotten. The feeling comes over us that we're in the best outfit ever organized and that every man in it is a prince among princes. This esprit de corps is quite a nice feeling, putting a glow inside of you that you hope never to lose again. We can't leave the immediate area, so days are spent hiking nearby, playing checkers, bridge, rummy, poker, dice, reading, and the like. There is absolutely no responsibility as soldier or physician.

I hope you miss Jeanette's flu and that she is over it by the time this reaches you. I've had a Christmas letter from Margaret but none from the rest of you, as yet. Suzanne had a big time with her tree and toys, and Margaret and Johne D like Texas lots better than they do Washington.

JANUARY 22, 1944. You might find it interesting to compare this date with your newspaper of the same date. You'll sure get lots more news that way than I can give you in a letter, now or later. [The landing on the Anzio beachhead was made that day, January 22, 1944, and we had been told we were headed up there but censorship forbade my mentioning either event.]

We're still bivouacked outside of a large city whose name I wrote recently but can't mention now. We're very comfortable in our tents since installation of stoves in each one. However in spite of this, we continue to go to bed at eight o'clock every night, I suppose for lack of anything else to do. Expect to move to the new setup in a few days, and when we do, we'll probably earn our money as usual after a move.

We didn't think we'd have an opportunity to send out mail today, but the announcement was made a few minutes ago that letters would go out in twenty minutes. Now everybody in the tent is writing as fast as he can to get a letter ready.

JANUARY 29, 1944. I don't believe I've written you since January 22. This won't get off for quite a while, either, but I hope you won't be worried. We've been involved in a lot of activity since my last letter, but the details will have to keep for awhile longer.

We're setting up in tents again today and are in a flat, sandy area for a change. It's quite a relief to get out of the valley where the mountains moved in a little closer on all four sides each day, giving all of us claustrophobia. There's no mud here, there having been no rain in the area in the past two weeks, fortunately. Pappy had a swell case of mal de mer again, as did everyone else, but that was cured yesterday morning about eight o'clock.

We all thought we were going to move into swell buildings this time—buildings with all plumbing in order, with good roofs, and with only a single broken window. An advance detail did go into the building, and it was just as nice as we'd expected. However, it underwent the usual radical alterations night before last so is no "fitten'" place for a hospital now. Nobody got hurt, and we're all together again in this meadow and have had a good rest. Probably start taking patients again tomorrow.

FEBRUARY 2, 1944. I don't know when I last wrote you and still don't know if our letters get out, but will try again.

We have been busier this time than at any other since coming into the army and will likely stay so for a bit longer. Colonel Carter had me transferred back to his service the first day we opened up, and I've been doing surgery ever since. Next day, all officers on the medical service were also transferred over to surgery, and they've been taking care of the wards while we stay in the operating rooms. I'm not on a team, but Johnson and I have a sixty-five-bed ward and one operating table. We do any cases we want to without supervision. We're both enjoying that arrangement very much, but I can tell you we're tired, and so is everyone else in the Baylor unit. We select our cases, but have done a few big ones and haven't lost a patient yet. Our worst was a soldier with a compound spiral fracture of his femur with a severed femoral artery. Fortunately, (with timely prodding by Turnbow who happened to pass by—clean living, as usual) we'd anticipated that severed artery and applied a tourniquet before making an incision through the very tight skin of that swollen and turgid thigh. Turnbow stayed to give the anesthetic, I operated, and Johnson assisted. We finished in an hour and five minutes, which is very good time for us.

Honey, please don't worry when you don't hear from me. This is the hottest place the hospital has ever been to—or ever will be again—and we're all safe and sound. We've not lost a bit of equipment and have not had a single casualty among our own personnel. I hardly have time to eat, haven't had a bath since we left our last setup, but do manage to get enough sleep. I simply can't write every day with things as they are. Don't worry ever.

FEBRUARY 3, 1944. Yesterday I wrote that we were all working our heads off, and that from the looks of things we'd continue to do so for some time to come. Well, not only Johnson and I but the entire staff got caught up about 11:00 this morning and now have nothing to do. Talk about your sudden change! The explanation is simple—a hospital ship docked and took out all the patients who could be moved, whether they'd been operated on or not. We now have less than two hundred patients in the hospital, and all of them have now been operated on. It is a mighty welcome rest, I can tell you.

I haven't had a chance to write you about our trip, and I didn't get to keep the usual diary letter while on board. I'll describe as much as I can remember.

We left Dragoni on January 19 with the usual "tarfu" ("things are really fouled up"), being ready to move early in the morning and not getting transportation until 6:00 P.M. We rode for a couple of hours to Caivano, near our port of embarkation. We bivouacked there until January 24. Italian kids kept the area besieged to sell us oranges, walnuts, and peanuts, upon which all of us gorged ourselves. Real good oranges were two for a nickel. We finally embarked on British LCIs, the nurses on one and the officers on another, at 11:30 P.M. on Thursday. These landing crafts turned out to be only a fourth as large as the LSTs but four times as rough. We were all crowded below decks in bunks tiered four high, with such narrow aisles between them it was hard to pass anyone. Our CO and other ranking officers shared the same accommodations and took it in good grace. Being British, there was no heat of course. As our bedding was inaccessible, we slept in our clothes—shoes and all—on the bare bunks. The ship being shy of water with so many on board, we couldn't even wash our hands. There was no mess, but we each had adequate C-rations and bread. We fared well enough, the British sometimes toasting our bread and frequently bringing us hot chocolate at night.

Our first hours were uneventful, but by morning the sea got rough, making everyone except Turnbow sick, as usual. Sometime before dawn, the skipper on the nurses' LCI signaled an LST to come alongside and take the nurses off. How that transfer was ever made in a storm I can't understand. I wish I'd seen it. We continued on to our destination, but the heavy weather prevented our docking. The harbor was a hot spot, tactically, and had no place for us to sit out the storm. The skipper had no choice but to turn around and take us back to our port of embarkation. When things settled down again, we completed our trip after spending five days on the LCI.

The buildings we were supposed to set up in had been bombed out during our stay on the LCI, so we moved out about five miles from the

German planes attacking convoy as it nears Anzio. Ack-ack puffs dot the sky.

Anzio harbor, D+4.

harbor and set up in tents, once more. Our equipment was on four separate ships, and every piece has reached us safely. That in itself is a miracle, but so are all the coordinated efforts of a huge army.

We're in the Pontine Marshes, allegedly drained by Mussolini, but the location is flat, sandy, and damp. Maybe we're too pessimistic, but the ground is so soft we expect lots of blown-down tentage if a stiff rain or wind blows up.

This building in Anzio, chosen for the 56th Evac to set up in, was wrecked by the Luftwaffe the second night the 56th's advance detail spent there. One German bomb made the hole above this window while the Baylor Unit's men huddled in the basement.

I feel that you're bound to know where we are from your papers. Since I've no idea what sort of stories they tell, I'm always worried that you'll fear for my safety. Be reassured that the jerries respect our red crosses and that their marksmanship is good, so we're always safe. We're where we hear lots of racket from both our own and jerry artillery but are a safe distance from where casualties occur. We always will be.

We've worked harder here than we ever did before. In our first twenty-four hours, we received more than a fourth as many patients as we did in three months on maneuvers. Had very few deaths, as usual.

First group of nurses to land on the beachhead at Anzio.

I sure do wish I could hear from you. We just don't get any mail and certainly won't for a while yet.

FEBRUARY 4, 1944. Have had a rather easy day of it again today. Johnson, Martinak, and I are now working together, two of us operating while the other gives the anesthetic. We rotate all three positions—anesthetist, surgeon, and assistant—and it's quite a satisfactory arrangement. We don't have a ward at all now and spend all of our time in the operating room. This also is a satisfactory way to function. Beginning tonight we'll work from 7:00 P.M. until 7:00 A.M. daily. There's no telling how long the schedule will hold and even less certainty about my ever going back on the medical service. As long as I can keep busy, I'll be satisfied on either service, but I sure don't fancy being on some major's team with nothing to do but sit. We have the situation well in hand with no backlog of unoperated cases, but with a steady enough stream of casualties to keep everyone busy.

Officers' and Nurses' Mess at Anzio.

Enlisted Men's area at Anzio, looking towards the front.

Gee, I'll be glad when our mail starts coming through again. It seems like months since I've had a letter, but if a jackpot came in tonight, I guess it would take me twenty-four hours' reading at odd moments to finish them all. We don't have lights yet but do have stoves. Maybe I'll read by firelight. We don't really need the stoves, as we're only in our tents long enough to sleep anyway. We're quite safe.

FEBRUARY 5, 1944. Quite a wind and rain last night, but contrary to general expectations, not a single tent stake pulled out. Everything held in spite of the soft sandy soil. I started to end that

Anzio.

Dug-out at Anzio, residence of two 56th Evac doctors.

33d Field Hospital after shelling by German 88s at Anzio.

Crater caused by A.P. bomb that killed Miss Ainsworth at Anzio.

*Major Sebastian and his foxhole at Anzio. Note the
bomb crater just behind him and the remains of a
tent in the background.*

sentence "in these pontine marshes," but we're told that words which are
capitalized seldom get by the censors. Ford had the words Ann Arbor,
Michigan censored out of one of his V-mails. I'll try to remember this
when I write.

We got about five hours sleep on our shift last night but are well
rested today. Lucky we are, too, as a backlog of cases now awaits us for
tonight.

We seem to have identified the outstanding feature of this location
already, and we've named it "Lonesome Polecat." Each location has its
own, the one at Bizerte being "Photo Joe," the jerry recon pilot who flew

Wounded Americans at Anzio dock, just prior to evacuation of ship to Naples.

over the harbor every afternoon. In the Dragoni Valley, it was the everlasting mud. Lonesome Polecat is a heavy jerry gun, which they say is self-propelled. We hear the Polecat fire off a few that whistle over our heads to explode about a minute later in the harbor. Then we don't hear him for some minutes until he starts up again from a new location, either to the right or left of the first. The whistle is different from that of all other American or German pieces, making it easily identifiable. It is heard each day—subconsciously for a bit—until someone remarks, "There goes the Polecat again. He kept me awake last night listening for him."

FEBRUARY 9, 1944. I've finally landed in a service from which I don't suppose I can be switched, at least for a while. We're having an epidemic of gas gangrene cases and have set up an isolation ward with me in charge for handling them. I feel settled, because once a man has worked on such a case, he's not allowed in the regular operating room or another ward for three days. This order is from the area command's surgeon's office and will be adhered to. I don't have many patients, but as I'm the only surgeon who can work on them, I have my hands full. Each one requires a great deal of care before, during, and after their surgery. Have done my first few amputations. Although they are the easiest operations I've ever done, I'm plenty provoked at the shortsightedness of my superiors for not seeing to it that I was trained for such things while still under supervision. I practically begged our CO to see that we were trained better while it was still possible, but he hooted at my idea that any junior officer would ever have to do major surgery unsupervised. By now everyone on surgery has had to.

Baby, don't worry about me. Newspapers have to print propaganda, and accidents do happen. Germany respects the red cross on hospitals, as they always have.

FEBRUARY 9, 1944 [to Mama]. I'm awfully busy but feel you've had some newspaper accounts of an accident that took place over here that might have caused you unnecessary worry. Our group is all safe and sound . . . [the punctuation mark and two full lines that followed were deleted by the base censor]. Now don't you ever worry about the things you read in the papers.

Along with everyone else in the unit, I'm awfully busy. Johnson, Martinak, and I did twenty-one operations on our twelve-hour shift the other night. I'm now in charge of all cases of gas gangrene on the beachhead and that's a job. Have done several extremity amputations and will do more. I'm having to work alone as the surgical service can't spare anyone to help. Uncle Rush and Charley will be interested to learn that we seem to be having phenomenal success with a new drug called penicillin. Most cases recover but not without radical surgery. Since they want to evaluate its use on cases of gangrene, the Mediterranean sector's entire supply of penicillin has been consigned to me. We have to give it intravenously in doses of 10,000 units every three hours. That certainly keeps me hopping as I'm the only one on the ward who can keep the solutions running.

Must go, Mom. Don't worry about us. A jerry aviator just made a mistake. He was shot down and is a patient in a hospital next door, where he tells a convincing story and is obviously distressed by what happened. Love to all.

FEBRUARY 10, 1944. Mail came through at last. Gee, I was glad to hear from you. Candy came, too, and at an ideal time, 'cause we've had no sweets and no bread for some time. We're eating C-rations and U-rations, which are okay. Thanks so much, darling.

Baby, I heard the BBC broadcast the news of an unfortunate accident that occurred to one of our neighbors day before yesterday. Your papers probably carried the story, so I must tell you that we're all safe and that the enemy in this sector respects the red cross. The pilot of the responsible plane had been hit by antiaircraft fire and was falling. He had to open his bomb bays and didn't realize he was over a hospital. It does all look like an unfortunate accident that won't likely repeat itself. You mustn't worry about it. Now if this doesn't make any sense, it's because our papers didn't really carry a story I was told they did, and I'm sorry I had to mention it.

Must get to bed. Wish I could write more often and answer your letters, but I can't.

FEBRUARY 11, 1944. Lots of mail from you today, and two little packages that have my curiosity aroused, but I've not had time to open anything yet.

Jabez Galt from the medical service has been assigned to the gas gangrene ward with me, and he's really a big help. But even with two working, we never catch up. Will have two nurses instead of one, starting tomorrow, and believe that will help, too. Baby, I'm well and working mighty hard and must get to bed. I love you dearly.

FEBRUARY 13, 1944. Another fairly easy day, but one patient we've been watching for three days developed gangrene under our eyes.

Surely enjoyed all of your letters, honey. Am sorry you have to pay so much for the reprints of my article, but if any one of them clicks it might turn out to be worth the cost. Enjoyed hearing of Suzanne's tricks, as I always do. Also enjoyed hearing about the rest of the folks and will try to write your dad. I've not written him before now, as I knew you'd keep him posted on any news I had, anyway. With you up in Washington, he might use some news from me. Your Valentines came today, exactly timed.

Galt and I have worked hard, but he remarked today that he'd never been as happy and fascinated with what he was doing as now. It is fascinating. So much so that one doesn't notice his fatigue until going to bed at night. And Galt is a better working partner than I ever dreamed anyone could be. Still, I can't understand why the work is so stimulating, when by its very nature it should be very depressing. The answer probably lies in the fact that within two days after we get a patient, he exudes the impression that he thinks we're almost gods. That is very flattering, particularly when the ward gets twelve to eighteen men in it. And it isn't because we amount to so much that the patients exude such feelings. No, I'm sure it is because our operating table is right on the ward, screened from the men by only a sheet. They are practically right in there with us and know we do lots of work on and for them, both by day and night. Also, most of them have come off crowded wards of sixty to seventy men where personalized care is impossible. They absolutely have to have such care, and we on our ward can give it. Then, too, they all come to us sick unto death and knowing that they're sick unto death, many of them delirious. By the time we've either amputated their gangrenous limbs or saturated them with penicillin, the majority are out of their delirium, fever-free, and feeling good again. So they feel that we've snatched them right out of the grave with our surgery. Sometimes we do just that, but more often they owe their lives to Fleming, the Englishman who did research on penicillin. Twenty percent of them are in coma when we receive them, and seventy-five percent of them survive. We're pleased, the survivors are pleased, and Colonel Carter seems to think we're doing well enough. So we're more exhilarated than depressed all of the time.

We do lots of surgery, debridements, and amputations, with me operating most of the time and Galt assisting. He did one thigh amputation with me assisting him—and did very well—but has not wanted to operate since. Being quarantined, we're completely on our own, and that's lots of responsibility for us, green as we are. Be sure you remember that gas gangrene is no hazard to the unwounded surgeons—we're in no danger at all.

P.S. The shaky writing is because my hands are cold.

FEBRUARY 14, 1944. Martinak hasn't had a regular berth since we've been here, and hasn't had much to do while the rest of us have worked our heads off. This has kept him pretty discontented, but he was put on Bussey's team two days ago and is much happier again. Of course, he's jealous that my Valentines came and his didn't.

I got a bath today! And don't ever think that statement not startling enough to justify an exclamation point—it's the first I've had in a long, long time. Not only have I had no baths, but as all civilians left the area ahead of us, I've had no laundry done either. There's a laundry in Naples that does up the clothes worn by our patients when they're admitted, but we do not have access to it. Our supply section exchanges clean uniforms for the dirty ones of patients, but we can't exchange nor buy from supply. I'm wearing nurses' summer fatigue uniforms at present, being forced to take whatever I could get when all of my own clothing became too blood soaked to put up with. It looks like I might have to draw a uniform in my size for some patient, turning in my bloody one instead of his and sending him out in the clothes he had on when he was admitted. Better not tell anybody I harbor such criminal thoughts, but I really don't know what else I can do.

'Night, honeybabe. I'm glad you miss me but will be gladder when you don't. [The above was written between blackouts during some of the twenty-six red alerts we survived on the beachhead on February 14, 1944.]

FEBRUARY 16, 1944. I sent a patient out today who will eventually wind up in Walter Reed Hospital there in Washington. I gave him Randolph's name and your address and told him to look you up when he gets there. I guess you'll be back in Alvin, but maybe Randolph will still be stationed there.

My work has slacked off a great deal compared to what it was for a while, but I'm still plenty busy. I spent the morning digging down to sink my cot below ground level. I feel like it was really wasted effort, but it seems silly not to do it anyway. We still get quite a few "heavenly burps" from the jerries, but in spite of what you may read in the papers, they aren't really directed at us. We were hit in those three unfortunate accidents when we first set up, but none since. Our coordinates, i.e., map coordinators, were sent to the German high command, and we've had no more problems. Tragedy did come to our organization in the last mistake. One of our nurses whom you do not know had been hit, and she died today.

Baby, don't worry. We're quite safe—Jerry does respect the red cross, and I've mentioned all of this only because we're told your papers have played it up so.

FEBRUARY 17, 1944 [to sister Mary]. I'm still awfully busy but have a minute between cases and will try to get a letter off. I've received a batch or two of letters from Mama and Margaret but won't attempt an answer to any of them now. I think when I do try to answer, you'll have forgotten what you'd written anyway. The round trip for comments and response usually takes no less than six weeks, as you know.

Most of us now sleep below ground level and with protection from falling flak over us, but it's probably an unnecessary precaution now. I didn't get around to digging in until yesterday and can't say I slept any better last night than usual, but I am certainly safe in my bed now.

Sis, apply the enclosed hundred dollars on whatever I owe you. I'll try to send you another hundred dollars out of my next check, but I can't remember our ever having decided on a total figure. I do remember I owe two hundred dollars for the Buick I got from you, and somebody owes me two hundred dollars for the Ford I traded in on the new Chevrolet. Then you and Mama took it off my hands and finished paying it out so I could go to medical school. I can't remember whether the new Chevrolet cost $395 or $495 but probably the latter, and I probably made no payments after the down payment with the Ford. Whatever it is, I can finish paying you now, and thanks.

FEBRUARY 17, 1944. Well, I didn't get any mail today for the first time in several days. I'm hoping the pictures you sent will get here tomorrow and that the captain's bars won't be far behind. The bars Hannigan loaned me are about to come apart, welcome as they were when he pinned them on me eight days late.

Did I write you about burning my sleeping bag the other night? Dadgum, I was asleep and got a corner of it against the stove about 6:00 A.M. while it was still pitch dark outside. Sure enough, Martinak had been up about every hour through the night to watch the antiaircraft and artillery fire and had kept the fire going all night. Of course the sleeping bag caught fire against that hot stove. I'd evidently been disturbed by the noise and flopped off my cot without waking up. When Martinak came back in, we had a pretty good blaze going, which I'd never felt. We threw the bag out into the total blackness before it harmed anything else, but all of that light scared folks some. I'm now sleeping on a mattress under blankets, finding that much more comfortable than sleeping bag, anyway.

Haven't had to work more than ten to twelve hours per day for several days now. Galt and I did our first surgery in several shifts tonight, debriding severe wounds of a man's leg and ankle. He has gas gangrene, but I'm hoping he won't loose his leg. We have really had marvelous results treating the stuff so far.

Honey, I'm all for living where they don't burn coal, too. Sorry you're having so much trouble with it in Washington. It does make a poor excuse for fuel, at best. As I recall I never saw a clean, white window curtain the whole time I lived in Memphis, where folks also burn coal.

Now wherever did you get the idea that I've so much patience, when I fly off the handle all the time? I guess maybe there's less to fly off about when I'm home than there is when I'm at work, so you just don't see me.

The picture developing sounds like a good hobby, and we'll put your darkroom out in my carpenter shop when we can be together.

FEBRUARY 20, 1944. I'm hoping there'll be some news from you when I get a chance to go see about it tonight, but am watching some gangrene antitoxin go in at the moment and can't leave.

Galt and I got in the first new case in a few days, today. He is a nineteen-year-old German youth, and I believe we got to him in time to save his life. Spent two hours doing an extensive debridement of his wounds, and he's the one now getting antitoxin.

We now have two more wards of minor cases to take care of, but they present no problems. All three wards are pitched in a row and tied together, making a convenient arrangement.

I started a letter to you last night but never did get to finish it. I've received yours telling me that you have reservations for February 16, so I guess you'll be home long before my letter reaches Alvin. Sorry I didn't learn sooner so I could have changed your address sooner. I did change it on the 15th.

No more news. We can't have lights in the area at night except in headquarters and in the operating rooms, so we simply work and go to bed. I usually stay on the ward until 9:00 P.M. and then turn in. I hardly ever see Martinak, both of us staying pretty busy these days. We seldom light our stove and never sit in our tent.

FEBRUARY 22, 1944. Surely you must already have guessed it, but now we're allowed to tell that we're on the Anzio beachhead. Things were tough enough when we first arrived but probably not as bad as your papers would lead you to believe. Except for Miss Ainesworth, there have been no deaths among our own personnel and few casualties. Her death was a tragedy following one of the attacks we were subjected to soon after our arrival. They really were accidents and were over almost before anybody realized they had started. I don't believe we'll have any more trouble, but our bunks are all below ground so we'll be safe if we do. We're annoyed almost hourly by "red alerts" sounded whenever an enemy plane is spotted, but we're never the target. The annoying thing about those alerts is that all lights except those over the operating tables are cut off each time, and we lose lots of time. I've seldom written you a letter without having to turn out my lights sometime during the writing. I have the same difficulty when writing up the necessary records. We also hear lots of artillery fire since the targets of the two sides lie one to the west of us and one to the east, and the shells go back and forth over our heads. Fortunately, the noise doesn't make me nervous as I'd expected it would, and I never hear a thing after I go to bed at night; that is, I never wake up.

Galt and I still have the gangrene ward, and I've done quite a lot of surgery. We both enjoy the arrangement, and the powers that be have apparently been well satisfied with our work. In fact, they are quite flattering at times.

The pictures came today, and I'm enjoying them a lot. Suzanne has grown unbelievably! Kiss her and your mirror, too.

FEBRUARY 22, 1944 [second letter]. I got through that first letter without having to douse the lights a time, so I'll keep writing.

Reprints of my article still have not come, and I'm anxious to see them.

Say, you have on a new coat suit and also new slacks in your pictures. I wish I could see them.

Your January 30 and February 9 V-mails came today. That's mighty good mail service for so near the fighting front, don't you think? I get a kick out of your descriptions of your furnace troubles, but I feel for you, too. I'm sure if we ever have to have a furnace, it will either burn gas or fuel oil.

I know I send few messages to those family members concentrated with you in Washington, but tell all of them the news and that I think of them often. The same goes for your mother and father when you get back to Alvin. I'm not working myself to death by any means, but I sure can't write many letters.

Martinak and I don't see much of each other these days. He's in the operating room daily from midnight until 8:00 A.M., but he's getting along all right. He gets pretty homesick at times, and I believe the spurt of long hours we've had has been good for him. He got some very good pictures of Jean and Macy last week, and Jean grows by leaps and bounds just like Suzy.

FEBRUARY 23, 1944. I'm glad the box from Capri reached you satisfactorily, but I'd really hoped it might get there for your birthday. I started to send it to Dallas but was afraid it would arrive too late. The tortoise elephant and the plates came from the island, and I got the basket from an island girl who had a boatload of them at the entrance to the Blue Grotto. The other things came from a single store in Naples.

Today, for the fifth time in the past three weeks, I evacuated every patient I had back to a general hospital. We're so unclean (quarantined) that we cause more problems than pariah dogs around primitive campfires, but our patients aren't really dangerous to handle.

The engineers have excavated a new location for our ward, and we'll be a good hundred yards closer to the pharmacy and central supply, a boon to my wardmen who make many trips to each place every day. The floor is now two feet below ground level, and the moved dirt was used to make a two-foot embankment all around it. Patients are much safer and much less anxious to get back to the front where they've felt safer in their foxholes. They really have been scared here—too scared to ever goldbrick.

FEBRUARY 26, 1944 [her birthday]. I've never written to you much about the life here have I? Well, it isn't really bad, although our hours are long at times. Martinak and I seldom see each other. In fact, with my ward quarantined I seldom see any of the others in the outfit. I can seldom leave the ward before bedtime. I get to work by 8:30 A.M. and change dressings until noon. Then after a thirty minute break, I'm either doing surgery or getting the never-ending transfusions and anti-toxins given. Taking off another thirty minutes between 4:30 and 8:30 P.M., I eat supper then go back to the ward to recheck the wounds and do more surgery. A wound may look fine in the morning then develop gangrene that can destroy the limb or even kill the patient within twelve hours, although such catastrophes typically may take a day or even two. Galt and I are still working together and still enjoying the work.

We live in tents, of course. Martinak's and mine is quite a mess because neither of us has time to keep it otherwise. We each have our cots sunk down below ground level, a result of our own digging. The dugout areas are lined with boards of one sort or another that we've bird-dogged from wherever we could lift them. I have an old kitchen table—also bird-dogged—over my cot with a heavy box lid nailed to its top and sand bags over that. Martinak couldn't find a table so filled U-ration boxes with sand, thus making 12 x 12 x 18 inch building blocks with which to wall himself in on three sides. Boards laid from end to end over these with sand bags on top, give him the same flak cover I have and with premium table space on top. Thus we each have a veritable vault in which to sleep and table space on which to scatter our belongings. We're just about impregnable to anything except direct hits, and the chances of these are quite remote—believe me. We don't have any lights, but have no need for them anyway.

Our meals each week are "same as Monday," but I always eat like a horse and never gain. We haven't been able to get any fresh meat but do have good bakery bread most of the time, good pies pretty often, and lots of good canned fruit. I had a navy cook for a patient a while back, and he earned the undying gratitude of all of us by teaching our cooks how to make whipped cream out of canned milk. We had some with canned fruit this evening, and it really was worth writing home about—hence, I mention it.

There have been some funny experiences with laundry around here, other than just having it not come back. White and several others sent some out a couple of weeks ago. It all came back clean, ironed, carefully folded. The only hitch was none of it could be used. It had all been completely riddled by flak and shell fragments.

Main personal problems are baths and laundry. There is not enough water to spare for showers more than once a week, and then for only an hour at a time. Each group has an hour—enlisted men, nurses, and finally us—and there are always some who could not make it during their hour. I've had no laundry done since we arrived a month ago but did send some out last week and have not heard from that Italian woman since—she may have been evacuated with all my clothes. I do manage to "liberate" clean uniforms from supply now and then, but I can't buy them.

The degree of activity on the front, and thus in the hospital, can be easily gauged by how many days' growth of beard and how many layers of cosmetics can be seen in the mess hall on the faces of the officers and nurses, respectively. We probably have gone more than five days without shaving, but not much more. For the past two days the officers have been clean shaven, and the nurses' faces are spick-and-span. Nobody's been busy. When we get rushed again the whole mess will be repeated. Also, as beards and cosmetics accumulate, mealtimes become less and less noisy until they are too, too quiet. In our biggest rush we did over eight hundred operations in a week, and I promise you, had no time for the niceties of life.

General Truscott awarded Miss Roberts, our operating room supervisor, the nation's third highest decoration, the Silver Star. Hers was the first ever awarded a woman, and the supervisors of the other three evacuation hospitals on the beachhead followed her to receive the same award. I'm sure hers was first because we've handled more patients than the other hospitals. I can't think of anyone more entitled to the award than Mary Roberts herself, but of course, it went to her rather than to all of the other nurses as she was their supervisor. All were entitled to recognition for their carrying on in spite of fire, on several occasions. Actually, it was three times and for no more than a few minutes, involving areas of no more than a hundred feet square each time. As I've told you before, the three attacks were accidents, incidentally coming on three consecutive days. The first and last were bombings, a single bomb falling in our area each time. The middle one was a single artillery shell that dropped from somewhere, possibly from one of our own guns. On such short notice, folks don't have time for being either cowards or heroes, but decorations awarded the military have always inspired civilians back home to support the wars.

Incidentally, Turnbow, Merrick, and Martinak dug a foxhole for the four of us. It was the only sensible thing to do at the time, but I was always too dead by the time I'd gotten to bed to get up and use it. The others kept themselves in such a lather with so much loss of sleep that the place was abandoned, and we just sank our cots below surface level. I was on my ward a good three hundred feet from the last bomb that fell and didn't even know we'd had an alert. It fell only ten feet from our big foxhole, and Turnbow, Merrick, and Martinak were pretty dirty when they came out. I'm sure Martinak gets exasperated with me, but I get lots more sleep than he does and I simply could not function without it.

On the day the last random shell hit the area—a good two hundred yards from the nearest ward—someone who had access to the loudspeaker used it to order all patients placed on the ground. My word, we must have had over a thousand patients on our wards. Many of them were in body casts, and many others—pre- and post-op—were at considerable risk if that order were actively responded to. I was in the pre-op tent when that announcement came and was afraid my seventeen patients, all of whom were critical and in casts or dressings, would be in a panic. I tore out for the ward to find one scrawny nurse and one equally scrawny wardman struggling to get the first man on the floor. I told everybody what had happened and explained that I didn't feel we could get them all on the floor in less than an hour, and that some probably wouldn't survive the trauma if we did.

Things had gotten pretty quiet so I asked if any of them wanted to be moved. I was flattered when one spoke out and said they'd be satisfied to stay wherever I thought best. With that, even the scared ones chimed in that they all felt the same way. They all stayed on their cots. There were no more shells, fortunately, and after about twenty minutes, an order came over the loudspeaker to get all of the patients back into bed. Pandemonium reigned supreme on the wards that had attempted to carry out the first order. Nobody yet has admitted to its origin.

I seem to have written too much, but the newspapers—or so we're told—have sensationalized our experience. For instance, today a letter came to our Red Cross lady. It stated that a Mr. and Mrs. So-and-So of Someplace, North Carolina, hadn't heard from a son since December. They wanted our Red Cross lady to tell them if he'd been a patient in the unit evacuation hospital when it had been bombed. I hope those accounts missed you while you were in Washington. We're told they threw the gals and wives in Dallas into fits. We're all pretty angry at the Associated Press and think if they're going to print such stories, they should print a complete list of all casualties as they did in the last war.

FEBRUARY 29, 1944. January 31 airmail and February 11 V-mail came today. Glad you enjoyed sending out the reprints and glad it's finished. Mine have not arrived, as yet, but probably will in a day or two if you sent them first class. If not, please send me a couple more first class, on different days.

Haven't been so busy today and got a chance to buy some clothes and wash my old ones. I washed out everything I own except for the new stuff, which I'm wearing. With my recently reduced wardrobe, the washing wasn't much of a task. Dadgum that Italian woman, anyway, unless she got hit. Today's is the first washing I've done since January 15, if you can imagine such a thing. Had a bath, too, and a shave, and if I'd had any toothpaste, I might have brushed my teeth.

One of my patients isn't doing too well tonight. I guess I'll go back over to the ward and operate on him. I'm trying hard to save this boy's leg, but it's a tough problem. With gas gangrene it's pretty hard to tell when you're risking their life in trying to save a limb. So far, we've saved several that had gas gangrene in them, but we did lose one German by that method while we were so busy. He was okay in the morning but died just ten hours later while we were getting him on the table to operate. Tell Suzanne I'll be ready for that ice cream and chicken.

MARCH 5, 1944. I can't remember when I've written but hope it hasn't been too long. We've had another rush of gangrene cases for the past five days, keeping us on the job for twelve to fifteen hours daily. Things have settled down again, or I'd not be able to write.

The letter telling of Randolph's transfer to Springfield has not come yet, but the V-mail announcing your arrival came yesterday.

Ever since hundreds upon hundreds of our flying fortresses started coming over us a couple of days ago, hour after hour, heading for enemy airfields, there have been no more enemy sorties. Lonesome Polecat is still around, but we're becoming accustomed to the whistle as his shells go over our heads to land in Anzio Harbor.

Galt and I have several enemy prisoners from the famous Hermann Göring Division lately. Most of them are eighteen years old and seem like babies. They make appreciative patients and have so much faith in us it is pitiful, not to say flatteringly touching.

We have a fine looking and appealing eighteen-year-old German prisoner named Fritz. He's so trusting that he wrings the heart of both Galt and myself. It was his leg Galt amputated today, and if Fritz realizes it's gone he certainly took it like a man. When he woke up and found that the operation was all over, he regained the smile he'd had before toxicity and extreme pain had robbed him of it. He greeted us with a "Ja, ja, das ist ser goot. Das Fuss smerzen nicht," all of which is to say, "That's fine. My leg doesn't hurt." These cases are remarkable—Fritz was doing fine when we went home last night but was having too much pain this morning. Within a few hours his blood pressure dropped way down, and he looked like he'd die any minute. Just as soon as Galt got that leg off, his blood pressure bounced back to normal, and he looked like a different person. He'll be all right now.

I'm hoping to get lots of mail today. I only know that you're in Springfield, knowing none of the details. Am glad Suzanne has a big back yard and hope you're through with coal furnaces but doubt that you are. I'm also curious to know if you like the Missouri people any better than some of those in Washington. You'd better, since both of our mothers came from Missouri. A nurse, new to our hospital—and presently functioning as our ward nurse, anesthetist, surgical assistant, and what-have-you—is from Springfield. She thinks you're very lucky to be there. I hope you enjoy it and that Randolph and Johne D are settled for a bit. Let me know what his assignment is if you haven't already.

My February *Reader's Digest* came some time ago, and I plan to read it by candle light tonight. I've not yet written to thank your dad for sending it. I know there's a lot going on around here that he'd be interested in hearing about if I really knew just what is going on. I've not listened to Axis Sally in weeks and haven't read a paper since January 27, so I don't know. I do know by the sound of it, we're holding our own on this narrow beachhead as Lonesome Polecat stays at the same distance. If he came any closer, we'd smell him. I'll try to write Mr. Sentell tomorrow.

MARCH 5, 1944 [second letter]. Two letters to you in one day. That's news, and here's some more: I'm writing by candlelight in my tent and have a fire going for the first time in days or weeks. Galt and I have had a light day, even though he did his second amputation this afternoon—which two cases constituted our total surgery for the day. Another patient who'd been on our critical list, requiring lots of attention day and night, expired last night leaving us with much leisure for a change.

Today, I turned in a summary of our activity since February 11. The figures look like we've done next to nothing all these weeks with only forty-nine cases of actual gas gangrene, but there are many mitigating facts that make the looks deceiving. I believe it no exaggeration to say that each case requires as much time as any ten other cases in its treatment. Then of course, many suspected cases had to be treated, although not gangrenous. We've had fifteen deaths among those forty-nine, nine of them before we could give them any definitive treatment. So, for the forty actually given more than supportive treatment, only six died. Also six of our deaths were among German prisoners, upon whom we're not allowed to use penicillin that is in short supply, nor volunteered blood, also in short supply. The discrimination can't be helped, and no one doubts that war is hell.

Martinak just walked in—he's had an easy day, too. He's working with Bussey and stays provoked at him most of the time for his imposing a relationship too much like medical student and professor. It's sad the major does have such a personality because fundamentally he's a good fellow, a fine surgeon, and not too hard to work with if his subordinate can just keep reminding himself of these facts. Of course, you'll remember I didn't find him easy to work with, either.

MARCH 7, 1944. Things are mighty quiet on this beachhead. All of those bombers that flew over us the other day must have done the trick, or maybe a rumor we heard today that Germany has pulled back its Luftwaffe to protect the Vaterland is right—suits me either way.

Your February 14 and 16 V-mails came today. Also received *Pygmalion* and *American Short Stories.* Thanks, darling. You must read "Johnny Py and the Fool Killer" 'cause it's unusual and so good.

I have taken a day off for a change. Finished everything about nine last night, and there hasn't been more today than Galt could handle, so I'm resting up my cold. Must have done the cold some good, too, as my nose is much less drippy. The weather is so changeable that I'm sure we'll all have our share. Nights are cold as in North Africa, with one day cold and rainy, and the next day, warm. And I can't see that Mussolini did much for the Pontine Marshes when he drained them. Even with his ditches, the water is a bare six inches below the surface.

Martinak wrote Macy that he had trouble keeping up their correspondence since we've been here. He says he can't get his mind to working properly when he goes to write, but I expect the trouble is he tries too hard to keep things from her that he'd as well tell—or do I worry you when I give along the bad news?

MARCH 8, 1944. Your February 22 airmail came today. That would have been good time even for a V-mail.

So, Randolph's major is the same doctor my class had as our neurosurgery instructor in med school! Tell Randolph he is quite a bird and unloved by his students. Wright's textbook of physiology was not our designated textbook, but we felt sure he gave pop quizzes to which answers were available nowhere else. He was probably just trying to show us how little we knew, but we didn't like it anyway. Also tell Randolph that Miller was a resident under Dr. A—, whom we all knew in Dallas, and A—said Miller was an excellent resident. I'm surprised that such an experienced neurosurgeon didn't get a higher rank. I'm sure he will before he gets out. He was young and was not head of the department at school.

Work is still slack, and I've sat and nursed my cold most of the day. I can't imagine what's happened to the Krauts, but the rest is most welcome. We've had only two red alerts in the past four or five days, each lasting only a few minutes and neither honored by more than a few haphazard bursts of ack-ack fire.

I've been interested in all of your trips, and your daily schedule in Springfield sounds good to me. I can hardly imagine being able to go into a Chuck-Wagon at any hour and order a meal. In fact, it's hard for me to imagine being able to spend money anywhere. The very last time I spent even one lira was on January 25 when I bought a shave from an Italian barber. Imagine!

MARCH 11, 1944. Your February 27 airmail came today—I can't get over what good service we're getting. Of course, ours is the hottest front at the moment, and these are always the spots with the best of everything while they last.

As far as getting Mom to forward letters to you, I didn't know where to send your letters so they'd be sure to reach you. Also, I sure didn't have time to write duplicates. Besides, we were getting some pretty lurid stories on what the Dallas papers were printing. I figured she'd see those stories before you would and would see that you did hear from me. I guess I got worked up more than the situation justified since I have the sort of wife I do, but some of the Dallas gals wrote pitiful letters—I'm proud you didn't.

My cold is almost well. But with work about at a standstill, I came in as a patient yesterday, where I could be made to drink plenty of water, gargle my throat, and the like. Must have been a good idea as I'm fever-free today and feel much better.

Honey, I can't understand how you'd go over two weeks without hearing from me. It could be that no mail went out of here for at least that long when we first arrived. I also have no idea how long we'd been here before I had a chance to write. It was for several days I'm sure.

I've been listening to a German propaganda broadcast in English tonight. It's a regular feature called "George and Sally." They pose as Americans but their English is too, too carefully correct, and the things they say are transparently German propaganda. They are probably from Rome, and no American soldier in his right mind would be fooled for a minute. Sally says she feels like she's talking to her brothers or a boyfriend at the front, "just like any other American girl." She says, "Hi, fellows!", only she pronounces it,"Hee, fellows." She's "so sorry decent American boys are being made to do such terrible things," etc. One night she invited "a bunch of American nurses from the 56th Evacuation to come on over to the German lines, so near now, and enjoy dates with good-looking German officers."

MARCH 13, 1944. Three reprints of "Foundation for the Adequate Distribution of Postwar Medical Care" came today. I hadn't known that I was director of the outpatient department at Baylor, but I guess I am. Dean Moursund evidently added that title when he sent the manuscript in for me. The paper looks better in print than I'd anticipated, so I'm elated. On the negative side, though, several typographic errors and a few completely jumbled sentences are in it, and I'm sure I'd have straightened them out if I'd had a chance to proofread it before it went to press. After my experiences of the past year, I'm surprised I could have gotten so worked up over the subject. I'm also surprised that the editor made no changes, but he must be short of help with a war going on. The article seems to jolt here and there, but smoothing it out would have required more wordiness, and it's a mite wordy already.

This is a beautiful spring day—we do get one along. I guess winter is about over, which suits me fine. Really, the elements have been about as good as possible to the Baylor unit, but I'm ready for warm and dry weather.

I was discharged from the hospital this morning but won't go back to work until tomorrow. I'm not really needed as Galt has only three patients, none requiring surgery. I'm feeling about normal and put out a big laundry this morning, once again owning nothing dirty except what I'm wearing.

Things on the beachhead stay very quiet. Even 'ole Lonesome Polecat has stopped whistling over our heads, and it's even rumored that he was sent to glory a few days ago. This could be true. Incidentally, the same rumor says he wasn't so lonesome, three of them having been knocked out just this side of Rome. We'll see how long it takes Jerry to bring in some more.

MARCH 15, 1944. Your February 24 airmail came today, my first letter in three days.

Honey, please send a reprint to Senators Wagner, Murray, O'Daniel, Connally, and to Congressman Dingell. Ask the two Texas senators to vote against the Wagner-Murray-Dingell bill. We might have some fun out of those reprints yet.

The rest of the hospital is quiet, but Galt and I are pretty busy again the past few days. We got a German soldier this morning who had been wounded on February 29. He had lain out in no man's land, untreated and unattended until two days ago. He is in remarkably good shape to have gone through what he did, part of it having been to drink his own urine. He had a badly shattered leg which I had to take off today, and I can't imagine how he survived the entire ordeal.

Martinak and I don't see much of each other again. His team is on duty from midnight until 8:00 A.M. They're pretty busy, but he came over to our ward for a while today. He admits that he is learning a good many things but stays upset because his major tries to handle him as he would a junior medical student. I would still be glad for that particular surgeon to operate on me for any of those conditions described in the books, but I'd rather have someone else if my case required more horse sense than book learning. And I mean no reflection on the man. His long residence training aimed successfully at teaching him everything there was to know about ordinary abdominal surgery, and he learned it well. The trouble with that sort of training is that a man never gets in over his head, and his common sense tends to atrophy. In the terrible business of military surgery, everyone is in over his head most of the time. He has to move on through uncharted seas, each case likely to encompass overlapping surgical specialties, and no one man can learn all of them down pat. Neither can a wounded man be shuffled from one specialist to another in forward areas such as ours. Whatever horse sense can be mustered is the sole answer, I'm sure.

MARCH 18, 1944. Gee, I got lots of mail today—three airs and two V's. I enjoyed your description of Springfield and the "Shepherd of the Hills country" and am willing to get a cabin up there just any time.

Weren't you the lucky one, getting the silver cup and spoon back that you'd left in St. Louis? It would never have occurred to me to seek the aid of the Red Cross to get something like that back. I'd hate to lose the cup the Baylor teachers' wives gave Suzanne. Maybe we should write the New Orleans chapter and ask them to look for the weekend bag we left at the airport on our honeymoon.

No, you aren't antisocial, and I'm glad you aren't around the rest of the unit wives much. I've a sneaky feeling they all feed each other's anxieties and keep upset most of the time. Had you lived in Dallas you'd never have escaped all of the gory details from over here, and that would have been hard, I'm sure. Letters to some of the fellows were written by very scared wives, and you should see some of the newspaper clippings that accompanied them. The newspapers sensationalized the events, and I'm glad Johne D and Randolph kept them hidden from you.

Do you know we've been on the beachhead almost two months? It just doesn't seem possible that it could have been more than two weeks. And yet it's hard to remember there ever was a different setup. It now looks like things are going to settle down here, like they have everywhere else. If so, it will mean a long wait between jumps and with very little to do. I did work until midnight last night but hadn't done anything through the day, and haven't had much today, either. Could be there'd be time for drinking "moose milk" again. Moose milk, you will recall, results from mixing the ever abundant grapefruit juice with medicinal alcohol. None has been consumed around here in a couple of months now.

We have one German patient forty years old, who provided us respite from tension during an amputation high up on his thigh. He had hopeless gangrene in the limb, and it had to come off. Everyone around our operating table is tense in such situations. Usually at such times, the patients are "out of their heads," and this man definitely was. So there we were, Galt and I, discussing the situation most seriously. Everything was so quiet you could hear a pin drop, when suddenly the patient burst forth with probably the only English he knew: "Hi diddle de diddle, der cat vas a fiddle, der cow jumped over der moon!" You can't imagine how ridiculous that nursery rhyme sounded on the lips of an enemy who was about to lose an entire lower extremity, and who was in such poor condition I was afraid he'd not survive the surgery. But he didn't die— he lived. It was hilarious.

Before I forget, no reason not to immunize Suzanne with tetanus toxoid. As she'll be running around the farm barefooted, it should be done.

MARCH 19, 1944. I got an airmail today that you'd mailed in Washington on February 7. I don't see how they keep from losing more like that than they do.

Had a long letter as usual from Ruth, today. She got real mad at the jerries last month and sold the oil stock she'd had for twenty years, using the money to buy war bonds. Lots of folks must have shared her feelings as we hear bond sales broke all previous records in February. She is also raising a bunch of chickens, she says to increase production. My guess is she's raising them because she likes them.

Uncle Rush and Charley apparently didn't object to my paper, and I am surprised. Ruth thinks they're anxious for us to settle in Waco. I do feel like a dog for not planning to do exactly that, though it just never has seemed to me like the best plan. My job at Baylor is available by law when I get out of the army, and maybe I'd like that better than having to practice.

Did I ever tell you that I owe Uncle Rush a great deal? If it had not been for his applying pressure, I'd never have gone to medical school. He convinced me that age twenty-eight was not too old to start and that I'd not really be imposing on anybody if I went. Except for this effort on his part, I'd never have gone. I'd either still be fighting a drug store too many hours each week, or I'd be an army noncom. And besides, I'd never have found you, and where would Suzanne be? I do indeed owe him a lot, and all of us owe Charley a lot. Disappointing either of them will not be easy for me.

This has actually seemed like Sunday—and it is. I even went to church this morning, but since there were no benches in the chapel I backed out on staying. It's the first time I've had a chance to go near the place since we've been here, but since I didn't have a helmet with me to sit on, staying would have been an ordeal. Guess it seemed like a Sunday because it was such a warm spring day. I even came out of my long undies. The front was absolutely quiet—no machine gunning, no artillery fire, no planes all day. Also, I had practically no work to do and was finished by 9:00 A.M.

I've been doing some medical reading of late and enjoying it a lot. Galt and I have both scoured the area for everything we could find on gas gangrene. Our responsibilities have stimulated us into studying a good many other phases of medicine, too. Too bad we don't have more current medical literature around here, but the textbooks can hold me for some time, I'm sure. We've probably seen more gas gangrene than any civilian doctor will come across in a lifetime of heavy practice, but we'd still get a lot out of current reports on the subject if we had them.

I'd never realized before that we're no more than a half mile from the seashore. We're several miles from town, and at the time we moved out I thought we were moving at right angles to the shoreline, when all the while we were travelling parallel to it. If I'd had my wits about me at the time, I'd have known we could not have ridden that way without being stopped by German soldiers. But I saw the water for the first time from the chapel this morning and was quite surprised. The blue Mediterranean is really blue, you know, and is very pretty. Incidentally, it is full of small islands which maps don't show. Most of them appear uninhabited, but a few have small houses on them.

You've always heard of the beautiful moonlight and sunsets in Italy. They are both about like those in Texas and are not overrated. The sunsets yesterday and today were beautiful, making me realize I was pretty fortunate in having the time to enjoy them. This wouldn't be a bad place to live if there were no war going on and if it were not so far from Alvin. The day we went through Anzio, I thought it about the prettiest town we'd seen since leaving home. They now say it is worse shot up than Battapaglia, the latter even worse damaged than Bizerte was.

Lonesome Polecat's successor has just now started making himself heard. Sounds just like the old one.

MARCH 22, 1944. Your airmail of March 13 came today—just nine days after it was written. I believe that's a record.

I see you got to Dallas all right, and I'm no more surprised nor worried about Suzanne's mischief-making than I know her grandmother is—i.e., not at all. She has certainly done a lot of travelling for such a little shaver. Do you know I'd never been farther than Chigger and Dickinson Bayous until I was nine and had to go to Galveston for glasses. I was twelve before I'd ever gone to Houston and then only because Papa wasn't about to drive the car in the city. I drove the twenty-five miles both ways and with no problems in town, traffic in those days being practically nil, anyway. And for your information, I'll bet I stick as close to home when I get back as I did before I was nine.

Before you hear exaggerated reports, I guess I'd better tell you that Brown was hit in the ankle by a piece of flak this morning. He said it sure did hurt at the time, and he was scared to look down where he hoped his foot still was. No bones broken, but he'll get a Purple Heart and a trip back to the general hospital in Naples and be gone some ten days.

Honey, spring must be here at last. I hear a whole chorus of frogs just going at it outside in our big ditch. Also, I must have seen half a dozen lizards along the path as I went back to the ward at noon. I've worn only a light sweater most of the day, adding a coat after supper. It always gets cool here when the sun goes down, and we need a fire at night. You know, we've spent the entire winter in tents—may sound like a rough way to live, but it hasn't been bad at all. Still, I'll be glad when we no longer need the fire.

Colonel Carter called a meeting of the staff tonight and had me give a talk on gas gangrene. He was hoping I could transmit information to our surgeons to help prevent it. Bussey came to me after the meeting to invite me to point out what I was finding wrong with his cases who were winding up on my ward. Gee, I was surprised, and it was big of him to do that. But good surgeons won't see more than one or two such cases in a lifetime, while I'm literally seeing them by the dozens. I probably do pick up knowledge—in fact I'm sure I do—that point up means of prevention.

MARCH 24, 1944. Your March 7 and 9 airmails came today.

Baby, I've never failed to scour shops in North Africa as well as in Italy for dolls. I've just never had much luck finding any. By the time we reach an area, it's pretty well shot up. What few shops still function don't have much merchandise, either. There are no civilians around here, so no shops. This silly little beachhead is a lot smaller than many a Texas ranch, and if we ever leave it, I'll look around some more. I'll also look for children's books, which I think is a good suggestion.

I enjoyed Charles McClure's letter. I'll write him tonight that he needn't waste time looking for me in Australia. Maybe the Walkers can't differentiate one continent from another so long as they're both foreign.

Galt has been pulled back to the medical service, much to his chagrin. I have the ward to myself again, but am not overworked as I've only three patients. We get down to three from time to time but never empty the ward completely. Usually three-patient totals seem to be a signal for getting five or six bad ones in a row. I hope that doesn't turn out to be the case this time.

I'm spending lots of hours every day trying to organize and assimilate the data we've accumulated on gas gangrene. I make slow headway but believe I'll eventually get it into shape to write up. I can see from a comparison of late records with earlier ones, that Galt and I have learned a considerable amount about treating it. I'm sure that some we lost earlier we could now save. We had to worry about each patient then but now can pretty well tell from our first encounter which ones we really need to worry about.

MARCH 26, 1944. Well, the beachhead is becoming civilized at last! We had good roast beef for dinner yesterday and steaks last night. Man, we enjoyed that meat! I wish there was some way I could get hold of a chocolate malt, a Coca-Cola, a quart of ice cream, a quart of cold milk, and some good fresh eggs, and the various kinds of salads. I could also use a big, comfortable chair in a "livey" living room with today's paper and the funnies. And while indulging myself in such dreams, I could use a bathroom with running water and a flush toilet! Of course, such inanimate objects are not missed as acutely nor as frequently—constantly— as are you and Suzanne. I've not been more than two hundred yards from where I'm sitting in months, so I miss strolls and car rides, too.

All in all, I'd say the blessings of peaceful living are priceless! As priceless as peace of mind, but no more so. Except for working up a new article on gas gangrene, I've practically nothing to do as there have been no new patients and we'll evacuate all of the old ones tonight.

MARCH 27, 1944. Well, it's happened. I've not had a single patient since 8:00 A.M., and this is the first time my ward has been empty in two months. I guess I'll be getting minor surgery on the ward, unless more gas cases start up again. I hope they don't, and I guess I'll never see an epidemic of them again, surely. We're to have a symposium on the subject this coming Friday, and I've been getting it worked up all day today. All of the hospitals on the beachhead are to attend as my ward was the only one set up for gas gangrene cases during the epidemic, and all military surgeons do need to learn about the disease. Adams will discuss the bacteriology, and Galt, the course and treatment of cases. I will have prevention and diagnosis, which places me in the unenviable position of having to criticize the work of much better surgeons than I'll ever be, all of whom outrank me. Some of the cases I received from other wards could have been prevented if their individual vulnerabilities had been recognized earlier. Such failures of recognitions are absolutely not the fault of personnel but simply a result of the chaos that is war. I have frequently been called upon to point out dirt and bits of clothing in the depths of wounds debrided by good surgeons who simply have a hard time ridding themselves of the laudable respect for tissue, which means everything in civilian practice but has no place in the treatment of many war wounds. The purpose of our symposium, of course, is to point out which wounds have proven most vulnerable to subsequent development of gas gangrene. If they can be described well enough for ward personnel to recognize them, they can be diagnosed earlier and the devastating effects of gangrene prevented.

No mail again today, two days in a row, and not much happened to break the monotony. We did have it broken for a little while this afternoon when about eight jerry planes made the mistake of coming over in daylight. The ack-ack was terrific, and four of the planes were knocked down. Of course the cheers here sounded like those at Bizerte when we watched our first enemy plane go down—just like the crowd at a football game over a sensational touchdown. We're too close to German artillery to permit use of searchlights—they'd not survive being turned on but once. Thus, today's sortie was the first in a long time where we'd seen planes fall.

So goes it on the beachhead—on this little bitty, stalemated beachhead. C'est la damn guerre!

MARCH 29, 1944. I'm over in our new recreational tent where Willis is playing all of our new classical records. Wouldn't you know I'd run out of ink right off the bat!

Your March 16 airmail came yesterday, and you're certainly right to assume that any ideas when we'll be coming home are strictly guesses. I've heard no predictions in months, but I'll stick with my original prediction of two years overseas. It would certainly tie up lots of ships if it happened, but Mallory thought the army would rotate men back after two years. Except for that transportation problem, it would indeed be criminal to leave some overseas for the duration while equal numbers of others stayed home the entire time. But the problems are real, and there's simply no way for a mass transfer of troops. For my part, I can't get excited over prospects of getting off the beachhead, let alone home, any time soon.

I'm glad you saw Dorothy and Charley, and I was interested in his views of the school situation. I've frequently heard Colonel Winans say it would have to have a full-time professor of medicine if it was ever to amount to anything, and I don't believe he has his eye on any such position. However, this group will be a strong clique the school will have to contend with when it gets home. I've a notion all shortcomings seen now will be promptly forgiven once we set foot on native soil, and the group will be clannish. Particularly difficult, I think, will be dealing open mindedly with young doctors who saw no military service, regardless of the reasons for such good fortune. Such an attitude may well be less than angelic, but it certainly is human, and this bunch can't be accused of being angelic nor less than human.

Galt and I have finished papers we're to give night after next. We've put in the hours on them, but even so, have a discouragingly small amount of firm information to pass on. The preparation has been interesting and has consumed otherwise idle hours. It should enable us to put solid information together within the next fifty cases we get. I hope our talks go over all right and suppose they will, seeing that doctors generally know even less about the disease than we do.

Jerry's very hardheaded, or he'd never have returned so soon with another daylight air raid. But he was back today, and it looked to me more than half of his participating planes were shot down. I know of no drama to compare with watching a plane plummet to earth. Such drama tears at your heart when it's one of our own bombers, but we've not been witness to one of ours going down for some weeks now. But in today's foray, a Messerschmitt fell not a quarter of a mile from my tent. He must have been going over three hundred miles per hour in that final dive— almost too fast to follow by eye—and with the same scream heard in the newsreels at home. The movies really have the sound down pat.

Spring has gone back on us with really chilly weather again. If it keeps up I'll be forced back into my longies and heavies. As soon as the mosquitoes come out, I'm sure we'll look back upon winter as a blessing. You know these marshes have been infamous for malaria since the time of the Caesars, and we're going to have to start taking Atabrine again any day now.

Gladys would think up the idea of keeping an album of my letters to the folks at home. I'm afraid I've written them very little to justify her efforts, what with censoring—both official and voluntary—and mediocre command of language. If you're saving them, you'd better cull them over carefully lest they return to haunt us both some day. Many of my spontaneous utterances are undoubtedly clouded by the limited view of situations accorded to a soldier.

Well, I ran out of ink, but am back in my own tent now where I have plenty. I also have a good fire, and nearby is a monstrous stack of ammunition crates for fuel. No fooling, I'll bet that stack is a hundred-foot square and twenty feet high. It serves our need for fuel but has to be replenished in our stoves every twenty minutes or so. Burning medicinal alcohol in our stoves sure was more convenient, although the supply depot accused us of sterilizing our jeeps and ambulances in the stuff, if you remember.

Captain Buck Somebody is company commander of black troops at a supply depot in Anzio. He says they came across about six thousand gallons of wine down there so he brought us a supply. After fortifying himself with some of it and loosening his tongue, he told us some good stories, too. He said some of his company was working on the docks a few days back when the jerries came in on a daylight raid. The men all took cover during the few minutes it lasted. As the planes disappeared, one man came out, took off his helmet, scratched his head a bit, and announced very matter-of-factly, "Mister Hitler, you has accomplished youah mission. You has harassed me."

Well, another bomb hit our area just now, and one of our nurses got a chest wound, and a doctor whom you don't know got a leg wound. It will hit your papers, so I must tell you about it. It was a phosphorous bomb, designed to harass rather than destroy, but it undoubtedly produced a good many patients for all of us.

MARCH 30, 1944. Can it possibly have been only a year ago, today, that I spent my last full day at home? Seems like an eternity has gone by. Still, it seems only yesterday, too. The year has absolutely flown by in spite of all the waters that have gone under the bridge. New York, Camp Shanks, Bayonne—the LST, Bermuda, Casablanca—the truck tour of North Africa—Bizerte with the flower gardens still in bloom in front of homes with caved-in roofs—Paestum, Pompeii, Naples, Capri—Anzio. Surely tomorrow, I hope, I'll start on the last half of time overseas. Only a year ago I watched you and Suzanne drive off from our troop train in San Antonio!

We've not taken any patients in the past two days. The engineers are digging ward floors down below surface level and stacking the dirt up into neat terraces around the outside walls of every tent. The patients really need the sense of security these walls will give them. Having been accustomed to sleeping in foxholes, many of our wounded men have begged release for duty after every bombing or shelling. Our eaves now are seven feet above our floors instead of the former three foot clearance.

The engineers haven't started on my ward yet, and it is full of the self-inflicted wounded transferred to me from other wards. The needs of a whole ward full of these men can be filled in less time than what one or two cases of gangrene require. Their wounds characteristically involve either the right or left heel, depending upon whether the man is right or left-handed. His act gets him out of combat still alive but crippled for life—likely crippled in more places than can be seen by the eye. The high casualty rates here on Anzio have spawned SIWs, as they're called. Their shattered heels can't be repaired, so a single cleaning and dressing of the wound is all that can be done for them medically.

The joint meeting of the beachhead surgical sections had to be postponed. I won't give my talk before next week, if ever.

Our food is good again, and we get two baths per week now.

MARCH 31, 1944. I sat around practically all day with nothing to do and then got in two new cases of gas gangrene. I also had to see a third man on Bussey's ward, but I don't believe he has it. It does not seem to bother Bussey, his having to get consultation from me, but it's a clumsy situation at best.

I'm no doubt somewhat intimidated by his gold leaves, but there's more to it than that. When we were classmates he was always a topnotch student—never very close to the rest of us—but we all liked him well enough and respected him even more. We lost contact when he went straight from Baylor into medical school and from there to Mayo's for several years' postgraduate work in surgery. I'd gotten a license as a pharmacist and a job. Our paths didn't cross again until the year I came to Baylor Hospital as an intern and he came to Dallas as a well-trained surgeon in solo practice. Oh well, we'll both survive the present situation. He was obviously relieved at my opinion that his patient did not have gas and that we could safely wait and not disturb his dressings. I'll bet Bussey hates war surgery as much as I do. I hope he has no more problems.

When I got back to the ward after lunch today, it was gone—lock, stock, and barrel. The engineers had dismantled it in about an hour and will have it back together again by tomorrow. My two cases of gangrene are on two separate wards and sure can't get all the care they need until they're back on my ward with my trained personnel.

APRIL 1, 1944. Postman is treating us shabbily again with no mail for the past three days.

We ran our watches up an hour today. I guess we'll have sunlight until eight o'clock tonight and until nine in June, as we did in Bizerte.

The engineers didn't quite finish digging my ward yesterday. Looks like they'll finish by noon tomorrow, and I'll have it functioning by the next day. It surely is going to be nice, and I'll have room for more beds. I'll probably get all of the prisoners of war on my ward now. It's logical that I do, as I've always had a few along, anyway. They frequently reach us in pretty bad shape, making them vulnerable to infections of all kinds.

One of my patients died last night, leaving me with practically nothing to do all day. The man was doomed from the moment he was hit with the type wounds he had. Bussey's patient is much improved today. He and I are much relieved that I didn't advise removing that man's cast last night. Just two months ago, I'd have had no more idea than a rabbit whether that cast should have been disturbed or not and would have been as panic-stricken as Bussey was. I've evidently learned some things about the disease, but it does seem that hard facts are mighty elusive. I'm sure we could do better if we could get our hands on recent literature on the subject. I really doubt that much literature is available, and of course, this beachhead does not have the library Baylor had.

I had to do another amputation in the middle of the night, and as usual, such cases are a signal for Jerry to act up. It never fails, but this time it was Lonesome Polecat himself that misfired a couple. Luckily, our mess hall was empty at the time because one shell struck the center pole causing an aerial burst, sending the fragments far and wide. Had it not been for the embankments put around us by the engineers, we'd have had many casualties among personnel and patients. With our embankments, hardly more than twenty-foot circles can ever get involved in such accidents.

Common to a good many of us I'm afraid, is the far away look in the eyes called "anziating." Neither "daydreaming" nor "meditating" express it so well, so a new word had to be coined. Then, too, we've discovered a new disease called "anziopectoris," easily diagnosed on anyone in the outfit who becomes a bit indisposed. Such people! Such a group of people, if you will.

Did I tell you I'm mildly excited about a phenomenon in medicine that is entirely new so far as we know? As yet I've no way to check up on it to see if it's an old one known to all others except me, but I sure never heard of it before. It has to do with sensitivity to horse serum, which I must frequently inject into the veins of critically ill gangrene patients. I always do skin tests before hand but frequently go ahead with the injection in spite of a positive test. So far, nothing more serious than chills have followed, and subsequent skin tests on these patients are negative. Whether or not I've made a new discovery or simply reconfirmed old ones will have to await a review of medical literature some day.

Mallory, the lucky stiff, is being transferred to the States tomorrow. We're all envious but hate to lose him. He has been one good executive officer.

Colonel Winans is presently in a city in Italy south of us, so I've not had a chance to talk to him about the new dean at Baylor. I do know and can now tell you he wrote in December, criticizing the new setup for not taking some notice of us. He asked for a statement of just what they assumed our status was as to faculty positions and hospital staff assignments. Colonel Carter told me this morning that the letter has never been answered. I'm afraid some resentments are being built up that will outlast the war.

I hope you didn't leave Dallas without seeing Mrs. Carter and some of the other unit wives, although I hear some of the girls are throwing one cat fit after another over our being on the beachhead. The names of four or five reach us with whom we're completely unsympathetic.

Haines, a man I knew during our student days in Tennessee, has been on detached service with us for some time. He belongs to a surgical outfit that supplies surgeons on temporary duty wherever needed—like Connally and Peyton. He'd been with four other evacuation hospitals before ours and says we're by far the best he's seen. Does make us feel good.

APRIL 5, 1944. Martinak and I had to get up at 6:00 A.M. so we could empty our tent for the engineers. The nurses' quarters were finished yesterday, and most of ours, today. Our tent is not only more secure but also neater and roomier. I can start sleeping on a cot again as well as above ground. Ever since the big air raid six weeks ago drove me to dig a hole to sleep in, I've slept on a six-foot litter that is about twenty inches wide. I was perfectly satisfied with that arrangement, but this one really is roomier and more convenient. Things on the ward have been quiet, and I've spent most of today putting living quarters back together and rebuilding the flak shack over my cot. Am all set for a good night's sleep.

APRIL 6, 1944. Your March 20 and 23 V-mails came today, and Martinak got two of the same date from Macy. Both of you mentioned the other, but you apparently hadn't gotten together at the time you wrote.

Our daughter must be a character, and I know her grandmother is tickled to have her around. Mama always was crazy about her grandchildren and evidently hasn't changed much.

We're reduced to candlelight again. Somebody snatched our bulb in yesterday's confusion, and I've not had a chance to replace it. Martinak would already have had a new one, but he's working nights and hasn't missed the old one yet. Candlelight really isn't as dim as you might think. Two of them in a small tent do very well for reading.

I've not had a chance to do any more checking on serum reactions since the one patient I wrote you about. I did skin-test him again today out of curiosity, and he's still negative. I'd like to keep him around longer than I'll be able to, but that would only satisfy idle curiosity. Along similar lines, it does seem to me we were taught that positive tuberculin reactors lose their sensitivity to the test if they break down with massive tuberculosis. I don't know why.

A new censorship regulation forbids the mention of any war experience less than a month old. I guess it won't have much effect on our correspondence as you already know where I am, and I don't have many war experiences, anyway.

Did I tell you McCauley's promotion came through? He and Hahn are going to a rest area, and I'll take over the receiving section in addition to my other light duties. I sure hope gangrene remains scarce or that Galt gets transferred back to surgery while they are gone. I'll have to get up earlier than usual to hold sick call for our personnel. Mitchell says he's trained his men to pretty well handle the section without much input from him.

McCleary and Craven got their captaincies this afternoon.

APRIL 7, 1944. Well, I've been receiving officer as well as ward officer all day today. I don't see how McCauley ever managed to seem so busy, as his enlisted men can do everything over here most of the time. We did have one unique emergency, but the details of that one must wait for at least a month according to our recent censorship order.

I'm expecting to get a week's leave on rotation far from the front lines as soon as McCauley gets back. I sure hope there are no slip-ups. I look forward to being in a quiet place once more, to being on pavement again, sleeping above ground and on sheets, and having hot and cold running water on demand. I dream.

Martinak got the only mail today, a diary that had been mailed to him before Christmas. He has been keeping one since the day we left San Antonio. Believe it or not, the last page in it is the one for tomorrow. Quite a coincidence, eh?

As I approached our tent tonight, the very first thing to catch my eye was a chicken coop in the passage between our tent and Merrick and Turnbow's. Inside, wonder of wonders, was a buff Orpington hen, alive and kicking. They have put a straw-filled nest box in with her in an attempt to get her to produce. Neither farmhouse nor domestic domicile of any type other than military is within sight around here, but there must be one someplace. A few civilians show up from time to time, and Merrick has a little Italian girl on his ward sick with malaria. Her father brought him the hen and some wine today. Some of Merrick's friends will probably make stew of that hen before she lays an egg. I expect she'll taste pretty good, and I do hope I don't make a pig of myself.

56th Evac Hospital at Nocelleto, one of the nicest sites they occupied.

Unwinding at Nocelleto   13
Spring 1944

APRIL 10, 1944. You'll be glad to know that we all spent Easter exactly as Turnbow, Johnson, Bowyer, White, and I spent last Easter. [Cryptic talk to get by the censors. We'd all spent the day on an LST leaving the Anzio beachhead. This letter had been opened by the base examiner but nothing was deleted from it.] We're in tents again but in a valley so quiet and peaceful our ears ring. I'm pretty tired from the trip but looking forward to a mighty good night's sleep. Don't know when we'll start taking patients again, nor even if we will, but don't expect many whenever we start.

Martinak and I have a small wall tent, as always, but this time with the added comfort of a good wooden floor. It also has a good on-end box with a shelf midway, which makes a nice piece of furniture. We're not at all accustomed to such luxury, nor to the green grass growing all over the area, nor to our gravel walks and gravel drives. There are scads of civilians around, and my laundry has already gone out to one of them. Best of all, there is a dandy garden all planted and ready to be cared for. I can watch the stuff come up and grow.

We swapped all of our equipment with the fresh outfit that was marking time here. All the setup was waiting for us when we arrived—lucky us! All in all, this place is heaven, and not the literal one that has been looming up as an imminent possibility for the cleaner living members here—for seventy-three days to be exact.

You remember I wrote you that we had an emergency come in while I was receiving officer last week? I'm sure I can tell you about it now. It materialized in the form of a rifle-carrying medic dropped off in our section by an ambulance, which drove hurriedly away as soon as its passenger hit the ground.

Although it was not unusual for us to receive uniformed soldiers still bearing their arms, all arms were collected on admission. But in this case two obvious incongruities were present. In the first place, medics aren't allowed to bear arms and this man was wearing the red cross armband of a medic. In the second place, ambulance drivers practically always love to stay awhile and help themselves to coffee and swap lies with our personnel. Something was clearly amiss.

At the first move by our personnel to take the patient's rifle, he squared off, pointing it at our men with a loud announcement that he aimed to go kill some Germans and would certainly kill anyone who tried to get his gun.

Well, of course, the man was mentally deranged, and everyone started reassuring him that killing Germans was a good idea and he could keep his rifle. They finally won his confidence while gently surrounding him. On signal from me, two jumped him and got his gun while enough others overpowered him. I'd heard somewhere that intravenous paraldehyde worked wonders in such cases, almost instantaneously, so I gave him a dose. It worked. He was asleep and limp on a litter in a matter of minutes, and two men carried him on over to the psychiatric ward. The receiving section personnel didn't seem particularly impressed by the incident, as I recall, but I sure was. I've been telling the story to anyone who would listen ever since.

The ambulance drivers came back for coffee as soon as they figured it would be safe. We learned the MPs in Anzio had accosted our patient walking aimlessly about town asking where "the front" was. When they suggested he give them the rifle, he had reacted like he did here. The MPs promised to let him keep his rifle but persuaded him to let them get some ambulance drivers "to take him on out to the front." The ruse worked and we're all glad nobody got killed in the process.

Haven't had any mail for several days. Hope it comes through tomorrow.

APRIL 11, 1944. More nice things about this place! The mess hall is infested, literally infested, with Italian waiters. Two waiters at each table of ten, and they wait on us hand and foot. For a whole year all of our meals have been served cafeteria-style. The tables were bare except for what we carried to them and equally bare when we left, as we scraped and stacked our own utensils. Here the tables are already set when we come in, and the food is served by the waiters. The change has encouraged practically everyone to wash his neck and ears again. Most of us are shaving every day, and a few of the more dashing are wearing their "pinks" and green shirts again.

The radishes that were barely green yesterday are thick and green today, having grown about half an inch through the night. Irish potatoes are looking fine, along with beans and English peas. One of the fig cuttings has a leaf at the top that is an inch wide, and a few grown peach trees are in bloom. There are flower beds around about half of the officers' tents with annuals in bloom that I can't identify and with violets, which I can. The latter look just like the ones at home. It's a nice place and spring is undoubtedly here.

I've been procrastinating all day trying to decide whether to write you a summary of the unit's experiences of the past nine weeks. I suppose I will, for as time goes on I'll forget them. But unless I'm frank, there's no reason to write, and if I'm frank, it may not make pleasant reading and might rile up the base censors. I hardly know what to do, but I sure don't want to forget.

APRIL 15, 1944. Since we're off the Anzio beachhead, I guess I'd better try to give you a more accurate, overall picture than censorship—both mine and the army's—would allow in the letters that I wrote from there. Do remember that anyone who tries to do so and tries to describe the experiences in such a way that his folks at home will understand them, is probably undertaking the impossible. But I can't resist butting my head against such a brick wall. That wall isn't going to crumble, but do be assured that the series of experiences weren't really as terrifying nor as nerve wracking as one might suppose. Also, remember that each incident was of such brief duration that it wasn't much of an experience while it lasted, assuming significance only when looked back upon.

Actually, I think most war experiences are less terrifying than something going wrong with the steering apparatus on a car. They are also less terrifying than almost putting a bare foot down on a snake—or having night's stillness suddenly shattered by a nearby train whistle, when one is eight and reaching for the knob of a door that stands between him and the haven of light around his parents. No, I'm sure the latter is more terrifying than anything we've gone through. And I know from the conversations of many patients that our experiences are not too different from those of fighting soldiers. Yes, and I'm sure that those who survive such experiences without serious wounds are no more affected by them than is the car driver who narrowly escapes a smashup. Now remember all of the above. Remember, too, as I go on that our psyches are intact.

Already you know, and I've not yet landed you on the beachhead. So I must hurry to recount that some time after 10:00 P.M. on January 24, we officers and nurses boarded a flat-bottomed delight of Satan known as HMS-LCI 316 and had our brains scrambled by a lulu of a storm, from Pozzuoli (Virgil's tomb is there) to Anzio. Everyone was seasick, the nurses violently so. Twenty-six of them who were strong enough to be moved were transferred in a pitch dark night to LST 178. This must have been some hazardous transfer while still at sea. But they, and Ed Rippy as medical officer, climbed up the Jacob's ladder without mishap. Our vessel made it to Anzio next morning, but the sea was too rough for landing. We returned to Pozzuoli to wait out the storm. This delayed our arrival on the beachhead until January 27, 1944.

All was quiet at first, and we had no inkling of what lay ahead until we saw White. He'd taken a detail of men up ahead of us to get our buildings ready for hospital occupancy. They had been bombed out the first night, rendering the buildings useless. So as usual, we had to set up in tents a few miles out of town.

By this time, I'm sure a vague uneasiness over personal safety troubled most of us. White's detail was obviously shaken, and their accounts banished any previously felt complacency on our parts. All who could, grabbed a shovel and started digging as soon as we unloaded from the trucks. This being a new attitude on our part, it was noticed by our commanding officer. With a wave of his hand toward the surrounding Alban hills, he announced loudly, "All those hills are ours, men! No need to dig foxholes!" That first sentence was destined to become a classic in the months ahead, yelled out by scores at the warning of each red alert on Anzio. "All those hills are ours, men!"

The CO's classic was barely out of his mouth when we all became aware of a great drone overhead. We looked up to witness what may well have been the greatest single air battle ever witnessed by uneasy people, before or since. In breathtaking agonies, watching both fighters and bombers of our own air force falling from the sky in great numbers, we forgot all yesterdays and gave no thought to any tomorrows. Possibly hundreds of fighters gyrated crazily, and with loud whines, plummeted to earth. I do not recall seeing a single parachute signaling the escape of a fighter pilot, their planes landing with loud crashes and bursting into flame.

The great bombers fell more slowly than the fighters, and it was not unusual that their eleven-man crews escaped at the rate of one every second or so as they fell. In fact, smoking bombers seemed to have been put on automatic pilot, heading toward the German lines even before they started falling. In such cases, the crews evidently had no trouble jumping out with parachutes. I must add that by no means did eleven men escape every falling bomber, although fairly often they did.

I confess I harbored nauseating doubts that our own war capability could survive such a rate of attrition as we were witnessing this first big air raid. Also I got to wondering how all of that flying hardware could fall over such a small strip of country without some of it landing on the exact spot where I stood. A most unsettling thought, but one that we later learned was pretty universal during shellings and bombings. One tends to become convinced that his enemy is centering his attention on the particular spot presently occupied by self, I, me! When this illusion becomes vivid enough that a soldier yields to it and begins seeking successive new spots, the activity is commonly known as running. It sometimes happens no matter how brave the man. Nobody in our outfit ran, but I'm sure each of us saw the mechanism by which a man under fire breaks.

We must have spent a couple of days getting a portion of our equipment and tents into a semblance of usability. I don't remember now why it took so much longer than usual, as our receiving section usually completed the task in eight to ten hours. Of course, they'd never attempted it before under almost constant enemy fire of one sort or another. Anyway, we received our first patient on January 30, 1944. As usual, the work started before we were ready, and some essential equipment did not arrive until February 2. By the time we had all of our equipment, this hospital was bulging with more than twelve hundred patients. Many of them were seriously wounded, penned down by enemy fire for days before reaching us.

Soon after opening, enemy fire struck us, inflicting a few casualties among our personnel and many more among our patients. Still worse, that same enemy fire knocked out all other hospitals completely. Our overload went on, and on, and on. Doctors, nurses, and enlisted men

worked and worked and then worked some more. Day crews worked on
into the night and night crews, into the day. Whenever it looked like we
might catch up, in would come more new cases, more than we could
handle in days or weeks. I don't really know the figures, but I assume
more Americans died here than did Union soldiers at Gettysburg. As
many of the wounded as possible were made shipshape and evacuated
back to Naples, but the active bombardments of Anzio Harbor precluded
this activity more days than not. Hospital ships just couldn't tarry long
enough to take on many patients. So we continued working under strain.
I think it unlikely that any of us will ever again work such hours and at
such a pace. Yet the need for our services was so great that we were
oblivious to fatigue or fear while at work—although not so after stopping
each day.

Still, very few grumbled and very few cried in spite of the fact that
a great many died. Least of all did the wounded grumble, delayed
treatments notwithstanding. They were completely committed to their
task at whatever the cost. You could read it in their eyes. They would not
have traded their country, their comrades, their officers, their medics,
their nurses, or their doctors during those hectic days. Not for anything
would they, nor we, have traded off the other, for those were days of
complete commitment, complete cooperation, complete teamwork, and
intense pride. Small wonder Churchill rated the ordeal of the English
during the blitz as their "finest hour!" I've no doubt our stint at Anzio
will ever remain as ours.

Whether or not those days provided our finest hour, when ours was
the only hospital on the beachhead, they certainly were our busiest. Our
pace kept up for more than a month before other hospitals could be
moved in to absorb our overload. During all of this time there were
frequent daylight air raids and almost constant night raids—721 enemy
sorties in one week, a single bombing of our hospital, two or three
artillery shellings, and daily showers of flak. Our own antiaircraft guns
put up barrages on an intensity that were said to be unsurpassed
anywhere in Europe. Also our position added to the pandemonium, as
we were between our own and the enemy's artillery. Shells from both
sides, by the thousands, screamed over our heads twenty-four hours per
day.

One or more of the German pieces were very heavy calibre, long-
range rifles, mounted on railroad flatcars. These beat out a regularly
spaced cadence day and night, overcoming the cacophony of Anzio. The

sounds of their shells as they whizzed over our heads were unique and recognizable. They soon become known by such nicknames as "Whistling Pete," "Anzio Express," and "Lonesome Polecat." And soon, too, all of us were unconsciously raising our shoulders and pulling our necks in with that five-minute cadence of the Polecat.

The fire lasted for ten weeks, and up until the last two, Jerry had been very careful. Also during the first two weeks of our exposure, the shells fell short a time or two and fell in our area. That sure didn't help our morale any, either. After we were told our map coordinates had been sent to the German high command, no more shells fell in the area.

Of course, reactions during that first month were as varied as the individuals reacting. When off duty, most of us were too tired to do more than sleep. While on duty, we were so intent upon the business at hand that neither cadence nor cacophony were at our conscious levels. Still, there were times of wakefulness and terror, the two going hand in hand. There were from four to ten red alerts nightly. Those who could not sleep responded with a trip to whatever shelter they'd contrived for themselves. The adjacent bank of the nearby Mussolini Canal made an ideal place for digging into, like prairie dogs. It was not long before everyone had dug some sort of shelter. These were usually covered with scrap lumber and sand bags to make a flak shack.

If the light sleepers had it rough, I was spared a great deal by having such a fatigue that I was insured sleep. But one night during an air raid this sort of good fortune nearly did me in. Martinak fired up our stove before responding to the alert this time, and I'd not waked up. I was zipped up like a cocoon in my sleeping bag. When the noise evidently disturbed me enough, I flopped reflexively to the ground, bag and all. When Martinak came back to bed, the foot of the bag, with me inside asleep, was against the hot stove. I didn't get a burn from the fire, but when we threw that bag out into the open, lighting up our complete blackout, my ears sure did burn. You never heard so much profanity, I hope, rising from anxious throats at such a compromise of our protective covering. I dug a hole that very night—one large enough to accommodate me and my cot—and saw other nights thereafter when I was glad I had.

I'd just gone to bed one night when the red alert sounded. I turned over on my stomach like always and put my pillow over my head to get down as far as possible. As I lay there, the ack-ack broke loose and I could hear the too familiar sound of a big bomber overhead. Enemy bombers liked to fly over the hospital area, just for the respite it gave them from our antiaircraft fire. Unless they got into trouble, they flew on over to drop their bombs on target at no hazard to us. This knowledge was a comfort and I wasn't too scared for the moment, although this one had waked me up because it was louder and sounded closer than usual.

Now when a bomber is flying away and drops a bomb or two or three, it's easy to tell that each one is more remote than its predecessor. When coming toward you, each dropped bomb is heard as a bur-r-r-UMP. If a series is dropped, you hear this bur-r-r-UMP, bur-r-r-UMP, bur-r-r-UMP, closer and louder each time and accompanied by ground quakes of increasing intensity. This is never reassuring, being too much like a terrible monster bent on your destruction and taking relentless steps toward you. The bombs usually stop falling before getting too close, and you realize they were some distance away, like a mile or so. Oh, but this time was recognizably different. The enemy was closer, his motors louder than usually heard and his direction definitely toward us.

Well, about the time I was sure of the nearness of the bomber overhead, our ack-ack broke loose to remove any lingering hopes that it might be friendly. As yet no bombs had been dropped, but simultaneously with the noise of friendly fire, I heard a terrible thing. The German's motors started sputtering, a sign he'd been fatally hit and would jettison his bombload regardless of what might lay beneath. He was losing altitude with the whistling sound of falling aircraft, and I was sure he was barely to my right and headed my way. Then it happened. The bur-r-r-UMP came so close on my right that I knew the next one would be on my left or on top of my head. It came again, still to my right, but much, much closer and with ground shaking like I'd never felt before. I died once again, waiting for the next bomb to put me out of my misery, but it was still on my right as the machine passed over me to crash on my left. Wow!

Those bombs were falling at about five-second intervals, which gave time for my entire life to march through my mind for review and judgment—and according to me, the prosecution's chief witness, it could have stood some alterations. I prayed a little but had to abandon the effort because of lack of composure, lack of faith maybe, and a very definite and eerie feeling that the Krauts in that falling plane needed all lines of communication open for their own supplications. I had no doubts about the Omnipotent but simply could not grasp His noticing falling sparrows and young army doctors.

All of which brings me to the point of confessing that I was indeed scared. It's probably a mistake to admit it in writing that could possibly fall into the hands of future children or grandchildren, but that bomber scared me to within an inch of my life. The emotional upheaval must have caused me to hold my breath for some time, for as the plane roared over my head, I noticed my breath coming in great gasps. I was hyperventilating my lungs like a jilted schoolgirl and could not control it for some minutes.

Recovering from the fright, I was surprised to see my tent undamaged, my own body intact with all sphincters holding. I rushed out in great dread of what I might see, supposing most of my neighbors killed. It was as light as day from magnesium flares still floating high in the air—they give such a spooky light, bright as it always is. Soldiers were coming on the run from all directions. I was horrified to see the third tent from mine and others adjacent to it, which had been housing a total of eighteen of my compadres, all blown to bits. By that time our commanding officer, also on the run, had caught up with the soldiers. He bellowed out one of the few direct commands I'd ever heard him issue—"All right, men, get those bodies out of there!" No one ridiculed the order then, nor do I now. It certainly seemed appropriate under those spooky flares and in the midst of all of those demolished tents. The fact, however, was that there were no dead bodies and only one minor injury. All occupants in the area had been dug in with their cots below the surface, and although bomb three had demolished nine tents and made a three-foot crater an equal distance from Sebastian's head, his ruptured eardrum was the only injury. He came up grinning sheepishly and shaking his head like a swimmer trying to get water out.

I must say in passing that my tent was possibly the only one on the beachhead without a hole in it on the day we left. I could have sacked out the entire ten weeks in perfect safety well above those Pontine Marshes. However, I must point out that neither our nurses, patients, nor our enlisted men fared as well. Suffice it to say, they all conducted themselves at all times in a manner entitling them to the pride and gratitude of their country. Several were cited for the fact.

Now I'll attempt a description of some of my typical days at Anzio. Before doing so, I must explain as best I can why a budding internist should have ever had such days. And I've carped so much in my letters—forgive me—about surgical assignments, but I really must defend our very capable chief of surgery in the matter. Boiled down, the explanation is simple. He had no one else any better trained whom he could spare.

Be all that as it may, on February 7 I was assigned to what was to become my own surgical ward and operating room combined. Necessity forced such responsibility onto me, one with no more surgical training than I. The circumstances began with a sudden rash of gas gangrene cases in epidemic proportions on the beachhead. The Mediterranean command, fearing cross infections from the infected to the noninfected wounded, ordered suspected as well as diagnosed cases of this devastating disease of war casualties, all isolated. Next, not only were the patients isolated, but all who cared for them were to be kept out of the operating rooms for a period of three days. The command would have grounded the entire surgical section within a week had not one man been assigned as I was. It simply could not be helped that it was to fall my lot to provide all treatment available to these men. No surgeon could see the patient with me, badly as I sometimes needed consultation. The one exception was the chief of surgery who came through once daily but not while I was operating.

So much for my duties. When I arrived to take over the ward, which had been filled through the previous night, only eight men actually had gas gangrene, but all were wounded and most had had no definitive treatment. Also, all patients were on litters as there were no cots available. Neither was there an operating table. There was no medicine, no equipment of any kind—no surgical instruments—nothing but wounded men on litters, and their litters on the dirt floor. And there were no nurses and no anesthetists—only two medics and myself.

The sickest of the eight gangrene cases had been irrational for some hours before my arrival. Nevertheless, giving an anesthetic and doing surgery before improving his chances with intravenous fluids and multiple blood transfusions would have been his execution, no less. It took time, but I collected the necessary surgical instruments and medications, including the first penicillin I'd ever seen. [The drug had just been released, and the Mediterranean command had a very limited quantity to be tried on gas gangrene exclusively.]

The patient was still irrational and still lying on his litter on the dirt floor. He was not long for this world without radical intervention from those who knelt beside him. I had willing, but unskilled help, and had to put the man to sleep myself and do an upper thigh amputation. Stark reality left plenty of doubt that our patient could survive this ordeal, but survive he did.

When I went to bed at 3:00 A.M., after doing the surgery on the eight gas cases, the first patient was still unconscious. I dreaded coming back.

Guess what—but you couldn't. When I went back to the ward next morning, all of the previous day's patients were not only alive, but all were rational.

As nothing I did the day before had been screened from the other patients, all had witnessed each dilemma and each fortunate outcome. I was sure I sensed approval, and believe me, it was a heady wine such as I never expect to sense again. Similar heady wine, frequently renewed, kept me from ever tiring at Anzio. That particular tent full of wounded men never suspected they'd witnessed, right along with me, the first amputation any of us had ever seen.

On another night at Anzio, I lost my nerve for doing what obviously had to be done. I had learned to take a single step at a time with each patient rather than planning all of his surgery before starting. This would be inexcusable under ordinary circumstances, but at Anzio it undoubtedly did save time and exposure for treatment. The patients had all been tagged and their wounds dressed before we got them. A simple inspection of the size and location of dressings readily gave the answer of where to begin without exposing wounds to further infection. On this particular night, a patient had come in exuding the usual stench of gangrene, with multiple dressings on all four extremities. Beginning with the largest dressing, I saw that an amputation of an upper thigh had to be done. Finishing that and moving to the opposite thigh, I amputated it, also, and moved to an upper extremity, which I also amputated. Anxiety over what the opposite arm might reveal put me into a cold sweat as I worked on the third amputation. And well it might have, because removal of the dressing on that fourth extremity confirmed my worst fears—the poor soldier would have to be converted into a basket case— the first I'd been involved with.

My first thought was, "Could my judgment be in error?"—my second, "Could I spend the rest of my life wondering if I'd made a wrong decision?" Consultation was in order, and I set out to demand it from whatever source was available. Waking up our chief of surgery at 2:00 A.M. resulted in his assuring me I was able to make the decision and telling me to do whatever was indicated. Still balking, I walked over to Dunlap's tent and waked him up. Although he'd not had a full night's sleep in a week, Dunlap said sure, and got up and dressed. He violated quarantine, took one look at my patient, and turning to go, said, "Take it off." I was never faced with the same situation again. [Military surgery had been called an awful business. I did concur, doubled and in spades.]

My average day began about 7:00 A.M. with breakfast. It seldom ended before 10:00 P.M., and frequently not until well past midnight. All

of my patients were wounded, some of them seriously, and those who
had gas gangrene in their wounds, critically. The sick ones required
almost continuous intravenous fluids, antitoxin, and blood. This was
intensive care before the term had become common-place. At first, I was
the only one who could apply the nearly always required plaster casts.
It was a real headache for one busy junior medical officer, until a second
and then a third nurse was assigned to the ward. Things became eased
dramatically two or three weeks later when Jabez Galt, another medical
officer from the medical service, was assigned. Even so, it was about a
month before my ward personnel was really adequately trained to assist
with the surgery. By this time, surgery was performed in a pretty
satisfactory operating area screened from the rest of the ward, and upon
an excellent operating table. One nurse had been trained to pinch-hit as
anesthetist, and things were running smoothly. Any suspected, or real,
case of gas gangrene could be on that operating table on short notice at
any hour, day or night.

By about the sixth or seventh week things began slowing down.
Time began to hang heavily on my hands so that I again became
conscious, even while I was on the ward, of the Polecat's lobbing them
over.

APRIL 18, 1944. The Surgeon General of the Mediterranean
base section, came out today and read us a commendation we received
from Gen. Mark Clark for "outstanding devotion to duty and meritorious
conduct for the period from January 26, 1944, to February 28, 1944, etc.,
etc." Actually, we got it for doing what we were supposed to do and for
what we had to do. What we had to do, I'm sure, was less than what we'd
all supposed when we first got into the war. The British like to take a
crack at us now and then for the numerous campaign ribbons, decorations,
and the like, which all units receive. So if they say our commendations
have Hollywood value, I'm afraid we can't defend ourselves very well.
Our surgeon general next read out a citation that went with a Silver Star
awarded to our CO. I believe the Silver Star is the third highest decoration awarded by the nation and I hate to think it goes out at times for
Hollywood value. Yes, I do hate to think it.

Downright funny sidelights keep coming up to tragedies and near-
tragedies that happened while we were under fire on the beachhead.
Today I heard the following story for the first time from a Red Cross
worker.

During an artillery bombardment that blew our kitchen and the
Red Cross tent to smithereens (along with a few others) a group of British

soldiers were playing soccer. Their ball had been borrowed from our Red Cross. They all hit the dirt as soon as they heard the first shell coming and none of them were hurt; but as soon as the Red Cross worker recovered her wits, she went tearing out to see about them, supposing all of them dead. Before she could reach them, another shell coming in made her hit the dirt. When the smoke cleared and she got up, she was terrified, of course, and horrified at what she was expecting to see.

Holding the soccer ball aloft, here came all of the British boys. Trying to wipe the look of horror from her face with a reassuring statement, they said, "Hit ain't 'urt none, miss. Just a bit scratched on one side, ma'am."

Just as typical was the reaction of another British boy after one of our air raids. The Red Cross had a record player with a number of fine records. Popular records were kept out for anyone to use at any time, but the classics had to be checked out at the desk. Well, this boy had checked out three, one of which was playing. The other two were setting next to him. When the raid started, a piece of flak tore through the tent missing the boy by inches but smashing the records beside him. Forgetting he'd nearly been killed himself, he carried the pieces back to the checkout desk greatly concerned that the records had been broken. The Red Cross worker had a hard time reassuring him that it was okay about the broken records.

APRIL 22, 1944. Several of us took a nice trip yesterday. I wrote you about it in a V-mail last night but couldn't begin to do it justice in such limited space. I'll try again.

Turnbow, Merrick , Ford, and I borrowed the command car and its driver for a several-hour trip over the Amalfi Drive, which is reputed to be the most beautiful thoroughfare in the world. We're all willing to accept the description as it hugs the coastline for twenty or thirty miles from Naples to Amalfi, where mountains seem to rise right up from the Mediterranean. The highway, always in view of the blue water, cuts into their sides. The elevation at Naples, of course, is sea level, which rises only gradually to fourteen hundred feet at Amalfi. Very beautiful every foot of the way.

As in most towns around here, we were met by guides asking for work. Many Italians over here have lived in the States, and we got a guide who had lived several years in New Haven. He first took us to an Italian home where we were shown to a balcony overlooking the water. We were seated at the single table up there and served a sure-enough Italian dinner that was excellent. This was on the second floor of the home, above any structures that might have obstructed the view of beauty from an elevation of fourteen hundred feet. To our right and left were mountains. Ahead and down below were views of the nicest of many little beaches that dot the shoreline. All of this, plus the beautiful water. The Italian woman who served us waved her hand toward all of that scenery murmuring, "Bella panaroma!" So we learned a bit more of the language, as well as an apt expression to use around here.

Our dinner began with spaghetti with the native tomato and pepper sauce and strong grated cheese. You will be interested to know that neither a spoon nor trick winding fork were served with this—only a plain, everyday silver fork. In fact, I've seen a good many natives eat spaghetti and have yet to see one wind it up on a fork. Served at the same time was a wilted lettuce salad with some sort of olive oil dressing, which was good. I could have done with seconds on that spaghetti, but was afraid I'd miss something if I tarried so went on to the main course. This consisted of sure-enough good (boy, oh, boy!) French fried potatoes and five or six small fish of some sort, which were also very good. Don't know what they were, but they did have a faint hint of sardine taste only not nearly so strong. We just might have been eating fresh sardines for all I know. Of course, we had white wine along with the meal and an abundance of oranges and apples as dessert. The woman even gave us drinking water, a rarity, toward the end of the meal. We all ate and drank like starving men, much to the woman's delight. The cost was $2.50 each! And, oh yes, the wine all through the meal was by far the best we've had, both in North Africa or Italy.

APRIL 24, 1944 [to Mama] Guess this will about reach you on Mother's Day, so best wishes for the day. Our airmail has started coming through fairly well, but I've not had a letter from you in some time. I do hope your cold didn't leave you feeling below par.

Irving Berlin visited us today and entertained the local military contingents with a good many of his compositions. He must be sixty but doesn't look it by any means. He sings so-so but has a nice personality, and we enjoyed him a lot. He sang some of his songs that I remember from the community sings of World War I. I thought one incident here today was striking. He'd name a few songs and then have the audience clap for them as he named them again, singing whichever one received the most clapping. Two or three times he'd mention "God Bless America" as one of the choices, but no one applauded it. Finally, he sang it anyway as his closing number, and it was then obvious why nobody would admit they wanted to hear it. They're just too homesick and most eyes were on the ground.

You'll be interested in a letter I got from the Dean of the University of Georgia College of Pharmacy today. He says he is chairman of a committee appointed by their national organization to work out a new curriculum for all colleges of pharmacy in the United States. He seemed impressed by my article on premed curricula and expressed a desire to work with me—of all people—in creating about what I'd advocated. If there were no war and I was in the United States when it was published, something might have come of it, and I might have helped. If colleges of pharmacy did include such a curriculum, it would provide every country doctor in America with a competent assistant in the person of a combined pharmacist/laboratory technician/anesthetist who'd not be forced to sell fountain goods and tobacco to make his living. It seems to me the lives of both such professionals would be enriched, along with the health of the rural Americans being served. Who can say?

Had a letter from Margaret while she was in Waco. She said Harris took Suzanne out to see the chickens, and she was into practically everything in the yard before he could corral her. I'd certainly like to see those two girls and the rest of my family.

APRIL 27, 1944. The chaplain came over right after chow, and we've just ended a three-hour session with him. At heart, he is a lazy, practically good-for-nothing ne'er-do-well like your husband, so I always enjoy him. Ostensibly he came over to bring some dried shrimp, but we sat here eating them like peanuts and verbalizing our dreams about how we'd like to live when we get home. We figured out ways to enjoy lots of different lifestyles when we get home. Some of them would require more money than any of us will every likely make, but others would require practically no money and no effort on the part of anyone except our everlovin' wives and kids. He told us about his wife's uncle who leases a thousand acres of Louisiana swampland and gets trappers to go in and bring out muskrat furs and other pelts on shares. He seems to make a good living at this. And since the season lasts only three months, he is left another nine to simply enjoy living. We couldn't decide in a single three-hour session whether to give this uncle competition when we get back or whether to just live in a houseboat like another Louisiana uncle does and fish for a living.

This other life that sounds pretty good to us is the one lived by the chaplain's uncle. He has a two-room shack on four acres of land away back in the Louisiana woods some place. There being very little housework to do, his wife has a cow and some chickens, and a few hogs, and a garden. They also have fruit trees, and being in a woods, there is always plenty of fuel at hand for the gathering. By tending to all of this his wife and children provide all of their food, so that all the uncle has to provide is money for their clothes. This he can do easily as they seldom go to town or see anyone and thus have little need to dress up. Selling the hides of alligators shot now and then provides for the husband's portion of the living. The rest of the time he is free to hunt or fish or just sit under a tree and smell the flowers while he watches his wife work in the garden. Now this is nice for both of them 'cause it gives the wife company while she's working, and that makes them very happy.

Being at a loss as to which of the above lifestyles to adopt, we finally gave up and started discussing the merits of various small towns in Texas. We about narrowed down the attractive ones to either Columbus or Junction but, again, are at an impasse in choosing between them. You can appreciate the weightiness of our problem; while Junction provides excellent hunting and fishing opportunities year round, the soil there would be pretty rocky and hard for women to garden in. Also, we're not sure Kimble County would provide adequate shade trees for us to sit under to keep you company while you worked. On the other hand, Columbus does have a good type soil for our purposes and also has plenty of shade trees. But Colorado County is too far from the coast for much fishing, and the only good hunting is in the winter when the ducks and geese are flying. So, we finally had to give up on choosing a town, too. Of course we did have great fun—sort of like thumbing through a new Sears Roebuck catalog when we were boys.

As you can see, we're just not doing enough around here to earn our salt. We're getting lazier, fatter, and jollier by the day though, so all isn't a loss. Martinak has already gained ten pounds since leaving the beachhead, and I must have too. I haven't weighed to see, but my clothes are getting tight.

I wish I could help you get Suzanne "church-broke," but you really shouldn't feel on needles and pins when you're out with her. I'll admit it does something to a sermon whenever a little tyke pipes up with an irrelevant observation at a critical moment, as the preacher pauses to draw a breath. However, you know people universally are pretty tolerant of children just learning to conduct themselves in public, so parents can relax.

Well, I hope my overconfidence in Jerry's aim up at Anzio didn't worry you too much. I wasn't really all that overconfident, at that. When my letters sounded so, it was simply my effort to neutralize the exaggerated picture I believed your papers were giving.

If I haven't already told you this, Martinak and I could have slept on our cots above ground the whole time we were up there and been perfectly safe. There were no holes in our tent when we left except where a single spent piece of flak made a very small hole of harmless implication. Anyway, I didn't really take unnecessary risks, wearing my helmet everywhere as ordered, staying by my foxhole whenever not on duty, bolting my food down and getting to heck out of the mess hall like everyone else at mealtime, and being quite as scared as anybody during off-duty waking hours. I evidently just oversold you on our situation.

We're finally going to give our symposium on gas gangrene day after tomorrow if nothing happens. Quite coincidentally, the same topic is to be the subject at the regular Fifth Army medical meeting here next week, so the outfit should be pretty well primed for it. This week's Fifth Army meeting was on malaria and was by far the most informative one I've ever attended. I believe the malariologist was the best speaker I ever heard, and he gave out some excellent information.

Did you ever read any of Damon Runyon's stories? They resemble those of O'Henry, but I think them lots better. I read a paperback book full of them, yesterday and today, and think they're the best short stories I've ever read.

Hurry up and send the pictures and be sure to include a bunch of yourself. I sure do miss you, honey. Kiss Suzanne.

MAY 7, 1944. I'm having to sit still while I write as Ben is taking a picture of Martinak and me. Martinak is reading *Stars and Stripes*. I hope the Kodak does its job so I can send you a copy of the photo. There, he's clicked it. I can move.

One of our nurses who suffered a chest wound up at Anzio and has been in a hospital in Naples, came by today on her way back to the States. She commented on how much better we all look than when she last saw us, and it's true. We were a tired bunch when she was hit, and all had lost weight. I'm no judge for the rest of us, but I am certain our CO, Col. Carter, Devereux, Sebastian, Martinak, Brown, Bussey, McCauley, all of the enlisted men, and all of the nurses do look like new people.

Rowe and I are now rotating the combined night duties of pre-op and receiving section officers. This is a secret between us as long as

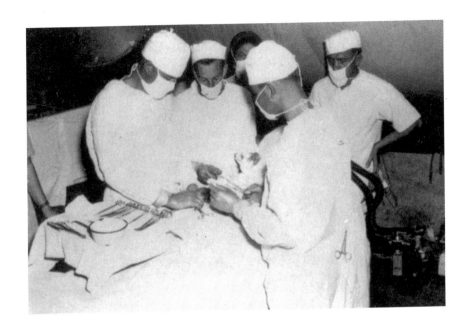

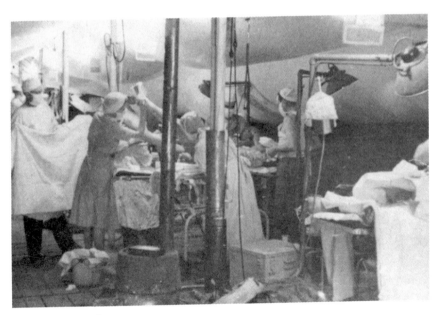

Surgery at Nocelleto.

nobody catches us at it because there is so little work, one man can easily handle both wards. I was kept up until 3:00 a.m. last night, not because there was so very much work but only because what little there was just kept dribbling in. The combined personnel of the two sections could easily handle both duties most of the time.

Martinak and one of his former patients are in here shooting the breeze about Anzio. I'm sure all of us involved in that little deal not only will reckon all time from it, but also will have to be on constant guard not to bore all who listen to us, for the rest of our lives. This visitor brings the only "first hand" information we've had as to how close we came to being captured the night of February 17. He tells us we were never more than three miles from the front lines, with nightly German patrols coming much nearer than that. The morning after that particular night, our own night crew told us that line officers had come in and said to pass the word for everyone to continue what they were doing unless ordered otherwise by German officers, who could be looked for at any moment.

Hospital ward at Fondi.

Soldier receiving a penicillin shot.

IN ROME ON
D-DAY   14
June 1944

MAY, 31, 1944. Fondi. Well, we're practically settled down again and have a few patients. Casualties in this campaign have not been nearly as heavy as anticipated, and I doubt we'll be busy until we move again. This is remarkable, too, in view of the terrain our army has moved through. Some of it looks like a few men could have held out indefinitely without heavy casualties. It is probable they would have if they could have been supplied. We see thousands of our own bombers to one German plane, and I suspect Jerry's supply lines have been kept in a terrible state most of the time. In fact, even the spot we left in Anzio has not been bombed or shelled since beachhead forces joined up with the main army a few days ago.

Our last move was really something. To begin with, White went with the Fifth Army Surgeon's Office official, who has charge of such matters, to pick out our new location. They picked one out but did not flag it at the time, White being assigned to that important detail next day after it had been cleared of mines and other booby traps. Ah, but places in a strange land don't always look the same for two days in a row, and ours didn't to White. He got confused and flagged the wrong spot for us. Not only was it already occupied by an antiaircraft squad when we arrived the following day, but we found that it was crisscrossed by irrigation ditches and levees. There was no way an entire convoy of vehicles—large enough to carry our hospital's tents and equipment—could even get off the route so more important material could pass on up to the front. And before bulldozers could level off the area, some battalion commander would have to order the antiaircraft squad to vacate their position. And before our two 6-ton generators could be unloaded off the trucks, a heavy crane would have to be provided.

One would naturally suppose those complications would be of no concern to a couple of junior medical officers. I certainly agree, as I'm sure E. K. Jones would. He and I had been assigned to ride up to the new location on the first personnel carrier from our hospital, and we assumed our functions were simply to provide any first aid treatments required by our own personnel. When we saw the place and analyzed its implications, we began chuckling to each other and could hardly wait for the first series of our convoy to arrive with poor old White, and perhaps a colonel or two to watch him straighten out the mess. Ha! Little did we reckon with the inscrutable ways of an army. The first series arrived with no officers but with the horrible news that Jones and I were in charge of the move.

We had been given absolutely no instructions, but we didn't need any to know that we had to get our trucks off Route 7 without delay. One medical officer arrived, Jabez Galt. White had told him of an engineers' outfit we were to call. We called, told them of our needs, and bulldozers arrived within minutes to get the weeds cleared off our location. And believe it or not, the exact crane we needed to unload the generators came ambling along the route just when we needed it, and we commandeered it around, enough to get them unloaded. Jabez knew of another engineers' outfit nearby and tore out to see them. He came back with two more bulldozers and a grader and we were all set.

Our convoy commander came up with the first small section, and he told us other units would arrive every two hours. We had enough equipment to keep levelling the ground ahead of their arrival and never did block the route. Our only problem that first day was getting rid of the antiaircraft guns that had been occupying the area for a week, but that wasn't really too bad—they wanted a hospital nearby about as much as we wanted their spot.

All of this started three days ago, and the last of the graders is just now pulling out. The wards are all up, and the living quarters for nurses and officers are up. The enlisted men's tents will be up presently, and everything is on nicely levelled ground. Jones and I sure did sweat blood for a couple of days and were really expecting a chewing out from the CO whenever he arrived. Not that we deserved any, but somebody usually has to be the goat for such snafus as this one has been.

Well, the CO arrived and did no chewing. He did opine that the place was a little small, but usable. If he has any conception that the impossible was accomplished he hasn't mentioned it. No telling what he said to White yesterday when he learned we'd set up in the wrong area, but I'll bet it was plenty. So, yep, yep, yep, the experiences of a junior medical officer can be quite varied.

JUNE 1, 1944. Your May 15 V-mail came today. I'm glad you sent Mama the Mother's Day candy and pin.

I've had my eye peeled for Italian handwork ever since I've been in Italy, but the only thing I've seen that I considered pretty was in a convent in Capri. A tablecloth and set of napkins were certainly of fine quality, but I couldn't afford to pay the eighty dollars asked for them. If such an opportunity presents itself again, I'll probably go ahead and buy them. The trouble with almost everything I've seen over here is that you can buy nicer than these, and at lower prices, at home. I would like souvenirs, and I'll certainly keep looking for them.

We're now north of the Gustav Line in country held by the Germans for months, if not years. General conditions here are much worse than they were south of the line, where nice crops were growing in well-cultivated fields everywhere. Here, the orchards and vineyards are all grown up in weeds, and not a crop seen anywhere except last year's frozen oranges still on the trees. Our Italian strikers who have been with us since last year say the "Tedescos"—the Germans—wouldn't let the people plant anything. Seems to me that's a lousy way to fight a war, but it does insure our having to feed these folks. The towns through here are in terrible shape, too. Much worse than Bizerte, if not destroyed entirely. Swarms of people, including children, beg for the hospital's leftover scraps of food. Little two- and three-year-olds go after our garbage cans with both hands, and they're pitifully undernourished. We hear they were told we'd slaughter them, so all the local civilians took to the hills as the Germans pulled out. Nothing up there for any of them to eat, so starvation made them willing to come back down to face us.

JUNE 2, 1944. Well, I'll probably take a trip about twenty miles inland in a few days, to a large and famous city. I can't imagine where your papers got the idea we're so busy, but we were for a few days, after the last drive started. Maybe that's what was being reported.

Something's gone wrong again and I'm accumulating money. I have fifty-six dollars right now, and come next payday I'll have more than twice that. I'm hoping to find something to spend it on in the next large city we take, but it's been occupied by the Italian's hated Tedescos, and they never leave much.

JUNE 3, 1944. Well, I'm assigned to the gangrene cases again, but there will not likely be any while we're here. It looks like I'm just going to be lazy for the duration of this setup. I'm betting I'll take another trip in a very few days. If I do, I'll be busy again.

I got a letter from Elise Parks yesterday, and she writes as she talks. She and J. K. seem very proud of their two little ones, and Elise says our little gal is mighty cute too. If I can get hold of more envelopes, I'll send you her letter. I still can't get envelopes around here.

Dunlap and I have a case together, and we enjoy scrapping as usual. I can't get around him without a scrap, but I always enjoy it and hope he does. Both fundamentally and professionally, he is one fine gentleman, and I hope I don't run him crazy. It's too bad the unit couldn't have spared one of the majors for the gas cases on the beachhead, but they were simply too badly needed for other things. He says he's willing for me to teach him what I know about gas gangrene, but most of what I have to pass on, at present, I can't really document without more statistics. No major is likely to accept mere impressions from an erstwhile lieutenant-internist. And dealing with them on the subject is pretty clumsy at best, even with those who were former classmates, which Dunlap wasn't. There is no such problem in talking to the nurses and enlisted men on the surgical wards. If what I think I know about the disease turns out to be valid, they will be searching for the early signs in every wounded man. That search has already picked up two cases before amputations were necessary. Should we ever face another epidemic of them, I'm convinced many extremities will be spared, the cases being picked up before the majors get out of the operating rooms to make their rounds.

JUNE 4, 1944. Well, I guess I'm sitting here with one of my rare moods of depression. I don't loaf well, and I miss you, and I miss home. I miss your talk, and your laugh, and the twinkle in your eye. And I could go on and on, but it would make a terrible letter, wouldn't it?

It's been quite a Sunday. I went to chapel this morning and heard the chaplain say we shouldn't drink moose milk. Sebastian and I were advised too late 'cause we sat in his tent and imbibed a bit last evening. Imbibed and talked. Decided that the only solution to our troubles was to hurry up and get the war over with. He's pretty depressed, having suffered indignities last Christmas day that he resents. He confided the CO's reaction to my paper, which I'd not heard before. Sebastian said he (the CO) was so mad when he read it, he was about fit to be tied. He had equated my position as favoring "socialized medicine" for the service—which I never did—to which he, as a regular army officer, had devoted his life. Anyway, he told Sebastian he'd have no such socialist in his organization. Sebastian told him he might better think twice before deciding to order a member of the original unit transferred out, lest he have more grief on his hands than it would be worth. Maybe Sebastian's reminder kept me here, who can say?

We've had a local trumpet player, an accordionist, and a local violinist playing for us during meals for the past two days. They all do very well, too. You know it does seem funny that this war has produced no AEF song [American Expeditionary Force] such as the "Parlez Vous" of the last one. Probably the one song sung and played by Allied troops this time is the "Lili Marlene" of the German army. If you've not heard it, I'm sure you will, as it is a beautiful and haunting piece of music. One of my very, very sick German patients in Bizerte wrote out the German words for me. It proved to be an exhausting task for him, and I regretted having asked him to do it.

I'm sitting on a five-gallon water can in the circle of a large bull ring. Good stories are coming from McCauley at the moment—stories of Captain Soper, our supply officer from Lawton, Oklahoma. I may tell some of them some day as Soper is one of our characters dragged out of civilian life.

JUNE 6, 1944. Rome. Well, I took a little jaunt today, a longer and much more interesting trip than I'd expected. I am in a large and beautiful city that has not been ravaged by war and has no evidence as far as I can see of the usual effects of war.

People by the thousands, the tens of thousands—and no doubt by the hundreds and hundreds of thousands—took to the streets as we came in by convoy. The happiness they exuded over our arrival could not possibly have been feigned. We were miles and hours behind the first segments of a great convoy moving forward, in pursuit of an enemy in retreat. The people had been exuding their happiness in celebration for hours. They'd run out of flowers when we came through but had both thrown flowers to the earlier troops as well as kissed them whenever the convoy stopped momentarily. We did get an occasional bouquet thrown at us, but nobody tried to kiss us. I was riding in the front seat of a truck, though, and every time we stopped, which had to be in every block or two, kids and elderly women swarmed over us. The kids wanted "caramelli, cho-co-lati, cigarettas and ghom Americana," and whether they got it or not seemed happy to be close to us. I'm sure no less than fifty kids and old women patted me on both cheeks during the trip on that main street, and don't think I didn't like it. I gobbled it up like a little tad who gets patted on the head by his hero!

Say, these people are fine looking folks. They're the best looking bunch we've seen since leaving the States. As a matter of fact, they look, dress, and act about like city folks in the U.S.A. Neither do they look hungry nor ragged. Except for the fact that most of the women wear no hose, most of them are just as well dressed as those in New York when we left. Gee, but it's good to see clean, well-fed, fine looking people again, and I'll never forget these.

The day has other never-ending wonders, as well. Not a smashed window is to be seen. The street cars still run, the lights burn, and the plumbing works. We've not seen such things since Casablanca, and of course that city can not compare with this one—not in size, not in cleanliness, and not in the looks of its people.

We are set up in a large and beautiful building that was built for a hospital. The Germans left it only yesterday, or the day before—without taking time to clean up, of course. We'll have it cleaned up in a day or two, and it will be fine. We even have window screens, wonder of wonders.

We passed right by landmarks of antiquity here in the city, one to which the Wolvertons, McDirks and Kilts of Alvin would all want to make a pilgrimage. [We'd passed Saint Peter's, and these were all Catholic families.] It is not over a mile from here, and I hope and hope and hope I'll have a chance to visit it.

We heard of the Normandy invasion this morning and are praying it won't be another Dunkirk. We were still the big war news this morning, but sure won't be by tomorrow.

JUNE 7, 1944. Well, I wrote you yesterday about moving. I still don't have an envelope to mail the letter in, so can't mail it. I'm afraid with things moving so fast, we won't ever be in one place very long again. But I do hope we'll be here at least for a bit. There is much to be seen.

It's pretty nice living in a building again. And we can use the experience for a change, although it's much easier to set up the hospital in tents. It is more convenient, too, as the various sections can be arranged in their most convenient proximities for our own particular needs. Maybe that makes sense to you, I hope.

Tunrbow, Gordon, Johnson, Barber, Roberts, Martinak, McCleary, and I have converted one of the hospital's wards into a dormitory. The rest of the captains live in a much larger one, and all the majors live two-to-a-room up the hall. If this hospital had been built more for private patients, I guess we'd all have had a room to ourselves, but it must have been designed for about twenty-five hundred charity patients. The wards are huge, and private rooms scarce. It is big, and new, and nice.

Two infantry officers just came in. They say the Germans are already seventy miles north of where they were yesterday. I'll bet we won't be here for long.

JUNE 8, 1944. I went into the city at 9:00 A.M. and stayed until 3:00 P.M. We decided this would be our shopping trip, and we'd sightsee next time if we had a chance. Well, wouldn't you know this would be Saint Somebody's Day and all shops would stay closed? We walked until noon before giving up and then went to the Albergo Excelsior, as swanky a hotel as you'll ever see I'll bet you. We had a couple of dry martinis at seventy-five cents each and then a very good meal prepared from GI food in their dining room. I can't understand how things in these places can become GI overnight, but they always do. Not true for the martinis, for they were as different from moose milk as the baked Alaska at Antoine's is from bread pudding.

Well, we did a bit of sightseeing after dinner. While I can't complain at what we saw, I was sorely disappointed at not getting to see the thing I most wanted to. Maybe I'll get to go in again. I sure do hope so, but we'll not be here long.

JUNE 10, 1944. We can now tell you that we're in Rome. Surprised? I am night receiving officer again, and there have been enough admissions to keep me fairly busy for the past two nights.

I visited the Vatican yesterday and had an audience with the Pope! Beginning at 12:00 noon, he held audience after audience with American soldiers, only a few being let in at a time. He began by saying a prayer in English that sounded about like any Methodist minister at home. I waited, along with two or three thousand others, for my turn into the small chapel at the Vatican, but it was certainly worth the wait. He had the personality of a most excellent politician, making all of us feel that he was very glad we came. He shook hands with all of us, asking where each was from. When I told him I was from Texas, he simply said, "Oh, the big state," and passed on. After he said a benediction, the soldiers nearly mobbed him to kiss his ring and robe. It must have been an ordeal for him, although you'd never have believed it from his attitude, which was very gracious. His Swiss guards were obviously worried but could not begin to hold back the crowd.

Before I forget to mention it, while we were waiting to get into the chapel to see the Pope, a very dignified and altogether handsome gentleman of about sixty, dressed in a military uniform, was ushered in ahead of all of us for a short audience. It was Field Marshal Badoglio, the defeated commander-in-chief of the Italian armies, who is said to have been no friend of Mussolini and perhaps contributed to his downfall. Anyway, it was a nice bit of history to be witness to.

Of course I saw Saint Peter's, which is elaborate beyond description. Everything in that place that looks like gold, really is—and there is lots of it. I was impressed by the seated statue of Saint Peter, which rests on a pedestal a bit over waist high, just beyond the entrance. It is of bronze and so old that the big toe on its forward foot has been nearly worn away by the kissings of the multitudes. George Adams and I thought we should add our bit to the wear and tear, and we did. We hope we didn't pick up a fatal bug deposited there for us by a leper in the middle ages. I was also impressed, of course, by Michelangelo's masterpiece in white marble, the dead Christ lying across the knees of Mary, the Pietà. It is just inside the entrance and is marvelous. Saint Peter's tomb is also most impressive— whether the saint actually was buried beneath it or not, millions of the devout have never doubted it through the centuries.

JUNE 12, 1944. Our mail caught up with us today and I got two V-mails. I'm glad little John is doing nicely. I too am sorry that we didn't have Suzy baptized before I left home. I remember we were going to at Waco that time and can't remember why we didn't. We'll attend to it when I get back.

I'm still working nights and may not be able to get back to town. For the most part, the shoppers have come back as empty handed here as everywhere else. We've always had the same answer everywhere—"the Tedescos have taken everything." I did manage to get a rosary at the Vatican the day I was there, and held it up for the Pope to bless. I also jumped off the truck once, for a minute, while we were stopped outside a store on the main business street. Most showcases inside were empty, but I spied a couple of cheap, hand-carved wooden bread plates and bought them. One had "Unser Taglich Brot," German for "Our Daily Bread," carved around the edge, and I caught the clerk just as he was trying to hide it from me. He was embarrassed and didn't want me to see he'd sought trade with German soldiers only a few days before. I don't know why he thought I'd care. Anyway, I bought it and a couple more with similar phrases in Italian. I've also picked up some abandoned fairy tales in German off the floor of a room in this building. I'll send all of this home as soon as I can.

Unfortunately, we have neither the time nor the transportation to really visit Rome. Of course, anybody could easily spend a whole year looking it over, and I sure hope I at least get to see some of the catacombs before we pull out.

Dunlap and Brown went to town the other night and had too many dry martinis at the Excelsior. They tried to stop a jeep and talk the driver into bringing them the eight miles back to our hospital. They got it stopped all right, but most unfortunately it was the jeep of the provost marshal of Rome, a bird colonel, no less; and he was in it. Fighting words passed, but they finally got the ride out here. Who should show up today looking for them but the provost marshal, not to jail them, but to apologize. He'd been a heel and also drunk on the night encountered.

JUNE 13, 1944. Randy's report to you about the plans for making Houston a medical center sounds mighty good. Might not be a bad place to live.

I go on the pre-op service again tomorrow and am looking forward to it. Pinto and I will rotate the twelve-hour day and night shifts. We have the opportunity and duty to really examine every surgical case and will get them ready for surgery. This service usually lasts for two months, so guess I'm settled for a while.

I'm still hoping to get back to town one of these days. But unless the work slows down considerably, I won't be able to make it.

JUNE 16, 1944. Much has happened around here in the past few days that I want to tell you about. A minor detail is that I've been transferred back to the medical service. Usually when I transfer from one service to the other, I find a whole ward full of patients waiting for me, and a new record was set this time. I was given a ward with 104 patients—all new ones who had not been seen by a medical officer.

My transfer is part of the most upsetting shakeup of personnel we've ever had in the unit. Ben was relieved of his duties as assistant chief of medicine and transferred to surgery! I can possibly care for about ninety percent of the surgical cases that come in and am replacing Ben, who would be pressed to handle a fourth of them. Ben certainly has no par in this organization and possibly no par in the entire theater in internal medicine, and is replaced by me, rusty as I am. One of the nurse anesthetists has been sent in as a ward nurse, and Bill Brown replaces her as anesthetist. To heck with his college and medical school and internship training, and the fact that he could care for ninety percent of our surgical cases. The nurse who sat at our table that time at the Swann Hotel has been sent to a medical ward. She is by far the best help in the operating room some of us ever get, and her place is being taken by a good medical nurse with no operating room experience in years. Miss Raymond, another good operating room nurse, now serves on a medical ward. The blonde nurse, who was on the medical ward at Fort Jessup, is now in the operating room. The nurse, who has worked in the operating room since we were organized, has been moved to a ward on the medical service. Pre-op, which has always been handled by one captain on each twelve-hour shift, now has a complete, three-man surgical team assigned to each twelve-hour shift.

Why has all of this happened? It's a long story, which I'll tell you when I get home. It satisfies a good many grudges, the one against Ben probably originating from the fact that both Dr. Winans and Ed Rippy thought so much of him. You know Dr. Winans always stood his ground around here, but he was evacuated back to the States after his heart attack a few months ago. La Due is now assistant chief of medicine and will be a good one, although I'd think not as well informed nor as conscientious as Ben. Few are.

Part of the upheaval probably involves a situation I mentioned to you while we were in Bizerte. I don't mention this as idle gossip but simply to point out possibilities. There have been a few, a very few, of the married officers showing a rather consistent interest in three of the nurses. Only two of these were medical officers. I'm sure the situation has been less prevalent in our hospital than in most, and only one case represented infidelity. I needn't mention any names but will say none of them were intimates of yours and mine, and neither are the involved wives. As a matter of fact, it seems to me you rather detested one of the wives and didn't know the other two.

One of the couples did incur the wrath of one who is in a position to cause upheavals, the more so with Winans gone. The upheaval has separated all couples during working hours, at least. Golly Moses, it would have been so much simpler to transfer these three officers, either out of the unit or off their present services. And that's that and I herewith wash it from my mind and my letters.

Baby, we're in khakis at last, most welcome change. Living in buildings has been rather hot. I'm sending my duffle bag home with a number of clothing articles I've no more need for. There are also a few souvenirs, including the rosary blessed by Pope Pius himself. We're getting footlockers at last and will have to get rid of some stuff we've been lugging around.

Mary sent a swell picture of you and Suzanne that came today. Darling, you look like a million dollars—best looking girl I ever saw. Kiss Suzanne.

JUNE 17, 1944. Well, I've finally caught up with my work again. I told you in an airmail that I'd been transferred to medicine, and I've had plenty to do the past four days. I'll not be overworked, unless I have to empty my ward and fill it again on the same day.

My own morale is not as bad as at times in the past, but I do believe that the entire outfit is at its lowest ebb since leaving the States. We're no doubt feeling the loss of both Dr. Winans and Mallory, who each seemed to exert stabilizing effects on the unit. Any mistakes of a unit commander are likely to cut his subordinates about like a father's can cut his children. And mistakes are inevitable in both cases, of course. The best any of us can hope for in a leader is a level head, an understanding mind, sobriety at all times, and consistency. It does look like our unit's plunge in morale is a result of failure somewhere in the leadership, which I sure hope is corrected soon.

Moving north to Peccioli, Italy. Collins is half-seated, smiling toward the camera.

PREOCCUPATION WITH THE PACIFIC 15

Summer 1944

JUNE **29, 1944.** Piombino. We took a little trip last night between midnight and 7:00 A.M. and guess I won't be visiting Rome again soon. We went about three-fourths as far as from your house to Ruth's, and in the same direction [i.e., north for 150 miles]. We didn't pass through any large cities, but I'm not too far from a famous one I'd like to visit as soon as our troops take it. I don't see how we can be very busy here, and if we're not, we'll get in some swimming again.

Our mail hasn't caught up with us yet but probably will by tomorrow. I hope the biography of Vesalius arrives, for it sure looks like time on my hands is about all I can look forward to. I've been giving all of my books to our library as soon as I finish them but will send this one home.

I'm back on pre-op and had only six patients all day today. Only one of these was a battle casualty, a far cry from the time we got over a thousand in twenty-four hours. I can't say how long things will remain so quiet, but they certainly will until the Germans make more of a stand than they've made in the past month.

I don't believe I wrote you about the visit to the Raphael Room in the Vatican, the same day we visited the Sistine Chapel. Its ceiling is covered with Old Testament scenes, the paintings much brighter than those in the chapel. Unless they have been freshened up, I can't understand this. There is more light to fade paintings in the Raphael Room than in the Sistine Chapel. I saw a great many other masterpieces than just those of Raphael but can't begin to identify all of them.

There was one sixteenth-century painting that shows exactly what happened to most of the pagan statuary around Rome. It is of a scene inside the Pantheon, and there on a large pedestal stands a crucifix. Lest the world forgets what happened, the artist shows a masterpiece of marble statuary lying broken on the floor beneath the crucifix. The statue was of some pagan god or other, the head and limbs broken off and lying on the floor beside it. It does make you sick to look at it, but it isn't really surprising that a zealousness capable of burning Bruno at the stake could destroy masterpieces of statuary, as well.

Honey, I didn't write my folks much about Rome. I wish you'd copy the descriptive portions of my letters and send them to Mama. I don't quite see how anyone can afford to live a lifetime and not see the Eternal City. We're going to have to save our pennies and come over here some day. And we'd better make considerably more attempt at scholarliness than has been my wont heretofore. Maybe you'd better review your college Italian to the point of fluency and learn more ancient and early church history than I ever did, so you can absorb more of what is here than I could.

We don't have lights as yet, and I can barely see what I'm writing. This won't really be surprising when I tell you that it is 9:45 P.M. and still pretty light outside.

JULY 20, 1944 [to Mama]. It sure was nice of Dr. Winans to call you. It's too bad he couldn't have waited another month before having his heart attack, so he could have seen all of us regain the weight we'd lost. He must have had to stretch what he remembered as the truth in order to reassure all of our families.

I've about decided that the best way to get through a war is to think about it not at all, read about it seldom, listen to the news never, and consider prognostication even in your own mind as taboo. But in the face of so much good news of late, I'm finding that harder and harder to live up to. I don't see how Germany holds on as she does, and I feel more optimistic than at any time since I've been in the army. But I do have to face the possibility of our going straight to the Pacific if Germany collapses before the Japs. As many of us as there are, and as far from home as we are, I doubt that enough shipping space is available in the whole world to move all of us twice—once home and once again to the Pacific. I hate to think about it but believe there is simply no way we can be moved twice. Our only hope is that Japan collapses before we can be moved even once.

I'm glad Charles got into the navy instead of the army. All of the twenty-year-old navy personnel we see over here still look like twenty-year-olds. In contrast, all of the twenty-year-old infantrymen look like thirty-year-olds after they've been in combat a while. The infantrymen are the ones I think deserve all of the medals and ballyhoo.

JULY 28, 1944. Let me tell you about your picture. I've looked at it about every hour since it came, of course. I've also been showing it about, and the universal comment: "That's a swell picture of Margaret, and Suzanne looks like her daddy." Oh, boy!

Baby, wedding bands have a pretty high mortality among doctors over here—we have to take them off when we scrub for surgery. Bowyer keeps his in a box with his extra insignia so that he won't lose it. That seemed like a pretty good solution until his naked left finger got caught in a picture he sent to Rosie. Rosie noticed and got after him. Devereux lost his but is wearing its duplicate. Martinak wears his all the time, and if it's caused him any trouble, I've not been aware of it. I wear a size 8-1/2 and would love to have one if you're not afraid to risk it. [She wasn't afraid, and the ring came in due time. I wore it until one day I vaulted over the top rail of a fence, and it caught on a nail and nearly pulled my finger off. My finger had swollen so by the time I got back to the hospital, we had to cut the ring off. I hadn't been able to get it off immediately after the accident because it was twisted, so it wouldn't slip over my first joint. I sent it back home, and Margaret had it repaired and still wears it on a charm bracelet.]

I got another letter from Dean Wilson of Georgia University today. Among other things he says, "There has been considerable comment in the pharmaceutical journals on your published article. Most of these writers are critical because, or so they infer, an attempt is being made by organized medicine to absorb schools of pharmacy, thus putting an end to them as independent institutions." He still favors the plan and is getting a committee organized to talk it over with medical educators. I'll be surprised if both groups aren't at my throat before it is over; that is, if Dr. Wilson can really stir up much interest in it. My guess is the two groups will simply squabble and never let it come before the public. Maybe ten years from now I can review all of the comments and rewrite a more forceful article if it still seems indicated.

I saw my first live octopus this morning. Some Italian fishermen came by in a rowboat with about eight octopi, the largest one eighteen inches in diameter. They put one tentacle on my bare arm, and the suction cups held so fast I could pull their boat along without its coming loose. The man threw him into the clear water a time or two, and we could watch him squirt out his famous ink as he swam along. That ink would hide him for a few seconds, too. The fishermen told us octopus was very fine food—maybe so, but ugh!

Jabez and Sid came in last night after an evening with some French officers who command a company of Goums. Each had a South African tom-tom that they'd learned to play during the course of the evening. You can imagine the weird noises we were subjected to for an hour or so. Just the same, I'd love to have one of those tom-toms for a souvenir myself.

AUGUST 2, 1944. Peccioli. We're still in ward tents but expect to be settled in small walls by tomorrow night. This sort of living would eventually get pretty old but it's fine for a few days. Dunlap has kept this end amused with his wit and idiosyncrasies all day. At the moment, he is playing checkers with Sebastian and getting beat. I beat him a game, too, and he is very unhappy.

George Adams and Ford are back from three days in Rome. Ford gave George a rough time by going on his first dipsomaniacal spree since the time the Galts tied him to the flagpole at Bizerte.

AUGUST 4, 1944. We are set up in an almost empty but colorful spot, in an orchard some little distance from one of many Tuscany villages. The villages sit up on top of either small plateaus or mountain tops around here. The city of Peccioli isn't much, but the surrounding country is interesting.

We also are on a plateau and must be about four or five hundred feet above sea level. In the adjacent orchard, rows of grapes are about fifty yards apart but are about six hundred yards long. Between the rows of alfalfa, garden vegetables are planted and all seem to thrive. In other areas of the orchard, there are rows of fruit trees on either side of irrigation ditches, which are about two feet deep and only about a foot wide. There are rows of apples, plums, pears, and Lombardy poplars and willows ever so often, also. The whole layout makes for pretty fields that can't erode. Apples vary in maturity from quite green to ripe, and our closest tree is loaded with plenty of tummy aches. If we stay a few weeks we'll have lots of ripe grapes, but the plums are all gone, already. The days are much warmer than those on the seashore, but the nights are much cooler. This spot is by far the prettiest we've ever set up in except for the one at Nocelleto, and this compares favorably enough with that one.

Baby, I was afraid you'd worry about those "state of the nation" letters I wrote on our internal dissensions. I wish you wouldn't worry. They always settle down and don't particularly upset me while they last. I have to tell you about them before you read of them in the papers or hear worse things from some of the other wives. I'll keep writing about things as they occur, but don't let it worry you.

Actually, there is so little difference in what the army has to offer its doctors, regardless of rank, that the rank makes no difference. As far as job satisfactions go, I can't see that much difference in one job to another because this isn't really the type of work a doctor is cut out for, no matter what the army offers. The system is designed to help win wars—nothing else—and a doctor is about as well off in one place in it as another. I don't see how a doctor with a whit of ambition could accept any part of what he goes through during a war by choice. He'd hate the war regardless of his position, as all of us do.

And "war" is too abstract a thing to be hated with the intensity of our hatred. So the soldier drifts into the error of letting some individual personify the entire abominable situation for him.

The object of the soldier's paranoia will likely be some superior with whom he has had enough intimate contact to spotlight the latter's human imperfections, thus providing concrete objects to despise. I am satisfied that no man in uniform, regardless of rank, is totally free from time to time of this type paranoia. You do recall my telling you that Sebastian and I have agreed that the only solution for civilian doctors in the army is to win the war and regain civilian status as soon as possible.

Before leaving the subject, let me reassure you that things have stabilized again. Ben Merrick is back on medicine, where he is again assistant chief of the service. Charley Bussey, for what reason I don't know, thinks he saved the unit from total dissolution, and he may have. He does have a knack of administrative ability.

Your last letter sounds like I'm going to have to watch my English for Suzanne's sake. I'll try to work as hard on her grammar as I used to on my father's when I was about fourteen. Whether I'll feel as responsible for her's as I did for Papa's in those days is no certainty. I annoyed him considerably.

AUGUST 6, 1944. I was OD last night and didn't get to write. Not that I was so overworked, but there's always confusion of one sort or another in the receiving section and I can't write. It really does not look like we'll be overworked at this setup. The few patients we've had have been civilians.

Wars are plenty tough on civilians. The retreating army leaves land mines and booby traps everywhere. And when the civilians start coming back, they usually get into trouble. The conquering army has taught its personnel to keep off road shoulders, not to open doors and windows, and not to invade orchards and vineyards; but the unwary civilians, particularly children, don't learn until too late. Kids are very bad about picking up duds, grenades, and the like with pitiful results more often than not.

You needn't be surprised at Suzanne's attraction to and misuse of those bright brass spittoons on the interurban. Neither Arab, French, nor Italian kids have any modesty when calls of nature are concerned. All Mother Nature has to do is hint at any of them, and they'll answer promptly no matter where they are. Actually, their male elders aren't much better either.

McCleary bought some rabbits three weeks ago intending to eat them, but he only ate one. He decided the other two were too pretty to eat, so he still has them. He lets them run loose and they really go for the alfalfa around here. One of them has just hopped into my tent and is nibbling grass at my feet. In case you haven't eaten domestic rabbit, it tastes about like chicken. I guess we'll have to raise some when I get home.

'Bye now. I'm still reading thirty to fifty pages of H. G. Wells' *Outline of History* every day. If you see a copy, honey, better get one for our library.

AUGUST 21, 1944 [to Mama]. I don't know what I wrote that you interpreted as advice to just never think about the war. If I ever said that, I was probably trying to fool myself. War is certainly the biggest event in the lives of those affected by it, and I'd be disappointed in anybody who could actually put it out of his mind. You'd as well rest easy as far as my own situation is concerned for I'm as safe as I'd be at home in normal circumstances. And even if I wasn't, I can tell you that one life, even mine, isn't much more valuable in war than one drop of water in a cisternful. I don't believe I've ever seen a dying soldier attach much more value than that to his own life. Golly, I didn't intend to get so morbid, but really you needn't worry when you don't hear from me. Whereas it may take a letter two weeks or more to reach you, a cable goes through in a day or two. You'd know it quickly if anything ever happened to this unit or to me.

I'm just back from a four-day leave to the seashore. We stayed in the villa of some wealthy Italian and hated to leave it. It had been taken over by the army, of course, but sure was nice. It seems the wealthy Italians lived mighty well. We had good swimming, boating, sleeping, and eating for four days.

Funeral of a Hulon Lofton strafing victim in Scarperia, Italy.

SCARPERIA 16
September 1944–April 1945

SEPTEMBER 22, 1944. So, my hunch was right. I came up with the advance detail yesterday, Martinak and some others came up today, and the rest will be along tomorrow. We're in another grape vineyard about seventy-five miles north of Peccioli and are in pretty country again. We have mountains on four sides for the first time, none of them very high and all are five or six miles away. We're evidently on a high plateau and can see the Tower of Pisa again, and it is much closer this time.

We came through Florence, the Arno River running through its center. It is a very pretty city, all right, and the part I saw was not battle scarred. Both armies spared the Ponte Vecchio, but the Germans blew up all other bridges across the Arno. Our engineers have thrown temporary structures across it for military highways.

We're ahead of our own artillery again for the first time in months. We'll probably be far behind it in a very few days as the German armies are on the run. There's very little shooting during the day. Our guns fired all through the night, but it didn't interfere much with my sleep. There's one big fellow in the area that makes a louder noise than any we've heard, except once, when a flying bomb blew up an ammunition ship in Anzio Harbor. Our tent flaps come in with a swish every time our big neighbor fires. Also, our

236

clothes cling closely at the same time—a most peculiar feeling.

Baby, it's so dark I can't see. Kiss Suzy.

P. S.: Just after I finished the above, Merrick, Martinak, Dunlap, and I were sitting in a tent chewing the rag in the dark. Who should walk in but McCauley with a typically cynical remark. "Damn," he said, "I'm in terrible shape—I can't stand to be alone, but I hate people!" He stayed until bedtime.

SEPTEMBER 24, 1944. We're settled again and received a few patients today. Lowell Lebermann, Mack Bowyer, and I are on nights and will probably put in half of the coming one in the operating room. We set up our ward as usual but, as usual, will not use it unless the hospital becomes crowded. Two or three surgical teams are thrown onto one ward, along with each team's nurses and wardmen. This results in chaos most of the time, the ward overrun with more hospital personnel than patients. Everyone being responsible for everything results in nothing being done well. The wardmen become sullen taking orders from so many nurses; the nurses sulk from orders from so many doctors; the patients, from their treatments being overlooked so often; and the doctors stay mad with their orders not being carried out. This insanity—which it is—is to insure everybody putting in equal time on the surgical service. It never spreads to the medical service, although the equally insane idea of scrambling personnel did. And we're winning the war in spite of all this.

I wrote you that Festus Sebastian, Andrew Small, Byrd White, and Bill Brown went out on detached service a week or so ago. They're all back again with the interesting story that they'd been sent out as a punitive measure, but were enjoying the setup too much for the CO to carry out his threat to leave them there through Christmas. He'd gone over to see about them, and they say he was obviously unhappy with their enjoyment. So, they're back with us.

OCTOBER 14, 1944. We've been overworked again for the past week, and you've no idea how tired one can become of seeing men shot up. On the other hand, it is marvelous to see how well they get along and how free of pain most of them are. Very few who get back to us fail to recover. Our team must have taken care of five hundred in the past three weeks, and we've had only one death. I might add that when a team loses a patient, it becomes depressed for a day or so, but losses really are rare. It is also rare that more than one or two patients per day require morphine or any redressing of the wounds postoperatively.

Nerves are prone to get on the ragged edge after we've been overworked for a while. A major got all over a private last night without adequate justification—in fact he was 100% wrong and the private 100% right. Another major, who is ordinarily very considerate of both enlisted men and nurses, called our mess sergeant over to his table last night. The paisanos had served him one drumstick and one wing as his portion of the night's fried chicken. Said the major, "Sergeant, I just want to know where the good fried chicken goes. Do the mess sergeants get all of it? Or does it go to the MAC officers? It sure as hell doesn't come to the officer's table." The sergeant got a wicked expression in his eyes but could only boil inside. In the meantime, the paisanos kept bringing in chicken plates, each with at least one piece of white meat on it. It could be we officers, generally, need to carefully memorize a good definition of "subordinate" and "subservient" and keep their distinctions firmly in mind.

OCTOBER 17, 1944. In spite of some letup in casualties, we're still averaging five hundred operations a week in the unit. Our team manages to get most of every third day off, but a jerry with gas gangrene consumed most of my off time yesterday. Priorities for surgery used to be based on the seriousness of the case regardless of nationality, but no more. Somewhere up in the chain of command, that policy struck a heartless cord and was changed by order allowing no exceptions: Americans are to be treated first. So, back to my gangrene case, Carter couldn't allow me to operate on the man until sixteen hours after I'd first wanted to, when it would have been much simpler and with more hope of success. I was provoked all day yesterday, and again today, each time I checked him. And we just don't come off with a clean slate at all in our treatment of prisoners during rush periods. By a whole lot, we don't, but that sure is graveyard talk.

OCTOBER 18, 1944. It still rains almost every day and last night we had a hard wind. Martinak says it gave our tent a real test. He lost considerable sleep worrying about it, but I slept through most of it to his disgust.

My jerry that I've been so provoked about is much better tonight. He is rational and asking for pen and paper to write home. He's eating his head off and looks like he'll pull through okay. I guess for sure we'll have to say we operated on him, and the Lord cured him.

OCTOBER 23, 1944. More about human relationships. We're exactly like a small town of a few hundred people, each one knowing a great deal about the business of everyone else. Also like a small town, anything anyone says about anyone else is very likely to reach the ears of the one talked about. One of the majors is said to have remarked inadvertently that he thought our nurses as a whole were inferior. Of course his remark got back to them, and they're all sore at him, naturally. It won't add anything to his own equanimity or comfort for the rest of the war, which serves him right. Actually, I'm sure our nurses come as close to qualifying as the "salt of the earth" as any group their size. They've had no more consideration shown them in this organization than is shown to male officers. Also, some restrictions have been placed on them that nurses in other organizations don't have. In spite of it all, our nurses have done their work amazingly well and have maintained a sweet enough disposition to contribute a great deal to the morale of the wounded men. Some may be inferior, but so are some doctors and some enlisted men. All in all, I've a lot of respect for them and feel they've done a right good job. Certainly no group has exceeded them in their courage.

And now, more about our team. I told you Mack Bowyer and I think Lowell Lebermann does surprisingly well at times. In spite of that, Bowyer would prefer working with one of the other surgeons. He is undoubtedly by far the best surgeon of any of the former first lieutenants, and Lebermann needs the good assistance he can give. The problem may simply be that he plans to finish his residency training in surgery and is afraid he might have some of Lebermann's shortcomings rub off on him before he gets out. As for Lebermann, our superior, he swears we hound the life out of him, never backing his judgment. Says the only time he's ever able to get either of us to back him is when we two disagree. At those times, he says, one of us has to agree with him. Thus the operating room personnel refer to Bowyer and me as "Lebermann's yes men." I guess we do sort of hound him, but he takes it mighty well. And whether he realizes it or not, he's prone to do better work when hounded than when not. And so it goes in the unit.

Honey, I feel so cultured, I may have to clean up my vocabulary even before I start home. Lebermann, Festus Sebastian, and I attended *Rigoletto* at the Teatro Verdi in Florence yesterday. It was my very first time at grand opera. Frankly, I only went so I could say I'd been. But, oh my, how I did enjoy it! The entire company must surely have been exceptional. Of course I've no way of knowing that, but even I know that Kyra Mascherini, Rigoletto, along with Maestro E. Tieri, was most outstanding. With intermissions and encores, the opera lasted three and a half hours, and I think no one in the entire audience was even the least bit tired.

The opera house has six tiers of boxes along both sides and across the back, with orchestra seats in the center. It was full and must have accommodated two thousand people.

About half the audience was civilian, prone to excitement with their appreciation at times. They respond with "bravo" when the degree is slight to moderate. But after such a show-stopping performance as given by Mannucci and Mascherini in Act III, they used bis (rhymes with "peace"). A thousand enthusiastic Italian voices saying "bis" sounded like a hissing "boo" in English. Since I had never in my life been so moved by any musical rendition, sacred or secular, vocal or instrumental, imagine my shock at hearing what I thought were hisses and boos! But the more the audience reacted, the more Mascherini, Mannucci, and Tieri smiled and bowed. Of course, what was being shouted was, "Bis, bis!" and it evidently means encore. So, about three encores of the duet ensued before the show could proceed. Man, it was all fine.

Our box at the Verdi was near the stage in the second tier, shared with an air force captain and his nicely dressed Italian girlfriend. Our seats were only $2.50 each, and I'll certainly go back to as many operas as I can manage.

DECEMBER 26, 1944. And so, our second Christmas away from those things that matter has come and gone. I hardly know what to tell you about the Baylor unit except that it is much, much better adjusted to its role than it was a year ago. It was strikingly evident by the way we conducted ourselves yesterday. Last year there was an almost universal depression, accentuated by each drop of alcohol consumed, and much was consumed. On that first Christmas a big party had been planned for 20:00 hours, but by that time, a high percent of our officers and a sprinkling of our nurses were beyond attending. The place was like a morgue, and those who drank lacked a lot of being hilarious even though still able to be on their feet. Hudson Dunlap's classic remark on seeing the floor's maudlin crowd last year: "Gaiety, gaiety, nothing but forced gaiety." Not that he was any happier, bachelor that he is, than everybody else.

Now yesterday was so different, in every way. All of our parties for the past six months have been quite pleasant affairs, affairs none of us would have minded our wives attending. And I heard any number express the opinion that last night's and the one before were the best ever. We have one every month or so and evidently enjoy a good reputation in the area, as they are always attended. Not only do the young officers who date our nurses come, but we frequently host both colonels and generals, who have access to the best clubs in Florence. Last night we had two generals, as well as the usual sprinkling of colonels and "piccolo" colonels. I overheard one who had been overseas for his third Christmas say that he had dreaded the day, until he got here, adding that this had been the most pleasant thing that had happened to him since leaving home. Oh, there will always be some drinking, but no one was rowdy, and no one maudlin.

The party had been planned to last from 9:00 until midnight, but lasted until 1:00 A.M. While all would rather have been home, this Christmas away from home was not the hell it was last year. Everybody hopes, and hopes, and hopes we'll be home for the next one.

Christmas Eve we had a party for which everyone had drawn names like in grammar school. The only difference was that since there is no gift that anyone has any particular use for, the presents were understood to be of a droll nature and were opened in the presence of all. William R. Turnbow was the Santa Claus, and he was a good one. He distributed such items as a live puppy, cans of C-ration, soap, toys, a whiskey bottle filled with vinegar, and one piece of intimate wearing apparel. This last gift was somewhat the worse for wear and had been purloined from the nurse who received it. Her tentmate had swiped it and wrapped it very nicely and put it on the tree. The crowd sang carols for an hour afterward, everyone enjoying every bit of it.

I'm sending you our Christmas card-dinner menu, which our CO had at all of our plates yesterday. It was mighty fine. Also fine: the ostracism the outfit has imposed on the Colonel for several months broke down yesterday. I'm sure almost every officer and nurse went over to his quarters to call on him. And I must say that any man who can be as pleasant a host and as obviously pleased as he was, can't be 100% bad. He "ain't no cherub" and that's certain, but all in all, he's possibly as good as any of us who've felt we're any better. Morale is higher than at any time since Anzio as far as I'm concerned. It does look like Christmas has bridged over a few chasms in the organization. When it all boils down, I guess that's what Christmas is for anyway.

I used to worry about the changes our folks would see in us when we get back home, but after seeing the bunch through yesterday, I don't believe there'll be any change. I feel like we're all back on pre-Pearl Harbor norms, and I've not had that feeling within the past couple of years.

DECEMBER 29, 1944. Already it looks like the German drive in the Belgian bulge has played out. I sure hope it stays that way and am convinced it will. A quote from George Bernard Shaw in a recent *Time* magazine declares that this war is a mere bubble on the froth of history. I'd say it's at least one great, big bubble.

JANUARY 13, 1945. Have been reading Tolstoy's *War and Peace* in this time of idleness. It's too bad it requires the idleness available in a war to allow for such reading. He says the chief attraction of military service consists in its compulsory and irreproachable idleness. Not for us it doesn't. We do better when overworked.

FEBRUARY 24, 1945. Colonel Churchill and Colonel Michael DeBakey talked to us this afternoon. Colonel Churchill is a very imminent surgeon from Harvard who is surgical consultant for this theater and is just back from thirty days at home. DeBakey is only slightly less imminent, is from New Orleans, and is in the personnel service division of the surgeon general's office. You'll recall that DeBakey just a year ago was the Captain DeBakey who approved my paper for publication.

I guess we had hoped to find out from our visitors just what day, exactly, the war would end; just exactly when we'd be sent home; what sort of practice we could expect when we set it up; how many children we'd have; and possibly when we could expect the "Second Coming." If they knew, we couldn't tell, but they did tell us things we already knew and hated to have confirmed.

Colonel Churchill made some startling statements:

1. No more civilian doctors will be drafted.

2. He was anxious to get back overseas after a short time at home, although he has a wife and four children at home.

3. He was struck by the absence of young men on the staffs of Boston hospitals. He noted that the absence of young men denied the older ones the stimulation they formerly had for study and excellence (we've all noticed a deterioration of quality in published articles).

4. People in the States are so much on the move, he had a hard time getting hotel accommodations and transportation.

5. Strictly rationed New England had as many cars on the road as ever, and his wife's maid told him she knew where he could get as much gas as he wanted.

Colonel DeBakey told us:

1. There aren't enough doctors for rotation to work any faster.

2. Affiliated units can and will be broken up as necessary.

3. The War Manpower Commission won't let the army induct any more doctors, although it needs them.

4. Demobilization will be by individuals and not by units.

5. The surgery done in this theater has been the best anywhere in the world, our patients getting back in better shape than those from other theaters.

All very interesting and we hope DeBakey wasn't just flattering Dr. Churchill. The latter thought the only reason he was anxious to get back was because he had no job at home. We could have told him all of our personnel who have reported after going home, report a desire to get back here whether they're working or not. That does seem odd, but I suppose all of us fight off making the necessary adjustments as long as war continues.

Colonel Carter let us read a letter he had from a doctor who is back in Dallas after eighteen months in the Pacific. He reports that a good bed, accessibility to good night spots, good food, and even his job as chief of medicine in a service with nine hundred patients is not satisfying him. He'd rather be back in the Pacific.

Oh, but your everlovin' husband, he's not changed one bit from two years overseas. What I want is to come home and stay within five miles of the spot once I arrive! What's wrong with all these returnees anyway?

MARCH 21, 1945. Lots of mail today for the unit after some days without any. I do love to get your letters, and four from you and two from Mama were in today's mail, none of them more than fifteen days old.

In addition to letters not over two weeks old, an *Alvin Sun* of January 11 arrived. I'm enclosing the wrapper so you can show them what's wrong: wrong APO number and no city mentioned. Do tell them I enjoy and appreciate the *Sun*, but the errors in the address delay each issue and must be no end of trouble for the postal service.

Our new commanding officer seems to have the interests of his subordinates at heart. Our interests will be secondary to those of the army, of course, but he is certainly getting around the place to learn the score. If he doesn't turn out to be plenty all right, I'll be both surprised and disappointed. I'm sure, of course, that after he learns the aforementioned score, he'll set about changing some of it, inevitably stepping on toes in the process. But even if we should just as inevitably swear under our breaths from time to time, the man is going to run a good outfit, and I'd bet on it.

We had coffee for the new CO yesterday afternoon, at which he met everyone again and behaved quite genially. I've not smelled liquor on his breath a time yet, something we've come to believe unusual in a CO. He must be about forty, shakes hands firmly, and looks one in the eye while doing so—things to make up for some shortcomings, if he has any. He comes by pre-op frequently at night and stayed quite a while to talk last night. He talked about medical topics and is well informed.

A major policy change was ordered by our new CO yesterday and another one today, both excellent in my opinion. The first was that only denatured alcohol is used in sterilization of instruments. Surely he knows that's what has always been used for the purpose, notwithstanding all the requisitions for grain alcohol. In the same order, all or any whiskey prescribed in the future will be by the dose and not by the fifth of a gallon.

The second new order is rather minor, but is one several of us have tried to get across for months. It places a bed in the receiving section for the OD who must spend his night there, and puts a stop to all loitering and chitchat so he can actually get a night's sleep when not busy. Colonel Epton is surely a man after my own heart!

APRIL 16, 1945. After loafing for five weeks, we went to work again at 03:00 hours and had operated on 85 patients by 17:00 hours today. The new Allied drive against the Gothic Line has begun, but other hospitals are ahead of us and most of our casualties have been light ones. It's a relief that the spring drive has started, and we all expect it to end the war in Europe. I hope.

I'm sure you needn't worry about your husband's having changed by the time we get back home. The rumors you've heard probably originated from boys of eighteen entering the armed services, going overseas, and returning in two years or so as men. In fact, a boy in the front lines for a few months looks much older. It makes your heart ache to get a patient you suppose to be in his early thirty's, and look on his record to find he's nineteen or twenty years old. It is very striking.

German prisoner patients being evacuated after treatment in Bologna.

Deaths of Roosevelt, Mussolini, Hitler 17

Spring 1945

APRIL 23, 1945. Bologna. Dadgum, I caught the advance detail again, but I enjoyed it. Bologna is a large city, and we're living in a natatorium whose swimming pool is empty. It does make pretty good living quarters. The wards will be in tents again, set up inside the largest stadium I ever saw anywhere. I didn't know there was anything like this in Italy until the CO brought me up here a couple of days ago. We got here less than twenty-four hours after the last German soldier pulled out, and he has nearly walked my legs off. We've climbed up and down these stadium seats until my knees have nearly ached off, but it didn't seem to bother him any. My knees are still swollen some, but are better than they were yesterday, and will be all right in a day or two.

From the lack of attention paid us by the natives, you'd think American troops had been here since the day one. We've never seen anything like it before. It is not that they seem at all hostile; they simply ignore us completely. I sure can't figure it out, although we're told there are more Nazi and Fascists sympathizers here than anywhere else we've been. That might explain it, for it is certainly nothing like Rome with a million and a half citizens, or more, in the streets welcoming us.

We hear that not only are things going well here in Italy, but that also the Russians are fighting in the

56th Evac Hospital in Bologna, located in one of Mussolini's stadiums.

eastern outskirts of Berlin and the Americans in the western outskirts. Hope it's true.

We're about set up and will probably start taking patients at 7:00 P.M. today. Our team is on night duty and I dread this first night. The new CO evidently never did move a hospital before, and consequently he messed up a bit. Colonel Carter is sore at him for not turning it over to some of us who have moved before, but if he did that, he'd never learn. He's a bird that's going to learn everything there is to know about his command. I say more power to him. He didn't make as big a mess of things as our experienced movers sometimes do, at that. In fact, Chizek [new executive officer] is the only one who has ever made one go off very smoothly, and he was the least experienced of any at the time. I predict that our next move will be the best ever.

It seems so long ago that I almost forgot to tell you George Cook, Jr., came by to see me just before we left Scarperia. I sure was glad to see him. Tell Faye he looks good and says Charles Seton is fine, too.

APRIL 28, 1945. Well, it's 10:00 P.M., and we've just this minute run out of patients after three very busy nights. Practically all of our patients have been Germans, most of whom are quite docile. All are pitiful, and most are in terrible shape from neglect. Many die before surgery, and some after. Not quite all are docile, for some of them really think we're going to execute them. Pitiful to see. Rumor has it that we've captured a thousand-bed hospital, and that it was in the charge of a single medical officer, and that most of our patients came out of that one hospital. Our ambulance drivers tell us that unwounded Germans are wandering in droves all over the front in a state of shock and offering no resistance. This is certainly not hard to believe.

I talked to a German lieutenant this afternoon on the ward. I asked him why they didn't give up, and his answer is a classic: "Well, you shoot at us, and so we shoot at you—that's war." Then last night, another officer told us Germany would give up whenever Hitler is captured, but I'm not sure I believe that. Their route hereabouts is by far the worst we've ever seen and their morale is gone, but still they don't give up. Oh well, some day it will be over.

Time magazine came today, filled with details of the President's death. He surely must have been the greatest our nation and the times ever combined to produce. I'd like to be around in fifty years to get history's verdict.

APRIL 29, 1945. We all feel mighty depressed about the President's death—probably worse than the English did when King Edward abdicated. We don't expect his death to alter the course of the war, but are afraid it might alter the peace a whole lot. I still believe he will go down in history as one of our greatest leaders, but I think we were wrong to lean on him for more than those first eight years. Had we elected someone else in 1940, whether he had been strong or weak at first, he'd likely have become strong by now when strength is needed. At this point, my hopes for Truman are simply that he'll do no more harm than Calvin Cooledge did in office.

Colonel Carter's remark to me when we heard the news was, "Man, I feel terrible." Dunlap's was, "I feel like crying." Those were pretty well the gist of the feelings over here.

I should tell you Colonel Carter looks ten years younger since free of having to room with the old CO. He is all over the wards and interested in what's going on. He won't even drink beer.

APRIL 30, 1945. Lord, but I'm tired, tired, tired. I wrote you that things had slowed down, but that was for only one night. The Krauts started pouring in again on that very day and have not stopped. I do believe a disintegrating enemy army means more work for the conqueror's medical corps than does a functioning enemy. After working a full twelve hours in the operating room, we have so many sick patients on the ward that we can't just go off to bed without checking on them, and working on many. If we find eight hours for the poor quality sleep available to day sleepers, we're lucky. It will certainly be a relief to get back on days after two more nights of this.

The entire Fifth Army had less than 150 casualties in the past two days. Can you imagine? But during this same two days, I'm sure this one hospital has admitted around six hundred Germans. That is four to one, and many of these have come in German ambulances driven by uniformed German drivers, and without guards. Our motor pools refill them with gas and oil and our receiving sections trade them our clean blankets and litters, their German drivers then returning to the front to bring us more. Oh, this war is a funny business. Our Germans even had fresh eggs for breakfast a couple of mornings and were quite impressed.

Our prisoners included two young German doctors who were quite willing to work in our operating rooms. We tried them for one day, but they weren't really any help. The almost unbelievable truth is that they weren't any good as military surgeons. They still want to treat their wounded just as our surgeons did during the Civil War. The French learned how to treat to keep down infection in World War I and were the first ever to learn the trick. They taught the British, who then taught us, but the Germans simply refused to learn it. I suppose it must be a matter of national pride with them because they've enjoyed leadership in both science and medicine for so long. It's too bad, and we've marveled at it each time we've taken over one of their hospitals. It was the French who gave us their word "debridement," which we still use, and it simply means the cutting away of all contaminated flesh from wounds. The wounds are then simply left open until all local infection clears naturally. Only then are they subjected to the "secondary" suturing, a term I've used frequently.

We don't know for sure what happened to German leadership in medicine after the turn of the century. What we do know, however, is that Chancellor Bismarck ushered in state socialism about that time. He socialized the medical profession at the same time and something catastrophic happened to it. We've been witnessing some of the results of that catastrophe here in Bologna for the past week.

MAY 1, 1945. I've so much to tell you, I hardly know where to begin. I'm sure I can't begin to exhaust the possibilities but can at least tell you some of it.

To begin with, we've moved, as I'm sure I've told you before. It was about like other moves, except that two of our trucks, one carrying goods and the other latrines, were delayed by an eight-hour traffic jam. The Germans had demolished a bridge when they pulled out. Those of us who had come up at 5:00 A.M. with the advance detail were a little bit provoked and a whole lot hungry by the time the food truck arrived at 4:00 P.M.

We finally got set up as we eventually do each time we move. Our new CO planned and executed the move himself, and although it didn't go as well as some, it went better than several others. I predict that the next one he plans will go much better, and the one following that will be the smoothest we've ever made. I'm still convinced he's that sort of fellow. He knows he messed the move up and had the grace to admit it to those of us on the advance detail. However, most of his command criticized him severely but not to his face.

Our team drew night duty and put in the most hectic week I've ever spent, not even excepting Anzio. We got one night off, too. But I started off exhausted from the work I did on the move and I never did get rested up. At least 95% of our patients have been German prisoners and have come in droves every night, except one, since we set up. There were so many that we could only care for the most seriously injured—a strain on everyone. Twelve consecutive hours spent operating on such cases is too much. I do believe the intelligent weighing of a policy will result in limiting such work to eight hours. I'd hate for anyone to operate on me even after eight such hours. Regardless of how much compassion one may have left after two years' war surgery, working on the captured enemy is infinitely more of a drudgery than working on your own. Frequent remarks made while the work lasted: "It's a screwy war where you shoot them up and then work your head off trying to save their lives." And, "They wouldn't do this for us. Look at the way they've treated captured Americans."

Several German doctors have brought patients in, and we've managed to keep them to work on the wards; but they're no good in the operating rooms. Two of them speak real good English, and Bowyer, McCauley, Johnson, Chizek, and I spent quite a while talking to them today. They had been captured first by the Brazilians, whom they thought pretty wild. They said the Brazilians had lined them up and stripped them of rings, watches, insignia, money, etc. We'd likely have done them the same way, although I didn't tell them so. They weren't complaining and even bragged about what a gentleman one of the Brazilian doctors had been.

We talked to the Germans about medicine and found that in the German army most of their problems had been similar to ours and handled in about the same way. One big difference is striking, if they're telling us the truth, for they say they've had very few psychiatric casualties. They said they had plenty of them in World War I but not this time, and they couldn't understand why—neither do we. Another difference: they've never seen penicillin, although they've heard of it. They've plenty yet to learn about debriding wounds, also. They complained, even as we do, that the German army does not always give commissions commensurate with the doctor's ability.

Promotions in their army are automatic at regular intervals, but all German doctors go in as second lieutenants. Peculiarly enough, the second lieutenants may have captains and majors serving under them as their assistants. The first lieutenant telling us this had evidently been a well-trained surgeon and bemoaned the fact that he'd had to say, "Vil you please do dis?" and, "Von't you please do dot?" I guess they're about as human in their army as we are in ours.

Baby, I wish I could really describe the situation as we're seeing it here. We're convinced the war in Europe is over. We're also convinced that there is no chaos like that of a disintegrating army. We saw the same thing on a smaller scale in the Italian army, but this is much worse. The prisoners we get are very docile and pretty glad their war is over. Now

Captured German ambulances hauled their own wounded to the 56th in Bologna.

and then one is provoked that some American shot him after he'd surrendered—trigger-happy. And some think we're pretty bad for demolishing their cities and killing their women and children in the process. Someone reminded a colonel that the jerries did the same thing in England, Poland, Czechoslovakia, and Russia. His reply, "Ja, ja, ja, I know, I know, I know, stupid, stupid, stupid!" Several others say we and England started the war.

We're going to move one day soon. We've torn down once to do just that but had to set up immediately to take in more Germans. That didn't help morale any. When we finally do move, it will likely be a long one, and I'm sure ready to go. That is literally true, as I've not unpacked since we got here. It is also figuratively true, this setup being like Dragoni and Anzio and one I'll be glad to have behind me.

I guess at this stage of the game I can now tell you that the Luftwaffe managed to get a couple of planes off the ground, raiding the area for six or seven hours on our first night. The highway going by our stadium was the real target, but machine gun bullets danced across our field at least once. We suffered no casualties but were harassed enough that not much in the way of sleep went on. And while I'm at it, I may as well tell you that we've been witness to four or five small raids since leaving Anzio, all of them aimed at adjacent highways. I'm very glad to tell you that I believe all of that is over.

MAY 7, 1945. I meant to tell you in last night's letter I spent the winter in Scarperia, a village thirty-five miles north of Florence. It was also about the same distance from the front and there was one hospital ahead of us.

Some of the fellows heard over the radio that the Germans gave up today. No one is very excited about it but hope it is true that the Japs will follow suit within the next eighteen months. There just isn't a bit of telling, but we all hope we either get back home in the next six months or our folks get to come over here. Ford, Ben Merrick, and Arnold have been sent on detached service to other hospitals, and more of us could be at any time.

McCauley and I took a four-hour walk this afternoon and sure did enjoy it. A stray dog took up with us as we left our gate. We enjoyed him, too, but he certainly earned his money. We did rest some at intervals, but it was a long walk.

MAY 8, 1945. All the time I thought yesterday was V-E Day, and now I find it is today. From where we've sat for the past ten days, the mass

A weary 56th Evac group reads the news in Bologna: "Nazi Armies in Italy Surrender."

disintegration of the Germans has made each day about the same, and all of them looked like victory. Maybe we're just emotionally exhausted, or maybe the preoccupation with the uppermost and unanswerable question of what comes next explains our phlegmatism. Also, the President's recent death has had a sobering influence. It is probably no exaggeration to say that that news put a big lump in every soldier's throat and tears in the eyes of many. Man, oh man! I'm glad it's over, over here—glad as can be, but not ecstatically glad as I've supposed I would be. Glad as can be, but not reverently glad somehow—there is no impulse to fall down on my knees about it. Glad as can be, but with no desire to get out and celebrate the victory. Just unemotionally glad, I guess, like everyone else seems to be. Glad, but nostalgic. I predict the emotions will remain pent up until news comes that a boat bound for home is waiting. Then I'm sure the ecstasy and the reverence, the desire to celebrate, and the other evidences of emotional upheaval will come. But I'm glad—I know I am— and it seems funny to be that glad and still nondemonstrably emotional at the same time. Yet, and yet, there is still the China-Burma-India theater to be faced.

Drat it. No mail for the past several days. I imagine we'll be in for a great many mail-less days, as well as C-ration days, and the like.

Redeployment of troops has always interfered with the routines of all remaining troops in the area. You know, we could usually predict the coming of drives and the like, by how we ate and how fast our mail arrived.

You'll be interested in the following copy of a letter distributed here a few days ago and bearing Mark Clark's signature:

PRESIDENTIAL MESSAGE

I take great pleasure in conveying to each American officer and enlisted man in the Fifth Army the following message received by me from the President of the United States:

ON OCCASION OF THE FINAL BRILLIANT VICTORY OF THE ALLIED ARMIES IN ITALY IN IMPOSING UNCONDITIONAL SURRENDER UPON THE ENEMY, I WISH TO CONVEY TO THE AMERI- CAN FORCES UNDER YOUR COMMAND AND TO YOU PERSONALLY THE APPRECIATION AND GRAT- ITUDE OF THE PRESIDENT AND THE PEOPLE OF THE UNITED STATES. NO PRAISE IS ADEQUATE FOR THE HISTORIC ACHIEVEMENTS AND MAG- NIFICENT COURAGE OF EVERY INDIVIDUAL UNDER YOUR COMMAND DURING THIS LONG AND TRYING CAMPAIGN.

AMERICA IS PROUD OF THE ESSENTIAL CONTRIBUTION MADE BY YOUR AMERICAN ARMIES TO THE FINAL ALLIED VICTORY IN ITALY. OUR THANKS FOR YOUR GALLANT LEADER- SHIP AND THE DEATHLESS VALOR OF YOUR MEN.

SIGNED: HARRY S. TRUMAN

MAY 19, 1945. Udine. As you see, we have moved from Bologna. We're completely set up in tents about eight miles outside the city. Udine is about the most American-looking city we've seen since leaving home. Its homes are single-family dwellings set back off the street, in contrast to block after block of apartment houses set right on the street of many Italian cities. Many of these homes are pretentious and beautiful.

Udine is a city of thirty or forty thousand, located in the extreme northeast corner of Italy. It is only eighteen miles from the Austrian frontier and about thirty from Trieste where Tito is reputed to be stirring up trouble. We're evidently here to back up troops brought in to discourage the gentleman. He's sure not popular with our unit. We're hoping his play does not have the backing of Stalin, but I'm sure you'll know how well founded these hopes are by the time you receive this letter.

Our trip up here covered more than two hundred miles, but the part from Bologna to Venice was over the same Po Valley route I've already described to you. I can now reaffirm all I told you, except Ferrara is not on the river's bank. It is really six or eight miles south of the Po. And we came through the business section this time and found it was not demolished as were the suburbs described in my last letter.

The country north of Venice is an absolute garden spot for seventy-five miles to Fiume Tagliamento [Tagliamento River]. It is thickly populated and very prosperous looking. It really isn't as beautiful as my recollection of a certain part of Algeria but is more beautiful than any other I've seen.

Only at river crossings is there any evidence of war up here. And it is only the ends or centers of most bridges in Italy that have been

The 56th Evac in Udine, 225 miles from Bologna.

destroyed, and these by a single bomb. It is the structures in every direction for a hundred or so yards that have suffered most, and that from hundreds of bombs. One is less impressed by the damage done by the hundreds than by the mute witness they provide as to the inaccuracy of aerial bombardment. We have concluded many times that the safest place to ride out a heavy air raid might well be in the very center of its objective. Certainly the bridges of Italy justify that conclusion. Maybe our bomb sights are better than the Germans'.

The country north of the Fiume Tagliamento is open, uncultivated prairie. It must either be used for grazing livestock or for hay, but I see neither haying equipment nor livestock at present. It is quite possible that all such items were sent to Germany earlier.

The people north of Venice sure are different looking from those we've been accustomed to. There seem to be four general types: first there is the blue or brown-eyed, Heddy Lamar-Austrian type; second, the dark-skinned, black-eyed, black-haired type that I label Yugoslav; third, the round to squared-headed, walrus-mustached, blue-eyed, fair-skinned type that I label Czech if short, or Austrian if larger; and fourth, the American-looking type, probably a mixture of all.

I hope we're not here for too long. Even so, I'd rather sit out our trip home right here than in some crowded redeployment area.

MAY 21, 1945. After being open for twenty-four hours, we have eight medical and five surgical patients. We'll probably keep those who come to us until they're well, so even five cases a day will eventually give us enough work to occupy us for four or five hours every day.

I hated to leave our cool buildings in Bologna, but I'll have to admit this is a much better setup and more interesting, too. The outfit on the whole was depressed after entering Bologna, but I believe our moving back into the country has stimulated us out of the pits. We seem normal again.

After supper last night, Jabez Galt and I walked down to a little village about two miles from here. We found it the cleanest, most picturesque little place ever, and enjoyed our trip. The people seemed genuinely friendly, and all of their homes have courtyards like those you've always seen in the pictures. The more pretentious homes were behind the courtyards, which were filled with formal plantings. The more modest ones, still picturesque, have their courtyards in the back, and house, barns, chicken and rabbit coops open off them. Being springtime, these are filled with baby chicks, geese, turkeys, ducks, and bambinos. You might guess I liked the village. The people told us we were the first Americans they'd seen but were not afraid of us.

So, you've been seeing films of the German atrocities? They certainly are terrible, aren't they? It seems peculiar that of the two or three dozen American wounded who have fallen back into my hands, I've never found one who thought his treatment had been atrocious. And I've never found one whose treatment indicated anything more atrocious than neglect. Neglect becomes the natural course of things when you're overworked on your own wounded. You know, there have been times when neglect of German prisoners contributed to their death in this very hospital. And I'm sure our fatigue necessitated some neglect of our own at times, possibly contributing to their death in some cases. In short, many atrocities are the inevitable result of war—an integral part of the fortunes of war—one of the risks of war. Some atrocities are simply a large scale expansion of those same forces existing in all countries to some degree, even in peacetime. Witness the occasional cases of institutional or police brutality our attention gets directed to at times by newspaper reports in our own country.

We've not seen the films referred to in your letter, nor have you seen the films of war specially prepared for us. I hope you don't. They show the actual killing, the actual agony, the actual stacks of decomposing bodies, and the like. We have seen the pictures of Buchenwald and the others, and we've read the accounts, and I heartily agree with you; they are horrible and doubtless true. If they impress the average soldier less— I am one—than they do most folks, maybe it's because of other pictures we've seen and other stories we've heard. I seriously doubt that the national conscience keeps the German people awake nights any more than ours does from our institutional atrocities. Darling, don't let these terrible things you've learned poison your mind with hatred. What they should do is humble us all with the realization that five thousand years of civilization haven't widened the gap between humans and brutes any more than they have.

Don't be angry with me about this paragraph nor about others I've written in similar vein, will you? I don't believe my feelings on many of the things I express to you are so intense that they'll be a source of friction when I get home. I express them only because I'm anxious to maintain our intimacies of thought through the years I'm gone. I simply don't want to undergo latent changes in thought or attitude to shock you when I return. Most of us have discussed similar anxieties ever since the matter of coming home became a plausible possibility.

And now for more. Fraternization between ourselves and our defeated enemy has not been confined to the generals of the several countries. In the earlier days of the war, we found it unwise or impossible to keep prisoners of war on the same wards with our own wounded. The latter's hatred for the German soldier was so intense, they'd threaten mutiny on seeing medical or nursing care given the wounded POWs. All had changed by May 2, 1945, when we had to mix them again on the wards in Bologna. There was no sign of hatred and no trouble at all between them. Fraternization must be the natural reaction after the enemy ceases to resist. Recall how we enjoyed talking to our captured German doctors.

The high command has been concerned enough about fraternization to issue a new directive on the subject. Our headquarters received one yesterday with orders that it be read to all officers, nurses, and enlisted men in the organization. It forbids any fraternization whatsoever and directs that associations and kindness be confined to the degree set out in the Geneva Convention and no more. It further forbids American women having anything at all to do with prisoners of war. Interesting.

I took my laundry over to a neighboring farmhouse yesterday, and the farmer showed me a litter of rabbits only three days old. Did you ever see any? They were the shriveldest, skinniest, ugliest little buggers you ever saw, whereas another litter ten days old was as cute as could be. I believe I've seen the young of every domestic animal and fowl up here, except calves and pigs. I'll bet they're around somewhere under cover.

DEFEAT OF JAPAN   18
August 1945

AUGUST 5, 1945. Montecatini. We turned our few patients and all of our equipment over to the 16th Evacuation Hospital a couple of days ago and moved up here yesterday. Montecatini is an old winter resort near the Mediterranean some thirty-five miles from Pisa and has been taken over by the army as a redeployment and training center. We are quartered in one of the city's hundred hotels, but not lavishly so. We do have running water in our rooms, which is certainly an unaccustomed luxury for us, but we still have army cots for our beds. It certainly does beat tents, but our location has the drawback of being some six blocks or so from our mess hall.

No way to tell how busy we'll be here, but I'd think we'll probably do physicals on a great many soldiers headed for new landscapes, either in the Pacific or the States. I do know that I'm to give a lecture for an hour tomorrow. The title will be "Life in the Pacific," and I've never been west of Lubbock, Texas. And the Pacific covers a fourth of the globe and houses such life styles as those of the Chinese, as well as those of multiple Polynesians. A pretty broad subject for 2:00 P.M. on hot afternoons. Of course, the army has thoughtfully provided me with a technical bulletin entitled "Medical and Sanitary Data on Hainan" [island in China]. If that really qualifies as "life" in the broad area, I qualify as a rabbi. Sylvester Ford, listening to my comments makes another classical statement: "Most of us were born somewhat cynical and in the past three years have suffered many, many relapses." Mea culpa.

AUGUST 8, 1945. Show time arrived before I finished my last letter. This certainly was a favor to you, as I'm much less grumpy this time. I did talk to those poor, hot, sleepy troops at 2:00 P.M. and for a whole hour. They asked questions at the end but surely must have been ordered to beforehand. Maybe the talk went over all right, but if so, I can't imagine why.

We're getting up a sort of college annual-type book of the Baylor unit's activities overseas. One of our enlisted men who is otherwise very intelligent will be the editor-in-chief. I am to be business manager in name, but really Ben Merrick is the actual ramrod. I believe it will be a very nice souvenir of all of us, and I hope nothing happens to prevent its publication. In addition to being a diary of our activities since we were activated, it will contain about three hundred snapshots of the people and places we've seen. There will also be cartoons done by some of our talented personnel. Should be pretty good.

AUGUST 9, 1945. I had a letter from Mama today. Dr. Carter called her about as soon as he got back to Dallas. I'm glad he did, and of course she thinks he's one of the finest people ever. Well, he really is above average.

Today's *Stars and Stripes* carry the news of the atomic bomb and of Russia's entry into the war. That bomb is a terrible thing even in its unperfected state, and its potentialities so unlimited as to defy the imagination. I do regret its principle was ever discovered but am certainly glad we discovered it instead of the Germans or Japs. I guess no modern nation ever before sent an ambassador for peace to its intended victim as part of a surprise attack plan, but that's what Japan did. She deserves not a particle of sympathy, and her rulers get none from me. But Hiroshima must have contained about a hundred thousand children who are as innocent of crime as Suzanne. It's just too bad such methods for stopping a war have to be used, and it's too bad such a method was ever discovered. So while I'm glad we're the ones who discovered it, at this point I'm sorry, sick, and humiliated that we'll go down in history as the ones who unleashed it. Haven't we proudly advertised we're much too humane to use poison gas in the war—we, who are so scandalized at the inhumane things our enemies do to conquered people while we're so good?

Mad at me, honey? Don't be. I know Japan has to be whipped. I know Germany had to be whipped. I was just born with the pernicious habit of idealizing my country, my family, and my friends. I know I put them all on an unrealistic pedestal, and I also know that is a foolish thing to do. Now of course, even as a child I knew I didn't belong on any such pedestal, but I somehow took comfort in the belief my friends did. Then I'd see them display weaknesses similar to my own, and I'd be sorry, and sick, and humiliated. Long ago, of course, I learned to enjoy friends and family on a more mature and realistic basis. It has been only much more recent that my feelings for my country have become more realistic. I guess it took "the Bomb" to complete the process.

We profiled about three hundred soldiers this morning in a couple of hours. The routine for our day seems to have established itself thus:

· up at 7:30 and walk to the hospital for breakfast;

· start profiling troops at the hospital at 8:00;

· back to hotel by 10:00 or 11:00 to read *Stars and Stripes* until noon;

· back to hotel for nap until 2:00 or 3:00, except for those lecturing at 2:00;

· either a cold tub bath in the hotel or a fresh hot mineral bath at one of the local spas until 4:00;

· beer and gab until 6:00;

· letters home until each of five shows start at 8:00;

· to bed at 11:00 and read until 12:00.

The evening routine may be varied by sipping mixed drinks at one of the local bars at thirty-five cents each, or attending a nightly dance at one of the spas where there are a few nurses and a few "paisettes." On Friday and Sunday nights is a big dance with lots of paisettes at the very beautiful Red Cross Club. Me, I just go to the shows, although a couple of us spent one night at the bar and danced a couple of times with nurses who came along later from the unit. I judge six weeks of this will get old.

AUGUST 10, 1945. Rumors persist that Japan has surrendered. I guess like everyone else, I haven't allowed myself to get too sold on its authenticity. Now, at 10:00 P.M., I'm slipping into an acceptance. There has been no hilarity over the news, but if it is confirmed by tomorrow's *Stars and Stripes*, I'm sure the lid will be off.

My first contact with the news came about 3:00 P.M. when an Italian who was shining my shoes looked up and casually announced, "La guerra finita. Si, si, si, troppa bomba Americana novella. Troppo Russe, Giappone finito." He swore the news had been broadcast over the Italian radio. Back at our hotel the Eytie manager was more conservative, but he'd also heard the announcement. He was willing to cede its possibility but with a "possibile—non sicuro." I'd sure blow the lid off if I knew I'd be home soon, soon, soon and it was over.

The local G-3 hasn't liked the lectures we've been giving and has told the CO so. For my part, they can all go to hades. But I am revising mine somewhat and getting some visual aids to go with it. Had I been able, I'd have done that in the first place. But only after everyone had flopped on the outlandish subject did G-3 make such things available. They've been having the talks since May without a single chart, blackboard, printed material, or outline available to us. In civilian life, a $125 clerk with one stenographer would have attended to all such details with no further instructions than that the talks were to be given. But here, the army had a few $600 per month colonels, a few $500 per month lieutenant colonels, a few $400 majors, and a bevy of $300 captains working on the matter for three months. They turn it over to our CO who delegates it to one of his lieutenant colonels and a major, none of whom makes the materials for preparation available. Then the captains are given less than a day's notice before having to present the subject to thousands of uninterested, hot, sleepy soldiers. Wowie! And such an army whips the heck out of its enemies. I'll have to give up trying to understand such matters and fall back on Tolstoy's belief that every army is flawed and the winners are determined largely by chance.

AUGUST 11, 1945. Oh, boy! Lots of letters from you. And confirmation just now at 6:30 P.M. that the war is over!

The radio says that the second bomb was so much more powerful than the first, it makes the first one out of date. It sure is hard to believe that a single plane could carry that much destruction in such a small parcel. By the time that thing is developed over another twenty-five years, whoever uses it in a war will undoubtedly wipe out civilization and a large part of the life on this globe. The United Nations will just have to work, that's all.

Our shipping date has been moved up to the next month, if it means anything. We may or may not be on our way home in a month, but I sure do have high hopes. And I've always hoped that congress would declare the national emergency over within a couple of months after Japan's surrender—an added blessing. I do have high hopes of being out of the army within a year but not much before that.

Here there's nowhere near the elation over today's news that it deserves—but infinitely more than there was over V-E Day, at that. Kiss Suzanne.

AUGUST 12, 1945. Major Lebermann, our plans and training officer, has been transferred to the 38th Evac and I'm assigned to his place. It's lots of work and I dread it, but it won't amount to much if the Japs surrender. We do have quite a training program here, not the least of which is teaching our nurses to handle a pistol.

I've been OD today. It hasn't amounted to anything other than staying at headquarters until 6:00 P.M. and staying in the hotel until midnight. I've spent the day reading up on my new job. I've read every order on the subject issued by the Fifth Army, as well as a great many suggestions that have come from Pacific commanders. I've learned a lot more than I ever knew about what goes on out there, and it isn't reassuring. The Japs never did sign the Geneva Convention, and it seems their general lousiness is phenomenal.

Our news reports our sinking eighteen more Jap ships yesterday and continued bomber raids over Japan. I'll certainly be low if they don't throw in the sponge pretty soon. Surely it can't take much more to bring them to their senses. I dread to think what might happen to them if they don't give up. A realistic history of it might not be very pretty.

AUGUST 26, 1945. We're to leave for Pisa or Leghorn about Friday, but it may or may not mean much. We still don't have a shipping number, simply because the entire center will be closed out by August 31. I had reserved the rifle and pistol ranges for our unit, but G-3 called to cancel it last night as the equipment is being dismantled. I'm still hoping to make it home in September, but that's probably too optimistic.

An ordinance captain, who came across in the same LST I did, is here from Florence and came by to see me this afternoon. He is commanding officer of a large machine shop there and has had his majority for a year. He has now been promoted to lieutenant colonel and is only twenty-eight years old, but he's fed up with the army. He has 109 points but knows he can't get home before January and is griped about that, too. It does seem that practically everyone is fed up, regardless of their branch of service and regardless of rank. Even if I've griped more than anyone else, the above seems to me adequate cause for sober reflection. If ten million discharged soldiers carry their bitterness into civilian life and demand revolutionary changes in the organization and conduct of our army, I'd be uneasy. Feudal system or not, it has always won our battles for national survival.

I got next week's training program out yesterday, and I hope it is surely the last one. I've been expecting orders each day to stop the program, but no such luck. On the contrary, I got orders today to start everything thirty minutes earlier and stop thirty minutes later every day. It is very hard to sell enlisted men on the need for any such program.

AUGUST 28, 1945. Dadgum, I gave another lecture to three more organizations at 9:00 A.M. yesterday and then found out I need not have. The entire lecture has finally been canceled. All training films are out also. This does leave our scheduled programs for the rest of the week very slim, and that delights all concerned, most of all the plans and training officer. The men are miserable when not kept occupied and resentful when they are. Surely we'll not sit in a staging area for long.

Something has happened to our mail again. The unit has not received any mail in four or five days and I can't imagine why, unless the APO has simply lost track of us again. I've sent a couple of boxes of clothes and papers home, and everything I have left will go into a single footlocker. I hope the APO doesn't lose track of any of that, but they might. We've been warned footlockers may sit in a warehouse at either end of the line for months.

AUGUST 29, 1945. Whoops! We got a shipping number today! That sure is a step in the right direction. And I guess that takes our going straight home out of the rumor stage. You wouldn't believe a little old number could do so much for morale. The laughing and talking at supper tonight was so obvious, I'm sure there must not have been any for some time.

Honey, a notice on the bulletin board says there will be no mail out after tomorrow. Whether that means all of Italy or just Montecatini, I don't know, so be prepared. In any event, it means we're nearer shipping out. Don't worry if you don't hear from me. I'll not be able to give you a specific date ever, as security censoring is still in effect. Also, a directive has come in that we've not to discuss the atom bomb with anyone. Can you imagine?

PISA, ROME, NAPLES   19
September 1945

SEPTEMBER 2, 1945. Pisa. We left Montecatini yesterday and are at the peninsula base section staging area, which is about three miles out of Pisa. We got a directive just before leaving that we were not to let civilians know when or where we're going. But the surest way to confuse any listening enemy would be for him to listen to what any of us believe and say on the subject. For all of that, I took clothes into a tailor shop just before we left and the lady who waited on me congratulated me that we were going home. She went on to say buono for us but malo for the Italians, and all those in the tailor shop seemed to feel that way. I believe we're liked by the majority of the Italian civilians. And my guess is that at least half of the American soldiers like them as well as I do, which is a lot, but the remainder think "eye-ties" are scum of the earth.

Well, it looked like we were practically at home, but now nothing is settled. All units have been frozen in their tracks pending yet another shuffling of personnel to let high point men go home first. And we may all go home as casual, rather than in units. In short, I may be home in two weeks or I may be lucky to get there by Christmas. So, do forgive me while I revert to type with a "damn it to hell, anyway." Never did I want so much to see you. Never have I been so miserable at not being able to. Never will I let you out of my sight once I do have you again.

Wideman, who lives in the pyramidal tent with Martinak, Merrick, and me, is making a chess board so he and I can play. He is about half through after working on it most of the day. And now Merrick is helping him and they're crowding me off this bunk where I'm trying to write.

I'm glad you didn't go to New York. I'm as likely to land in San Francisco as anywhere else, anyway.

SEPTEMBER 3, 1945. I guess we're foiled by the fickle finger of fate again. Not a sign of anyone leaving this place. The 24th General Hospital has been here and inactive for two months and was scheduled to leave tomorrow, but the new orders stopped them, too. Boy, are they burned up. Martinak says that at least we can be thankful we don't have to write Udine at the top of our letters anymore. Everyone did get fed up with that hayfield—it was so hot.

We sure have been getting good meals here. The kitchens have been turned over to a bunch of Krauts who can do unbelievable things with GI rations. We had roast chicken tonight, as good as any I ever ate. Even the dressing was good and it was the first in the army I've tasted that I could eat at all. Oh well, even good food isn't enough!

We're located in a big pine forest about three miles from Pisa and from the Mediterranean. They say it belongs to the King of Italy and used to be his private hunting grounds. It is quite sandy, quite pretty, quite hot in the afternoons, and cold at night. It is also quite a distance from home.

Points have been readjusted, with everyone overseas getting an additional eight. I now have 102—not that it has any meaning for medical officers. Wideman has just now remarked he believed he'd join the German army with an eye to reaching the States more quickly. It probably isn't all that bad, but folks are getting griped.

Oh, today's *Stars and Stripes* reports the army has announced it will release over a third of its medical officers by February. Wouldn't that be nice? I hope they do and that I'm in that lucky third.

SEPTEMBER 5, 1945. Your August 26, 27, and 28 letters arrived today. I'm sorry your morale suffers from our delays, but I'm sure we'll all get home before long. You'd just as well not be upset by the inequalities, injustices, and the like, which we seem to observe in the army. Consideration of the individual as an individual is not part of the army's mission, and all of its policies are designed to fit the overall mission. We might not really want it changed, either, much as we think we do. Of course, you feel and I feel that some of its policies aren't always formulated by the very highest calibre men, but most of them are. It has been so in all armies we ever learn about. No need to be upset by it—it won't affect us always, and society owes a big debt to its military just as it does to its other policemen.

However, for all of that rationalization, your husband is adequately griped that troop movements were frozen just as he reached the staging area. I hope Randolph got under the wire all right, but we're all glad an order came to freeze the European theater personnel so their units can't beat us home.

I went to Pisa yesterday, and the Leaning Tower, cathedral, and baptistry are interesting. There are many raised figures on one of the great bronze doors on the cathedral. All are green with the patina of age except for the head of a woman and two lizards, which shine like gold. As I meditated over this peculiarity, three different signorini came by, each rubbing a hand over the figures as she passed. Of course I had to ask why, but all I could understand was that it brought good luck. I've no doubt that a thousand years from now these figures will be completely worn away like the great toe on the statue of St. Peter in Rome.

Wideman, with characteristic humor, comes out with today's classic: "We've only three pleasant things we can do here in the course of each day: eat, play chess, and defecate, and I wish the bowel movements took up more time. They're all that give any satisfaction."

SEPTEMBER 8, 1945. Gee, I haven't written you in the past two days—too irritated over a clipping in *Stars and Stripes* of September 6. I didn't send it to you either, but it told the sad story that twenty thousand fewer men will leave the theater this month than left in August. DeArman and Martinak put it into letters to their wives last night, but I just went to the show instead of having to tell you about it.

You might know the news item didn't help morale much, particularly when a new latrine rumor has it that a liberty ship assigned for troop movement was loaded with scrap iron instead. Add to that an official report that one ship destined for our theater was diverted to the European theater, instead, when troop movements here were frozen. Ed Rippy wrote a bitter letter to his congressman and Ray Willis wrote an even more bitter one to his wife. I do believe there has been poor redeployment from this theater, particularly of medical officers, but I never did expect anything else, anyway. I hope I'm not too bitter about it.

There is also some good news today. Officers are to be discharged on a point basis and no mention of excepting medical officers. The news item says lieutenants and captains with eighty-five points and up will be discharged within the next sixty days, while majors and up must have one hundred points or more to get out in the same period. I'd readily trade my chances with 102 points for certain discharge by Christmas.

William Hahn got a letter from M. D. McCauley yesterday. McCauley is already out, but his pay continues until December 1. He will do ob-gyn about eighty miles from Fort Sam Houston and has probably already started.

Hudson Dunlap and I thumbed rides to Viareggio, an ocean resort about thirty miles up the coast. It is one more beautiful place with mountains, forests, and Mediterranean in a single view. The beach stretches as far as you can see for miles in both directions. That beach is the only one I ever saw equal to the one at Bizerte. We had lunch at the 92d division officers' mess and came back here about 3:30 P.M.

All of our nurses have been transferred out to other units. Some of them will probably have to go back to work. It just doesn't make any sense—no other group has worked so hard.

SEPTEMBER 10, 1945. We still sit, and sit, and sit, and find out just about nothing. Two of the fellows went over to the replacement depot to see about their old outfit, the 15th Evac, and found that many of the officers with lower points than theirs are scheduled to leave day after tomorrow. These two had been transferred to us from the 15th because they were the high point men in that outfit. It just doesn't make any sense. But I'll bet Bill Brown is tickled as he was our low point man transferred over there last month.

I wrote brother Charley today and hope he'll have time to answer my letter. I'm worried about his arthritis following his broken leg, and about his wife's circulatory problem if that's really what she has. Mama and my sisters try to keep me informed about the family's health, but they always give me just enough information to worry me. Don't ever let them know this, but they get symptoms across but never diagnoses. The symptoms they send me could fit half a dozen diseases, and this time they think Gladys may have to have both legs amputated. Sounds horrible, but my guess is they misunderstood and I certainly do hope so.

SEPTEMBER 11, 1945. Rumors run riot around here, as you already know. At least they are confined to a single subject these days—going home. They vary only as to the length of time before consummation. Today's "official" report, according to latrine information, is that high point men will leave for home before the end of the month. That's the first good one we've had, but don't you bank on it.

You might know there's been more griping than I've heard since the days in North Africa when it finally dawned on us that being overseas was just like being on Louisiana maneuvers, except that the natives speak a different language and our families aren't with us. For the most part, the officers had adjusted to peculiarities of the army, but adjustments seem to have been lost since our last move. The old wounds have reopened and we're chaffing at the injustices again. To tell the truth, the old members of the Baylor unit have much less to chaff about than the twenty-odd men who've been transferred in. All of them are still captains, and one is a board certified plastic surgeon with the required degrees in dentistry and medicine. He's been in an army that sorely needed plastic surgeons but has been a battalion surgeon for four years. A senior medical student could easily handle the job of battalion surgeon. Our tentmate Wideman's story is not quite as bad, but similar. On the day he finished requirements for certification in urological surgery, he came into the army as a first lieutenant. He's been in the 15th Evac ever since, subordinate to men less qualified than he, and his only promotion was the automatic one we all got for being overseas. "Happy, he ain't too." Then we have a fifty-year-old psychiatrist who has spent his army career in two battalion aid stations and one station hospital, never as a psychiatrist. Of course, I, with no training in surgery but board qualified in medicine—not psychiatry—spent a whole month in charge of the psychiatric ward at a time when it was kept full. My army classification now is general surgeon, the same as Dr. Carter and other outstanding teachers. We'd certainly have a talented staff if we reopened the hospital tomorrow and they kept me out of the operating room.

Honey, let me close by admitting that today's rumor peps me up a lot. I hope it pans out.

SEPTEMBER 12, 1945. Your September 3 arrived. Golly, Randolph was lucky to get out of Europe just under the wire, wasn't he? I hope he'll be able to get right out of the army. We still have no idea what will happen to us, but as far as we can tell, things are looking up. Our low point enlisted men have been ordered and will take over the entire 33d field hospital. It seems we will go home as a high point unit but no telling when.

Brown and Wideman are playing chess as I try to write, each swearing at the other after each telling move. Their terms were "fighting words" all through high school and college, but no more, having become simple adjectives and adverbs in all armies. Brown is from Ohio and

Wideman from Maine, and the three of us keep that chess board busy several hours a day. They are both swell fellows and brilliant, and I enjoy them a lot.

SEPTEMBER 14, 1945. Still lots of rumors, but no news. They transferred low point men out a day or two ago, but today a new bunch was transferred in with even lower points. This snafu yields to no logical explanation. Our personnel has been scrambled no less than four times to date, and we have personnel whose points go from less than 40 to above 120. Somewhere in this theater there must surely be an officer, likely of the regular army, with a rank of no less than major general, of about the calibre of our erstwhile CO, and responsible for it all. We all laugh about it and hope it stays funny for as long as it lasts, but I wish to heck they'd get me home.

Our days, as usual, are filled with reading, chess, and griping. Some West Point colonel in our mess hall made the mistake of observing aloud that he thought this thing of griping was being carried too far. He then added that a man's boss in civilian life wouldn't tolerate it. Boy! Did they let him have it, as if he'd been a private first class. It was emphatically pointed out to him that men picked their own bosses in civilian life and from men whose competence had been proved before they became boss. Colonel or not, it shut him up.

SEPTEMBER 17, 1945. The headquarters staff of Fifth Army arrived here yesterday, just about a thousand strong with no more points than ours. About a week ago the Fourth Corps Artillery, with about eighteen months overseas time, came here. But while we complied with the standing orders that all units turn in their transportation on arrival in this staging area, neither of these did so. They're lousy with vehicles running all over the place while we walk our legs off. We're angry about that and more. We've had chinawear in the mess hall ever since we've been here, but it disappeared simultaneously with Fifth Army's arrival—we now have metalware and rumor has our china gone to Fifth Army. We think that's pretty shoddy of them. Even worse, rumor also has Fifth Army leaving tomorrow or the day after on a ship that was supposed to take us along with Fourth Corps to the States.

Then, of course, the orders sending people home are always cut by high ranking officials but are only tentative and can be overriden by any officer of higher rank than the one who cut them. We think all generals and bird colonels of the medical corps have already gone home and they've left our destinies in the hands of a Lt. Col., M.A.C. He may be a good man, but lieutenant colonels around here come at a dime a dozen. Interesting situation.

September 20, 1945. Well, sure enough the Fourth Corps Artillery pulled out yesterday and Fifth Army headquarters left this morning. Whether justly or unjustly, they'll certainly be accused of playing their politics harder than they did their points. No doubt they've been screened and particularly low point men transferred out. But Bowyer and Dunlap ran into Colonel Skiles of whom I wrote you from Anzio. He has been consultant surgeon since Colonel Churchill was sent back to Boston. Bringing up the subject himself, Skiles said he supposed the units left here feel like it was dirty of headquarters to leave at this time.

They sure do—justly or unjustly. It was about as severe a blow as could have been dealt to the high point men left here. It seems like any dumb bunny would have known that and screened them out, letting them go home as individuals and leaving the headquarters here until every unit serving under it had gone home. But of course, the aggrandizement of a general or two is better served by bringing their unit home intact to parade it up Fifth Avenue. This needs be done early while people will still come out with ticker tape to welcome them.

September 27, 1945. Rome. Well, seven of us have reached here without our orders being rescinded and are quartered in the Excelsior Hotel, Rome's swankiest. The people are still cordial after fifteen months of American occupation and the city is clean. I've been to the Vatican Museum, which was closed when we were here before, and plan to see *Madame Butterfly* tonight. Our next move will be to Naples, and we're hoping to get on a ship within the next couple of weeks.

September 30, 1945. Naples. Still no hitches in our orders. I arrived at the nearby replacement depot last night and am already processed to go home whenever my time comes up. There are more than twelve thousand here with the same idea, so it may take a while.

I tried to call you from Rome but gave up at 11:30 P.M. There were about thirty soldiers still trying when I went to bed, but the New York operators hadn't been contacted for about two hours then. Ben Merrick never did get Mattie, but Martinak reached Macy and I believe it made him more blue than if he'd not reached her.

Charles Seton was here but left for Galveston on an oil tanker this morning. He said he'd call you as soon as he gets to Alvin. Adams had to go straight to the Pacific, he said.

Gee, I hated to leave Rome and may go back for another week while I'm waiting, if I can do it without jeopardizing my chances to board ship.

I visited the Capitolino Museum on this trip and saw the original *Romulus and Remus* bronze that was cast in about 500 B.C.

OCTOBER 2, 1945. Well, after looking it over, I find Naples has improved a bit in the past two years. The harbor certainly lives up to its reputation of "world's most beautiful." The long, wide street along the waterfront has been cleaned up and is still lined by picturesque buildings compatible with the setting. Then, the shops along Via Roma are the equal of any I've seen over here, instead of barren as they were two years ago.

Suzanne's pictures came yesterday but only because they were by registered mail. All other mail to us has been stopped. Gee, she grows, and grows, and grows. I sure am glad you sent her pictures so I'll have an idea what our daughter looks like when I start looking for her. She's a fine looking little girl if I do say so and shouldn't.

Wideman and I spent a couple of hours in the National Museum this morning. I'm sure I've now seen all of the Greek and Roman statuary pictured in our high school ancient history texts. Most of the masterpieces are from Greece of the fourth and fifth centuries, B.C., and are most interesting even to a country boy. Usually when I'm in one of the art galleries over here and see a painting which impresses me, the guide passes it by, either dismissing it completely as "nota moocha goota" or else damning it with faint praise. Sculpturing at least tries to make the figures as true to life as possible and any sap can pick out the masterpieces at a glance. Even I can pick them out. The Romans, by and large, were pitifully inferior to the Greeks in the art until Michelangelo's time. His Pietà in St. Peter's is certainly the equal of anything turned out in Athens. The surface anatomy of those Greek statues is astonishingly perfect, and I sure doubt such perfection was attained without the sculptor's dissecting cadavers beforehand.

White marble was not the only color used in Greek temples, but masterpieces weren't ever two-toned. There are many statues in the museum with clothing of black marble but with either white marble heads, hands, and feet or with these extremities made from brass. Although striking enough, these are obviously inferior to the masterpieces. The guide explained that they were built to order on a commercial scale.

The National Museum also contains any number of perfectly preserved bronze statues from Pompeii and Herculaneum. Their subjects vary from horses to wild boars, and of course, life-sized statues of several of the emperors. No noticeable changes in the physiques of men or animals are evident and wouldn't be expected over a twenty-five hundred period, but apples, pears, and other fruits are larger now. The three golden apples as held by Hercules are about the size of today's crab apples. On the other hand, Bacchus and the satyrs dance in drunken glee holding grapes no different in looks from today's.

Many elaborate urns and sarcophagi are in all museums, and a good many bronze tables from Pompeii are in the National. They are three-legged, ornate, and interesting. The patina on all bronze from Herculaneum is a darker green than that from Pompeii, easily identifying the source of the items.

OCTOBER 5, 1945. I'm enclosing a bit of news distributed to us today. It's the first such information we've had that wasn't qualified by the restrictive clause "except medical officers." Anyway, it sounds pretty optimistic for our getting home some time between now and Thanksgiving.

We learned today that the Baylor unit sailed for home on October 2 with a single medical officer and eighty-three nonmedical on their roster. Who can say why?

Wideman and I took a nice trip yesterday out to Herculaneum. About a fourth of the city has been excavated, all more recently than Pompeii. It is a few miles closer to Vesuvius than Pompeii, and for some reason its buildings are better preserved. It adds a few more pointers on the life of the people about the time of Christ. A good many pieces of wood have survived, among them one three-legged table in excellent condition. It still has a terra-cotta lamp resting on it, just as found. Several kitchens survive, fitted as found. Their utensils are in design and number about like ours today. Shelled beans in large shallow pans are easily identifiable. On dining room walls are paintings of fine looking meals of roast beef, fruits, salads, and pastries that can make your mouth water. The Phoenicians had conquered the city long before Roman times, bringing glass with them for vessels and windows. Some of the glass survives, their likenesses depicted in the dining room paintings.

In the inevitable house of prostitution there is a large covered glass bowl of walnuts, just as preserved as any of last year's ungathered crop. Wine, women, and walnuts.

What else survives? Oh, yes. A piece of four-strand, half-inch rope made just like today's but with an added spiral of fine cord that would prevent unraveling. Mosaic floors of marble with intricate designs built into them survive in perfect state. An often repeated design is the swastika, which was evidently a good luck figure. But another even more prevalent figure in both Pompeii and Herculaneum is the isolated external genitalia of man. Hardly a house exists without the figure in the mosaic floors, stuck around over doors or on walls. This figure, too, is the pointer used everywhere in lieu of the hand with pointing index finger used by printers and painters today.

One of the most interesting shops is a bakery whose buildings and equipment are in perfect condition. A large brick and mortar oven stands just as it did two thousand years ago, the usual "good luck" sign over the door. Two large grist mills of lava stone are intact, and stone shelves hold several bronze bread pans slightly smaller than today's loaves.

The colors in Herculaneum are in greater variety and preservation than those in Pompeii. Room walls in both cities are decorated with paintings, but faded reds and pinks are about all I recall in Pompeii. In Herculaneum bright colors predominate and are in reds, greens, blues, yellows, aquamarines. These people had good taste in such things.

Another interesting building was a public restaurant complete with a marble vomitorium, no less. Anorexia nervosa must have been commonplace for all who dined out. In this building are two wall mosaics of Neptune and some other pagan goddess, in the brightest greens, golds, and reds imaginable. Technically they are as perfect as later masterpieces. They look like paintings.

All of this and sewers too, among a people ancient and cultured when Christ was born. These ancestors of the Italians had all this when ours were courting caveman-style and screaming over the raw meat of their fresh kills.

OCTOBER 9, 1945 [two days out of Naples on the S.S. *John Breckenridge*]. Whee! And hot dawg! I'm on my way home at last and so surprised I can hardly believe it, let alone fully realize it.

We were told on Saturday night that we'd probably be in the replacement depot there in Naples for at least another ten days. They advised us to take the various trips now offered with army transportation.

But then at 9:30 A.M. Sunday, one man was called and told to be ready to ship out by 11:30 that morning. None of us could figure that out but we all envied him. Then at 10:00 A.M. on the same Sunday, we were ordered to be ready to board ship at 12:30 A.M. Man, oh, man!

Unfortunately, but with typical army efficiency, someone misplaced Bowyer's record. They failed to cut orders on him, and no amount of gnashing of teeth on his part could make them change the setup. He didn't get to come with us, and neither did Marshall Jones or Wideman. All others of the Baylor unit had gotten out several days before.

The whole thing is a fluke as this ship had been ordered to Marseilles to pick up troops there. Its orders were changed at the last minute. We all decided Bowyer had grounds for justifiable homicide. And if he knew that only two of the ten bunks in my cabin are occupied, he might really try it. Isn't it a rotten shame?

We're pulling into Oran, Algeria, tomorrow to take on ballast, and I hope to mail this while we're there. We'll then head for Hampton Roads, Virginia, expecting to dock about the 28th of this month. Oh, boy!

So far this trip has been the smoothest I've ever made on water. This is a victory ship, three times as large as the LST we sailed on so long ago. The meals are by far the best any of us have seen since we left home. Fresh milk again and the best light bread I've tasted in many a day. 'Bye now, and I expect to see you in about three weeks or less.

Epilogue

The letter mailed in Oran, Algeria, is the last letter to make it home. The unit had been scattered by degrees through the transfers mentioned in letters from Udine and Montecatini. Ben Merrick, Richard Martinak, Mack Bowyer and I were transferred out together for redeployment home, via Rome, Naples, and Oran. Bowyer and I hurried on to Naples to get our names on the first sailing list possible, leaving Merrick and Martinak in Rome to attempt transatlantic calls to their wives. As things turned out, I was the sole member of the Baylor unit on the S. S. *Breckenridge* due to the foul-up in Bowyer's orders.

This ship arrived at Newport, Virginia, some ten or twelve days after leaving Oran. Appropriately attractive WACs in dressy uniforms greeted us as we started down the gangplank, directing us to a gigantic army mess nearby. More than a few of the younger enlisted men, having no decorum to maintain, left the gangplank on the run to fall prostrate with yells. They kissed their native soil in ecstasy, scooping up its dust in both hands. Setting foot upon U. S. soil was an emotional moment for all of us, decorum or not.

Entering the mess hall, all were served in long chow lines, each receiving an overloaded tray. Each received a huge T-bone steak, a quart of fresh milk and as many hot rolls as we'd estimate we could con-

Lawrence D. Collins

sume. It was such food as we'd all dreamed of, but had not tasted, for years. After gorging ourselves we were herded onto waiting troop trains, mine headed for the separation center at Fort Sam Houston, Texas.

Our train had neither fixed route nor fixed schedule and simply went wherever and whenever appropriate railroad dispatchers had available package. Even so, we arrived at Fort Sam Houston in less than three days. Happily for me one of our more protracted stops came just outside Waco and I was able to contact a nearby doctor brother whom I'd not seen in over four years. He had time to meet me during the delay and I was absolutely shocked at how he had aged in the interim.

Although many wives had been phoned from Newport, we could not furnish them with an hour of our arrival at destination. Our train rolled into Fort Sam Houston without fanfare and no familiar faces were about as we marched into the separation center. My wife remembers waiting at the curb outside the center and seeing me come out and onto the walk leading to her. I only remember the terrific wave of relief as my own anxieties of several months faded in a flash the moment I saw her— I don't remember just where that was.

I have lost contact with all except medical officers of the Baylor Unit. I suppose Dean Moursund was the first personality associated with the unit to be overtaken by death and our CO was possibly the second.

They both died soon after the war. Colonel Winans had suffered a heart attack at Anzio and his death was soon after the CO's. Bussey, Lebermann, Sebastian, and Willis among the majors have died, and of the captains La Due, Alessandra, Martinak, McClung, and Brown are gone, and most recently Colonel Carter died at age eighty-six. Six or eight of the original group still practice in Dallas and I retired at age seventy-eight. Colonel Mallory retired as Major General and lives somewhere in the Southwest. The rest of the medical officers are scattered here and there and most are still in practice, although all must be past age sixty-five by now.

As I look back on the entire experience with the Baylor Unit, the first highlight was the nine weeks on the Anzio beachhead, and nothing after compared with it. As said earlier, it was a time of intense pride in our nation, in our organization, in our patients, and in each other. It was a time of consuming interest in our work and a dedication to it. Such pride and such consuming interest and such commitment, being rare qualities in even the best of lives and absent in many, really do seem to compensate for any and all miseries endured in gaining them. Stepping once more upon native soil and later walking out of the separation center to see my wife waiting at the end of a short walk, the end of thirty- one months separation, were the brightest highlights in the insanity of war.

 **INDEX**